Security Engineering for Embedded and Cyber-Physical Systems

Digital transformation, also known as Industry 4.0, Smart Industry, and Smart Manufacturing, is at the top of leaders' agendas. Such a transformation stimulates innovation in new products and services, the digital transformation of processes, and the creation of new business models and ecosystems. In the world of manufacturing, Industry 4.0 is based on various technological advances, among which we can mainly cite CPS (cyber-physical systems), IoT (Internet of Things), and IoS (internet of services).

While engaging, this fourth wave also brings significant challenges for manufacturers. Business operations and the supply chain are becoming more vulnerable to cyber threats.

Security Engineering for Embedded and Cyber-Physical Systems is an invaluable resource to discover cybersecurity and privacy techniques for embedded and cyber-physical systems. This book presents the latest studies and research results on all aspects of security engineering for embedded and cyber-physical systems. It also provides a premier interdisciplinary reference for researchers, practitioners, and educators to discover the most recent innovations, trends, concerns, and practical challenges encountered and solutions adopted in security engineering for embedded and cyber-physical systems.

The book offers comprehensive coverage of the essential topics, including the following:

- Embedded and cyber-physical systems threats and vulnerabilities
- Security engineering techniques for embedded and cyber-physical systems
- Security engineering for embedded and cyber-physical systems and potential future-use cases
- Artificial intelligence techniques for cybersecurity and privacy
- Security engineering for Internet of Things
- Blockchain for cybersecurity in embedded and cyber-physical systems

This book comprises a number of state-of-the-art contributions from both scientists and practitioners working in security engineering for embedded and cyber-physical systems. It aspires to provide a relevant reference for students, researchers, engineers, and professionals working in this area or those interested in grasping its diverse facets and exploring the latest advances and future trends related to security engineering for embedded and cyber-physical systems.

Security Engineering for Embedded and Cyber-Physical Systems

Edited by
Saad Motahhir
Yassine Maleh

CRC Press
Taylor & Francis Group
Boca Raton London New York

CRC Press is an imprint of the
Taylor & Francis Group, an **informa** business

First edition published 2023
by CRC Press
6000 Broken Sound Parkway NW, Suite 300, Boca Raton, FL 33487-2742

and by CRC Press
4 Park Square, Milton Park, Abingdon, Oxon, OX14 4RN

CRC Press is an imprint of Taylor & Francis Group, LLC

© 2023 selection and editorial matter, Saad Motahhir and Yassine Maleh; individual chapters, the contributors

ISBN: 978-1-032-57647-3 (hbk)
ISBN: 978-1-032-57649-7 (pbk)
ISBN: 978-1-003-27820-7 (ebk)

DOI: 10.1201/9781003278207

Contents

v

Editors

Saad Motahhir, PhD, IEEE Senior Member, has expertise as an embedded system engineer at Zodiac Aerospace Morocco (2014–2019) and a professor at the National School of Applied Sciences (ENSA), Sidi Mohamed Ben Abdellah (SMBA) University, Fez, Morocco since 2019. He earned an engineering degree in embedded system at ENSA Fez in 2014. He earned a PhD in electrical engineering from SMBA University in 2018. Dr. Motahhir has published a number of papers in journals and at conferences in recent years, most of which relate to photovoltaic (PV) solar energy and embedded systems. He published a number of patents in the Morocco patent office. He has edited one book and acted as guest editor of different special issues and topical collections. Dr. Motahhir is a reviewer and on the editorial boards of different journals. He has been associated with more than 30 international conferences as a program committee/advisory board/review board member.

Yassine Maleh is a cybersecurity professor and practitioner with industry and academic experience. He earned a PhD in computer sciences. Since 2019 he has been a professor of cybersecurity at Sultan Moulay Slimane University, Morocco. He worked for the National Port Agency (ANP) in Morocco as a Senior Security Analyst from 2012 to 2019. He is the founding chair of IEEE Consultant Network Morocco and founding president of the African Research Center of Information Technology and Cybersecurity. He is a senior member of IEEE and a member of the International Association of Engineers and the Machine Intelligence Research Labs. Dr. Maleh has made contributions in the fields of information security and privacy, Internet of Things security, and wireless and constrained networks security. His research interests include information security and privacy, Internet of Things, network security, information system, and IT governance. He has published over 120 papers (book chapters, international journals, conferences/workshops), 20 edited books, and 3 authored books. He is the editor-in-chief of *International Journal of Information Security and Privacy* (IJISP) and the *International Journal of Smart Security Technologies* (IJSST). He serves as an associate editor for IEEE Access (2019 Impact Factor 4.098), *International Journal of Digital Crime and Forensics*, and *International Journal of Information Security and Privacy*. He was also a guest editor of a special issue, "Recent Advances on Cyber Security and Privacy for Cloud-of-Things," of *International Journal of Digital Crime and Forensics*. He has served and continues to serve on executive and technical program committees and as a reviewer of numerous international conferences and journals such as Elsevier Ad Hoc Networks, IEEE Network Magazine, IEEE Sensor Journal, ICT Express, and Springer Cluster Computing. He was the publicity chair of BCCA 2019 and the general chair of the MLBDACP 19 symposium and ICI2C'21 Conference.

Preface

Industry 4.0 or IIoT (Industrial Internet of Things) is a discipline that combines industrial systems, the Internet of Things, the cloud, and data and analytics. In Factory 4.0, industrial production systems (IoT) are instrumented to feed data about their operation to the cloud through dedicated communication networks. The data in the cloud is analyzed and cross-referenced with other external data by intelligent systems to make production and supply chain optimization decisions. The decisions made are fed back to the industrial systems to drive the industrial processes automatically and remotely.

Most critical infrastructures such as the power grid, rail or air traffic control, industrial automation in manufacturing, water/wastewater infrastructure, banking system, etc., are cyber-physical systems (CPS). Due to the cyber-physical nature of most of these systems and the increasing use of networks, embedded computing, attack surfaces have increased. Given that the continued availability of their core functions is critical to people's every day and economic lives, there is widespread concern that they could be subject to intense cyber-attacks. A number of these cases have occurred over the past decade. It is therefore essential to defend these systems against cyber threats.

IIoT solutions and industrial systems (IoT) are poorly prepared to operate in a connected environment that is more exposed to cyberattacks. This makes them potential targets for hackers and cybercriminals looking for notoriety, industrial secrets, or financial gain through ransomware and/or data exfiltration. Poorly protected, remote accesses implemented on supervision systems can constitute potential vulnerabilities and put at risk certain industrial applications for production control and monitoring.

With the introduction of IIoT, the boundary between enterprise information systems (IT) and industrial systems (IoT) is gradually disappearing and IoT systems no longer have the perimeter security (air gap) they originally enjoyed. Industrial automation systems (robots, numerically controlled machines, programmable logic controllers) are becoming much more interconnected, open and accessible from a company's management computer network, or even the Internet. Cyber-attacks targeting management networks would, therefore, easily spread to IoT systems.

This book presents the state-of-the-art and practices addressing the following unique challenges in cybersecurity and privacy in embedded and CPS. This book is ideal for policymakers, industrial engineers, researchers, academics, and professionals seeking a thorough understanding of security engineering principles for embedded and cyber-physical systems. They will learn promising solutions to these research problems and identify unresolved and challenging issues for their research.

SECTION ONE

Security Engineering for Embedded and Cyber-Physical Systems

Challenges and Applications

Algorithms and Security Concern in Blockchain Technology

A Brief Review

1

Rejwan Bin Sulaiman, Amer Kareem, and Muhammad Umer Farooq

School of Computer Science and Technology, University of Bedfordshire, Luton, UK

Contents

DOI: 10.1201/9781003278207-2

1.1 INTRODUCTION

The basic concept of blockchain technology is that it uses the process of the distributed database, which performs a number of transactions that are entirely open to the participants. The blockchain system verifies all the transactions that are made, and once the transaction is done, it keeps track of the transactions and it is not possible to destroy the records. The blockchain specifies that it gives pure verification to all the transactions and keeps a solid record that can never be misguided. In simple words, it is much easier to steal something placed in a specific place rather than stealing the same thing placed in front of thousands of people [1].

The blockchain is made up of blocks, each of which contains a record of all the exchanges made between its users at a given time. These different blocks thus provide a history of all the transactions since its creation and allow everyone to check the accuracy of the data exchanged.

The blockchain is a distributed register: it is the user who own and update the information, without the need for a central authority. This decentralized nature allows it to be used in many different ways, beyond digital currencies such as Bitcoin, for which it was invented in 2008. Bitcoin is one of the prominent examples introducing the world with a multi-billion market with all the anonymous transactions. It doesn't involve any centralized control. It is one of the famous cryptocurrencies that has attracted millions of people to participate, but, on the other hand, there are many controversies [2].

Let's analyze the current situation of the digital economy. It will be clear that all vendors providing the services are based on trustworthy sources. In simple words, it will be clear that there is always a centralized medium for management that gives the people the confidence to rely on these sources for their investment. For example, let's consider the banking system, just like any banking transaction we do. Bank confirms that a third-party agent always plays a centralized role if the transaction is processed successfully. But here, the compromised thing is that this third-party agent can be easily vulnerable to security threats, which creates a risk for the system to be hacked.

So, at this point, blockchain technology has an important consideration. This is one of the unique ways of securing all the relevant transactions of all time which can be verified easily. And this verification is done based on the privacy of the digital world and all the participants involved. In other words, the distributed nature of blockchain technology and anonymity are its unique features [1].

1.2 SECURITY CONCERN IN BLOCKCHAIN

Information security is correlated with social life, wherein it can run in the whole system of national informatization. The construction of national informatization is the central point of information security. People have invested vastly in information security due to security concerns in their social and work lives.

Blockchain can also be a strategic tool for cyber security. Indeed, the current wave of cyberattacks is becoming increasingly sophisticated, fueled by both sophisticated mechanisms and a proliferation of devices that offer hackers numerous entry points. Although solutions are developing in line with the evolution of attacks, they could nevertheless reach their limits when faced with a certain type of malicious act.

In addition, it is bringing a revolutionary change in information security and technology. This technology can identify and certify, stay strong against Distributed Denial of Service (DDOS) attacks, and assure data credibility and integrity to develop the information security technology. Blockchain technology is the base upon which foundation of Bitcoin data structure and the transaction of information-encrypted transmission is constructed [3].

Blockchain technology uses a cryptography form and provides an open, decentralized database of every transaction involving value, money, goods, property, work, or even notes. Cryptography ensures that no one can change the records. It was usually developed as the accounting method for Bitcoin and is used in many commercial applications today. The main purpose of the blockchain is to verify the transactions. It is straightforward to digitize code and insert any document into the blockchain [4].

The blockchain is made up of a vast network of nodes. The computers of the blockchain network use a different client that executes the transactions, i.e., validating and relaying transactions. When you join the blockchain network, the node automatically gets the complete copy of the blockchain. Every node is regarded as the administrator of the blockchain and every person can participate in this network and get the chance of winning Bitcoins. Each node in the network updates the record independently [5].

The blockchain is a type of database that the public holding encrypted ledger can access; this means a block is the current part of the blockchain which records the recent transactions. Once verified, it becomes a permanent part of the growing blockchain. The people who run the system use computers to hold bundles of records made by others, known as "blocks", as a chronological chain. The "block" is the main and important part of the blockchain, verifying and recording recent transactions. After the completion of the block, it gets saved in the permanent database of the blockchain. Whenever a block gets completed, it overrides the previous one. In this way, numbers of blocks are connected in a blockchain. The blockchain carries a complete set of information about a specific users' addresses until the last completed block [5, 6].

Every block contains some information, some of the new block and some of the last block.

- **Data**: Each piece of information present in the block depends on the type of blockchain.
- **Hash**: The block contains a hash in it, you can compare a hash to a fingerprint. Hash is very useful in detecting and upgrading the block [7]. It is always unique and it identifies the block. If you make changes inside the block, it will cause the hash to change.
- **Hash of the previous block**: This effectively creates blockchains and secures the blockchain. If the hash of previous blocks changes, it will make the following blocks invalid. The first block is known as the genesis block.

1.3 MINING IN BLOCKCHAIN

The blockchain is particularly the technological innovation of Bitcoin mining. The transaction which has been completed gets recorded into the blocks and then automatically into the blockchain, where first it is verified and then used by other Bitcoin users. On average, every 10 minutes, a new block is generated in the blockchain using the mining process. Bitcoin is just the beginning of the blockchain. In the future, blockchain will manage and verify online data.

Blockchain network lacks the centralized points that computer hackers can easily exploit. The Internet today has many security issues that are almost familiar to everyone in this world, as we all rely on simple "username/password" to protect our identity [8]. For security reasons, blockchain uses encryption technology. You can store your data on blockchain without any fear. It can solve a stock transaction in a few seconds if it takes place on a blockchain-based system. It can never get manipulated or hacked because of the basic structure of blockchain. Once the information has been saved inside a blockchain, it is very difficult to update the information [7].

The most transformative application of blockchain is the "Smart Contracts". These automate the payments and safe currency transfer as negotiated conditions are met. A company could signal via blockchain that a good has been received, automatically triggering the payment [8]. The implications of blockchain technology are fascinating. Many tech companies are adopting blockchain technology to disrupt a variety of industries. This technique would embed the Bitcoin mining chips into Internet of Things

(IoT) devices and cell phones, according to research. Some established firms are also interested in using this technology such as Microsoft Corporation. Blockchain also offers point-to-point (P2P) network as everyone can join this network. When a user joins this network, she/he gets a full copy of the blockchain, which the node can use to verify that everything is in order. When someone creates a new block, that block is sent to everyone in the network, and each node verifies the block to ensure it has not been tampered with. Then, every node adds the block to their blockchain [9].

The uses of blockchain technology are endless. You only have to download this app on your computing device, then you can transact with it without paying a single transaction fee. Some expect that in less than 10 years, it will be used to collect taxes. It will make easy for the immigrants to send money, back to countries where access to financial institutions is limited. It could also enable us to launch companies entirely run by algorithms making the self-driving car safer. It can also track billions of devices on the IoT. These innovations will change our lives forever and it's all just beginning [10]. The blockchain technique can add up to serious cost savings. The blockchain serves as a financial institution and each block in the blockchain is like an individual bank statement.

1.4 INNOVATION OF BITCOIN

Blockchain technology is the public ledger responsible for keeping all the records from the very first stage. It makes the transactions information available for keeping records and verification purposes. The backbone of the blockchain comprises a number of blocks linked to each other and every new block is generated and added to the chain in a sequence. For authentication purposes, Bitcoin uses special digital signatures, i.e., ECC [11]. And for verification, there are certain vendors in the Bitcoin-linked network known as *miners*. These miners are based on specially programmed software that utilizes computer power to verify the transactions. It uses the bandwidth and the electric power, where blockchain comes into action.

Every time, a block is generated repeatedly throughout the Bitcoin system with the help of a miner. This way, replicated copies of all the Bitcoin transactions are generated across the network for the last 10 minutes. So, in this way, the miner utilizes the computer power to ensure effective transition between the two parties without any issue. This is how Bitcoin is different from the normal traditional banking system. The largest amount of Bitcoin that has ever existed is 21 million. Due to this, all the payments made are like taking the currency free of limitation. That is how a transmission control protocol based on the "communication" protocol is different from the blockchain protocol, which is based on the "value exchange". So, the only way to add more Bitcoin to the network is to use the process of mining [12].

Nowadays, the world is leading toward using the new version of blockchain technology, indicating other ways of using this technology, which is not just limited to transferring money. There are a number of new protocols that have been introduced, i.e., Multichain or Ethereum, etc., that can be considered for using this technology in a better way. Most of them are normally based on the similar concept of distribution system, i.e., ledger and some of the better features are added like smart-contract and many other applications. Work is continuously being done to increase the boundaries of this technology and many new techniques and applications are introduced [11, 12].

1.5 BITCOIN

According to the report, there are around 110 types of cryptocurrency. Still, Bitcoin constitutes about 77% of the cryptocurrency's total market due to the highest number of available active users [12]. It is one of the famous forms of a digital currency run over the entire network. It points to a point-based system of payment that doesn't constitute any central medium.

The major backbone of Bitcoin is blockchain technology. And this technology comprises all the available features for the Bitcoin currency. One Australian businessman named Satoshi proposed the foundation of Bitcoin back in 2008 [13]. Figure 1.1 shows mining process in Bitcoin.

1.6 BACKGROUND TECHNOLOGIES

All the individuals who want to add the block must follow up with some work. So, for the proof of work (PoW), it requires a significant amount of computational power involved in giving the proof, like, in this way, all the participants in the network can

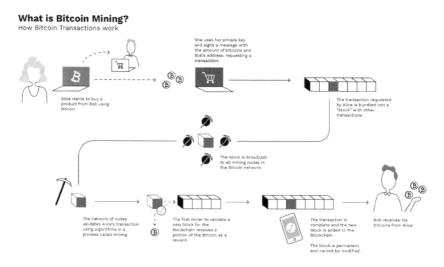

FIGURE 1.1   Bitcoin mining.

know that the work is done for generating more blocks in the chain. Therefore, this can prevent the bad users from manipulating the chain, thus ensuring the system's integrity.

Hash-cash is the function used to promise the verification of the system based on the PoW. It doesn't involve any kind of central medium, rather it is distributed effectively. It uses the method of symmetric key cryptography, i.e., SHA-1 or SHA-256 [14].

The major function of the hash value is that it takes the data that can be of an alternative size and because of that input, it transforms the data in a way that it is not possible to reserve it and makes it into a special string. In case of any changes in the data received, the hash function is changed very randomly. Thus, no one can make the same hash value with the various data blocks. So, every hash matches specific data, while in the case of Bitcoin, all the input data is more than the SHA-256 hash value [14]. Therefore, Bitcoin doesn't require any serial number as the specific hash value identifies each block. This strategy provides the identification and promises the integrity of the data. Adopting this kind of strategy allows us to verify the real owner of Bitcoin. It ensures the distributed database of a number of available transactions, which avoids the user for wrong spending.

1.7 POINT-TO-POINT NETWORK

In the Bitcoin framework, there are "nodes" involved in the operation of the whole system. In the P2P network, all the involved parties hold similar opportunities to start the communication process. That is how, all are involved in the processing of transactions, keeping the record updated in the system, and ensuring that all nodes in the network get the information effectively [15].

One special protocol used in the Bitcoin system is known as the Gossip protocol. The major functionality of this protocol is that it informs about the data to each node and in return, it receives data as well. By adopting this protocol strategy, data is disseminated throughout the entire network. Another major consideration about this protocol is that it follows up with the fault-tolerant mechanism, which means in case of any node failure in the network the availability of information via multiple places would not get affected. Other than that, it is worth considering this protocol because it is highly scalable. It can consider various nodes and adjust itself in the network irrespective of the changes while performing the configurations in the network [16].

1.8 CRYPTOGRAPHY IN BITCOIN

In case of public-key cryptography, every coin is linked with the real owner's public key, which means when the Bitcoin is sent to anyone, a message is created in terms of the transaction and as a result, the public key is attached to all the available Bitcoins and the private key verifies them. So, as a result, when it is publicly broadcasted, this

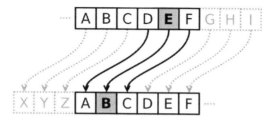

FIGURE 1.2   Cryptography in blockchain.

will cause other users to know that the owner of the Bitcoin is the same owner of the key. The owner's signatures are solid evidence that the message produced is trustworthy. Everyone holds all the previous records of transactions, so this strategy makes it possible to identify the real owner of the coins at any time [17]. Figure 1.2 shows the cryptography in blockchain.

To ensure the integrity of the whole blockchain system, every block in the chain promises the integrity of the last block (previous). And this process continues till the first block. So, in this way, no one can overwrite any one of the available records. This process is expensive as it is quite hard to fulfill all the special requirements.

1.9 CHALLENGES ASSOCIATED WITH BITCOINS

The major drawback in Bitcoin is that it doesn't involve any kind of central medium or authority for the transaction control. Instead, it is public, which brings up certain security concerns [18]. So, while considering this scenario, the following are some of the security aspects that should be considered.

1.9.1 Twice Spending on Coins

This term means that the user shouldn't be able to use similar coins two times and shouldn't be able to use the same coin for another user at once. Through the blockchain infrastructure, spending twice is prohibited; therefore, for this, everyone over the Bitcoin network must agree to the certain transaction before its confirmation. While adopting this strategy, it can be assured that the user didn't use the coin and whether the user is the actual owner of the coin. This identification is possible because the blockchain system keeps the record of all the available history of transactions; therefore, the real ownership of the Bitcoin can be traced easily. So, it can be concluded that the double spending of the coin simultaneously is not practically possible. If anyone manages to spend two blocks, just one of the transactions will work because of the nature of design of the algorithm [19, 20].

1.9.2 Access to the Network

It is tough to consider the whole network while using computational power. In the case of anyone who managed to get access to most of the network will allow him/her to do anything as he/she intended to do, which may fail the entire network. This can be avoided by adopting the PoW technique, assuring that none would alter Bitcoin as a whole network while considering the computational power. This process can be adopted if many people make a big pool but this has never happened yet.

The algorithm used in the block hash is made so that each block constitutes the hash value of the last block of the chain. The block configurations are shown in Figure 1.3.

In case someone wants to alter the data in the transaction, then they have to follow up with the PoW for that specific block and this follows up with all the interconnected blocks while considering the computational power, so that they could create the PoW of all the previous blocks and in the same way create the similar one for the newly generated blocks. At the same time, they are added to the ledger. Well, the only case in which the probability of success can be possible is when the overall control is more than 51% of the total value of computational power [21].

In usual circumstances, no one has the authority to access private key information. Still, in case of higher computational power, the access for changing the transaction can alternatively be possible. While, along with this, due to higher computational power, the creation of a large amount of cryptocurrency can also be possible by utilizing the process of mining.

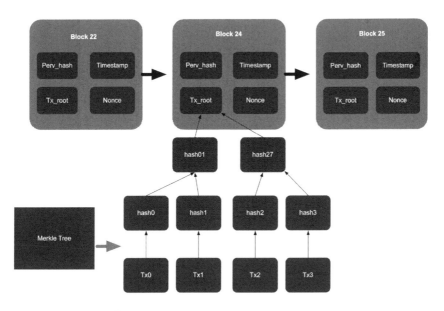

FIGURE 1.3   Block configurations.

1.9.3 Anonymous Users

This is one of the vital considerations in Bitcoin technology that the anonymity of all the participants is promised. Although the functionality of Bitcoin is based publicly, however, keeping the user identity confidential and private is necessary. Therefore, it becomes difficult instead of impossible for anyone to explore the relationship between the certain key and the person behind the key. This situation is achieved at a certain level by considering the utilization of public-key as the address.

1.9.4 Legal Issues in Bitcoin

The basic system of blockchain technology in Bitcoin is that there is no central system of management; therefore, the whole system will only stop working if the overall network is shut, which is practically not possible. Following are some of the legal considerations in the Bitcoin network:

- Practically, all the legal enforcement parties, including the government, failed to control the Bitcoin networking system. All the transactions and number of activities performed over the Bitcoin network cannot be traced over the normal circumstances. This has promoted some illegal things over this network. This can be understood by considering the example of buying drugs that can probably not be possible to buy via normal credit or debits cards, etc., but here cryptocurrency is the solution that can be used due to its feature of untraceability [22]. So, these kinds of issues made it impossible to use this platform under the legal boundary.
- There are certainly other legal concerns about the Bitcoin platform which are very confusing; for example, if the Bitcoin is treated as money or property, other than that if the owner of the Bitcoins is liable of paying tax, if "yes" what are the possible ways this can be implemented as there is no central controlling mechanism in Bitcoin [23].
- Another strange thing about Bitcoin is that its value or price changes frequently and in a wild way, and this trend is possible because of a limited number of participants and the transactions, and also because of social media. None of the government of any country, including a number of banks, would like to base their economy where there is no centrally controlled structure.

1.9.5 Technical Issues in Bitcoin

Apart from legal and security concerns in the Bitcoin technology, there are a number of technological issues in the Bitcoin network. Following are some of the issues based on Bitcoin technology:

- One of the significant challenges in the operation of a Bitcoin network is the power consumption used by the feature of PoW in Bitcoin which requires a significant amount of computational power for transaction verification. Therefore, it isn't worth wasting this much power on a small task.

- A total of 21 million coins are the total number of Bitcoins that can be possibly achieved and according to forecasting, this will take place by 2140 [23]. Afterward, there won't be any mining payment, and during this situation, the only possible way is the fee that is charged during the transaction and that will be the sole means for mining blocks by the miners. So, in this scenario, the Bitcoin system will be useless, when the transaction payment is the same as other centralized systems.

- In terms of safety, Bitcoin's overall network is quite safe and secure; however, if anyone or maybe some group gets control over the major computation power, this might cause the overall system to come down. However, this condition is quite impossible to achieve as mentioned before.

- Another major technical concern about the Bitcoin network is that if someone commits any mistake that might be unconscious, there is no way to get that fixed. In one way, this is an advantage, as this enhances the network's security, as no one will be able to perform any alterations or changes. However, on the other hand, this can create a problem when something is done just by human error.

- Many concerns are causing privacy issues in the Bitcoin infrastructure, including removing sensitive personal data from the Bitcoin system. While considering the other blockchain technologies, there are a number of situations where it keeps the data of the users at a certain time. Still, when there are alterations in the circumstances, this personal data is not kept the same way as before. This can be easily understood by considering the following example: the Unites States has recently published a law that states that the name of the company's CEO and date of birth must not be published on the company's website. However, other information like license holder, etc., can also be changed similarly. All this data is under the control of the government. However, blockchain technology gives the best chance to people to get together and make their data-sets throughout the end-to-end network without the involvement of any central medium [24].

1.10 THE CONSENSUS ALGORITHM IN BLOCKCHAIN

A consensus algorithm is a process in computer science used to achieve agreement among distributed processes or systems. There are various consensus algorithms like Paxos. Google implemented a distributed lock service called Chubby (based on Paxos), PoW, etc. Two of the general problems in blockchain technology that need to be solved are double-spending problems and Byzantine Generals' Problem [25].

Double-spending is an error in a digital cash scheme in which the same digital token is spent twice or more. This is possible because a digital token consists of a digital

TABLE 1.1   Comparison of the five consensus algorithms

	CONSENSUS ALGORITHMS				
CHARACTERISTICS	POW	POS	DPOS	BPFT	RAFT
Byzantine fault tolerance	50%	50%	50%	33%	
Crash fault tolerance	50%	50%	50%	33%	50%
Verification speed	>100s	<100s	<100s	<10s	<10s
Throughput (TPS)	<100	<1000	<1000	<2000	>10k
Scalability	Strong	Strong	Strong	Weak	Weak

file duplicated or falsified. The prevention of double-spending has taken two general forms: centralized and decentralized. It is usually implemented using an online central trusted third party to verify whether a token has been spent. This normally represents a single point of failure from both availability and trust point of view.

The second problem is the Byzantine Generals' Problem. We all know that blockchain is a decentralized network. There is no central authority in a decentralized network, and one node does not trust any other nodes. The question is how all the nodes can agree on the correct state of shared data. This is known as the Byzantine Generals' Problem. This problem is described as a group of generals of the Byzantine army camped with their troops surrounding an enemy city. The generals must agree upon a common battle plan and they can only communicate with each other using messengers. However, one or more of the generals may be traitors who will try to confuse the others. The problem is to find an algorithm that ensures the loyal generals will reach an agreement on the battle plan regardless of what the traitors do [25]. Table 1.1. shows a comparison of the five consensus algorithms.

The characteristics of the consensus algorithm include points discussed in subsections below.

1.10.1 Proof of Work (PoW)

A PoW is a remarkable piece of data that is very difficult to produce to satisfy basic requirements. It is a random process to generate PoW with low probability and efficiency so that the number of trials and errors is required before a valid PoW is produced. This mechanism could reach a consensus between many nodes on a network and secure the Bitcoin blockchain. However, the PoW algorithm works with all nodes to solve a cryptography puzzle. This cryptography puzzle is solved by all the miners and the first one to solve it gets the miner reward. PoW gives more rewards to people with better equipment. The higher your hash rate is, the higher is your chance of creating the next block and getting the miner reward. To increase chances any further, the miners can come together and form a mining pole; they combine their hashing power and distribute the rewards evenly across everyone in the pole. One of the disadvantages of PoW is that it uses a large amount of electricity. With PoW, rich people are more likely to enjoy

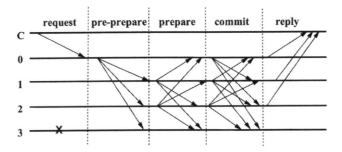

FIGURE 1.4   Steps of PBFT.

the power of economics at scale [26]. Figure 1.4 shows the Practical Byzantine Fault Tolerance (PBFT) consensus mechanism.

This method forces miners to have a stake in the Bitcoin network. Proof of stake does not have miners but instead validators. It does not allow people to mine new blocks but instead mint or forge blocks. To become a validator, a node must deposit a certain amount of coins into the network as a stake. The size of the stake determines the chances for the validator to be chosen to forge the next block. The validator chosen to validate the next block will check whether the transactions in the block are correctly made and if everything checks out, the node signs off the block and adds it into the blockchain. As a reward, the node receives the fees associated with the transactions related to this block. If the node no longer remains as the validator, his/her stake as well as all of his transaction fees which he/she has got will be released after a certain period. Proof of stake is environmentally friendly compared to PoW because it does not utilize a large amount of electricity [26].

1.10.2 Delegated Proof of Stake (DPoS)

DPoS users conduct a reputation system and real-time voting to create a panel of limited trusted parties, which are called witnesses. Witnesses have the right to create blocks to add them to the blockchain. You can consider this a representative democracy in which citizens elect officials to represent them while making decisions. In the model, people's worth strength depends on how many tokens they hold. This means the people with more tokens will influence the network more than people with very few tokens. The voting for the witnesses is a continuous process. Therefore, the witnesses must carry out their functions to a higher standard or lose their position. The DPoS is a decentralized consensus model, with a high transaction rate and low energy [26].

1.10.3 Practical Byzantine Fault Tolerance (PBFT)

It was a breakthrough in distributed computing that came out in 1999. It is a replication algorithm that can tolerate Byzantine faults and achieve variable consensus in a distributed computing network. It is a multi-stage verification process where at the beginning, the verification is done by a selected number of nodes. As it progresses through the verification process, it needs more and more confirmation. It is used in many distributed networks such as Ripple, Stellar, and Hyper ledger.

1.10.4 Raft Consensus Algorithm

The Raft is a characteristic of the consensus algorithm like Paxos in fault tolerance and performance. The main function of Raft is that all nodes in a group agree on the same transitions. In Raft, a person is selected from the group who acts as the leader. The leader's job is to accept the requests made by the clients and then manage the replication of the log to other servers. The data flows in one direction from the leader to the server [26]. Figure 1.5 shows RAFT consensus algorithm.

1.10.4.1 Technology behind blockchain

This is a basic issue that Lesley Lambert has developed to have a proper communication system between peer-to-peer [27]. The technology originated from a mathematical problem known as Byzantine failures. The point of the Byzantine question is to formulate consistency to message via the channel of information. Hence, the anticipation is that the channel is always reliable to communicate.

Blockchain technology is also known as the technology of distributed ledger and it also has an underlying technology that confirms the operation of Bitcoin. In the Bitcoin Forum, an essay written by Satoshi Nakamoto has been published in which the name "Bitcoin" first appeared in "Bitcoin: A Peer-to-Peer Electronic Cash System" [28]. Blockchain technology is an amalgamation of numerous technologies. The technologies are integrated into a database to maintain a reliable and unique database. This is a database technology that is distributed through the Internet. Storage is being done in a centralized data center. In blockchain technology, any person in this system can work in the data center. This technology can integrate, be continuous, and consistent through password verification of asymmetric mechanisms.

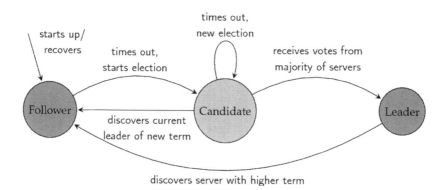

FIGURE 1.5   RAFT consensus algorithm.

1.10.4.2 Aspects of blockchain technology

Blockchain technology is one of the evolutionary technologies on the Internet. The core of blockchain consists of block-based data structure, the architecture of decentralized open-source, cryptographic asymmetric mechanism [29].

The blockchain is a distributed database technology that is entirely different from the traditional structure of the database. This technology is equipped with the innovative block as an important data component. Information of the data is being kept in the data record and the file that keeps and stores the data is known as a block.

Nakamoto has created a genesis block where every single block is responsible for recording the value in the case of the creation. The structure of the block keeps a header of the block and that block creates a link with the previous block.

The genesis blocks, as well as the block structure, are given in Figure 1.6.

That is why the block's structure consists of two distinctive characteristics. At first, the data information inside the block is an exchange of the activity recorded. In contrast, the creation of the previous block takes place to create the whole block to ensure the integrity of the database blockchain. Next, in the case of creating and linking to the ending point of the blockchain, the block data is ready to have assurance and the consistency of that blockchain database.

The block acts like a node based upon the value exchange agreement to create a blockchain. Before generating the latest block with the prior block, the index must have been known. That is why each block is needed to be linked with the prior block. Hence, it can be said that index of prior block creates the head of the following block and the data information creates the data block and here, the timestamp has to be fixed to the end [29].

"The magic of blockchain data structure: a block (complete history) + chain (full authentication) = a timestamp, which is the maximum innovation of the blockchain technology" [30]. Blockchain technology database can store complete data information starting from genesis block and it goes to the last block in the structure. Every data, as well as messages, can be traced and validated.

Since blockchain technology differs from many technologies, it does not record and store data in a centralized data center, instead of different nodes that are bound to work together. To begin with, blockchain technology is constructed with different sets of protocol mechanisms. Different nodes are used to do different tasks. One is used for maintaining the data information for its node, whereas the other is responsible for verifying other nodes.

The block data information depends on how almost all the nodes in that network can correctly consider information. Later, the comparison of the result and the authenticity is considered. In this technology, all data are regularly and spontaneously updated. In

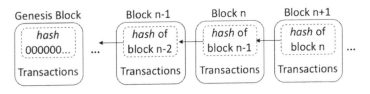

FIGURE 1.6 Genesis block and block structure.

addition, they are also stored in different nodes of the network that participate while the recording is going on. Though some of the nodes might be tampered with or damaged, it would not impact the recording of the database. The network system is purely stood upon the principles of volunteering. It also tries to establish a spread-out network system. Here, all persons can have accessibility to each other. By having so, total networking system will be decentralized as well. Data information is being validated as well as disseminated throughout the distribution network. In the case of blockchain technology, a different type of transaction is needed to be distributed in the distribution structure. For the P2P protocol, the messages are delivered to different nodes from a single node in the whole network. This is fully a decentralized architecture that is updated in real time in a single network node to ensure the security of the blockchain database [31].

The accounting distribution, storage, and dissemination of the blockchain depict that an organization can't have absolute control over this. The procedures regarding the storage of the data, transmission of the information, and the verification of the transaction are kept decentralized.

The blockchain technology can validate the ownership regarding the information that is purely based on the algorithms of asymmetric encryption. Two distinctive keys are required to encrypt and decrypt such as a public key and a private key. The public key is used to have the blockchain encrypted and remains open to anyone in the entire network. Anyone can use their public key in the case of encrypting data. On the contrary, the private key can only be owned by the information owner. To encrypt information, a private key can decrypt it to ensure the security and privacy of the data. Some common encryption algorithms are RSA, ElGamal, D-H, ECC, and many more. In the case of the blockchain technology transaction, the public key is responsible for encrypting the transaction. In contrast, the private key is responsible for decrypting it to utilize the value of the original data it has [32].

In a decentralized environment, all blockchain agreements are required to stay ahead of where the script is being taken as a programmable smart contract. This technology utilizes a script and in return, it ensures flexibility, practicability, and adaptability. The scripts are files that can be executable in some formats. This can also provide a list of different instruction for holding value on each exchange job.

1.11 EXHUMATION OF BLOCKCHAIN TECHNOLOGY IN THE CONCERN OF INFORMATION SECURITY

1.11.1 Authentication of Identity

The authentication process is a system that examines the identity of the users. It gives a mechanism for confirming the identity of the users [32]. The normality of the technology is to protect the users who are legitimate.

The authentication technology is regarded as the pillar of the security protocols like accessibility to the control, detection of the intrusion, security audit, etc. These are the important components of information security. The authentication technology includes different password-based technology, smart card-based authentication technology, and PKI-based authentication technology. In addition, different authentication technology has been introduced based on different biological characteristics of humans [33]. Traditional authentication technology has already adopted a centralized authentication method. The Certificate Authority (CA) is responsible for executing the authentication technology to realize the functions in terms of issuing, revoking, updating, and verifying certificates. Nowadays, web-based application systems like email, portal, and messaging applications purely stand upon the CA mode. On the other hand, it is a big risk since the crackers can crack the CA center to crack the encrypted information.

The authentication process of the identity is purely situated on the technology of blockchain. It has different characteristics of different decentralized authentication, whereas it does not create any threats to the CA. In addition, releasing a blockchain key can surely disrupt any action of the fake secret key. Now, a project from MIT named by "certain" is one of the best examples of implementing PKI created upon the blockchain technology. The certain can remove the centralized CA and replace the spread-out accounts by utilizing the blockchain. Moreover, Pomcor has already marketed an implementation of PKI based on the blockchain.

The approach permits the users to authenticate certification via decentralized and transparent sources of the user. IOTA project is used to leverage a lightweight, Tangle, block the less and scalable account and acts as the standing pillar of the IoT [34].

1.11.2 Protection of the Infrastructure

DDoS is responsible for attacking different computers as a platform with assistance provided by the Client/Server (C/S) technology [35].

Denial of Service (DoS) is responsible for targeting the availability of three components related to the security of the information: usability, confidentiality, and integrity. The attack mode uses the defect in the system network that is responsible for consuming the resources. Therefore, the target stays unable to give expected service to users.

The basic type of DoS attack can require huge resources to implement by utilizing the requests of the service. By doing so, the legitimate users might not have the prompt response of the service [34]. The attack might have a target on the memory, CPU, and bandwidth where the performance indicator is relatively low. The attack of DoS is made on a one-on-one respectively. Since the network and computer technology are developing day by day, DoS attacks are less likely to occur. The reason behind that is the increasing power of the computer processor, increased memory, and bandwidth.

1.12 DATA SECURITY IN BLOCKCHAIN

Data is being built on the exact foundation of that application system. For the method of cryptography, the digital signature creates a new set of information that depicts the integrity and the identity of the signer that is embedded into the data file [36]. The user is responsible for confirming the signature by using the public key of the signers to authenticate the information.

Generally, the intention of using a private key is because of the digital signature technique for the recipients. A problem is that the private key needs to be verified to see it has not been fabricated or tampered. As blockchain technology is developing, usage of this technology to replace the data signature can help to replace classified information with total transparency. That can increase the cost of the tampered data; hence, it is impossible to alter data without being sought [36].

1.13 DISCUSSION

Blockchain is one of the leading and emerging technologies in the 21st century. The overall theory of blockchain technology has given us insight into this decentralized technology. A number of previous literature reviews have helped us identify the number of possible improvements and concerns that can be considered in the future. Undoubtedly, Bitcoin technology has been researched and investigated on a broader scale. This has allowed studying further on this technology toward the future perspective while considering the number of blockchain applications.

According to the researchers and investigators, this technology constitutes a number of characteristics that are composite of many advantages which are fairly well to be used in the financial sector. Blockchain technology has already been implemented on a larger scale in cryptography and other information technology sectors. However, there are still limitations to implementing this technology on a large scale during this era of the modern world. The experts are still hopeful for blockchain technology to perform the future contribution due to the immense advancements and the development in the Internet industry.

Blockchain technology uses cryptography to make a system more secure and transparent. This technology was designed for digital currency such as Bitcoin, ripple. We can send this digital money to anyone. It doesn't have any physical worth. It stores information or data over the network to make it a centralized or distributed system so that anyone can access it. There are a number of blocks in blockchain technology that contain all data. It provides an open, decentralized database for money, goods, or work transactions. Blockchain has a vast network of nodes and for the execution of transactions, it uses different clients, transactions like relaying and validating. The blockchain is one of the emerging technologies of this century, and many researchers and investigators are putting their efforts into getting the best possible deal out of it. Its tremendous advantages and useful implications in a number of different areas can never be ignored.

1.14 ALGORITHMS

Blockchain technology uses different consensus algorithms. The consensus algorithm is a technique or a process in the computer field to attain the goal among distributed systems. Different consensus algorithms are used to achieve the results, i.e., Paxos,

Chubby (a google implemented distributed service) and PoW. The PoW algorithm is used in blockchain technology to secure the Bitcoin blockchain and it can be used to get consensus between different nodes. There are some other methods and algorithms used in blockchain technology for getting a good result: Proof of Stake, DPoS, and PBFT. The Proof of Stake method is used to mine the transactions according to your holding coins. It means that you have more power in mining if you have more coins. We can say that the Proof of Stake method works directly proportional to your coins. Peercoin was the first coin that used Proof of Stake method. DPoS method is used to solve the scalability issues that faced the users in the blockchain. EOS, BitShares, and Steam used this method. DPoS has also sped up the transactions and creation of blocks. Byzantine Fault Tolerance defines the system which permits the class of failure from Byzantine Generals' Problem. The most difficult class of failure modes is a Byzantine failure because a node can generate any garbage value during the transactions, which are very difficult to handle.

1.15 USER ROLES IN BLOCKCHAIN PROJECT

There are three different types of user roles in blockchain project: Application Developer, Solution Administrator, and Business Network Participant. Application Developer develops the application that interacts with the ledger, modeling the business network and implementing the script files that define transaction behavior. The Solution Administrator provides the target environment, deploying the business application and managing the blockchain.

The Business Network Participant runs an end-user application that invokes transactions, is aware of business concepts such as assets, participants, and transactions, but may not be aware of blockchain underpinning.

1.16 DEVELOPER CONCEPTS

The application concepts provide the user's front-end and may require different applications per participant. Furthermore, it interacts with the registries to add, delete, update, query, and registries that persist on the blockchain. It also connects to the blockchain via JavaScript client libraries (SDK) or REST. The model concept provides a domain-specific language (.CTO) that defines the type structure of assets, participants, and transactions.

Moreover, it aims to match how we talk about business networks in the real world. The script concept provides the implementation of transaction processor logic specified in JavaScript. Further, it is designed for any reasonable JavaScript developer to pick up easily.

In terms of security, blockchain technology constitutes a number of vulnerabilities, which must be considered. Although this technology is decentralized from the government agencies, however in terms of its dependence on the technology, it depends on the Internet platform for accessing resources like database and another authentication system. While blockchain technology has given big confidence to the people during its features of very strong cryptography, once the whole process of performing transactions is unchangeable, it is not possible to reverse.

Another major consideration about the blockchain infrastructure, which also includes the Bitcoin system, is that the system is highly available because the blockchain system is decentralized. It doesn't hold any centralized server, making it resistant to DDoS attacks. Therefore, this technology is highly acceptable for people.

1.17 CONCLUSION

This technology can devise a new perspective on trading technologies like the security of the password, decentralized coherence, sharing the public accounts, and the visibility of the control as well as the permissions. It surely can create a new society by exchanging different tangible or intangible assets. Due to its security features, it is getting better each day in terms of its acceptance toward the people and it is booming the users' confidence to get themselves involved.

In the past, Bitcoin technology used to be considered the only innovation in the Bitcoin platform; however, during the current era, it can be seen very clearly that blockchain technology is expanding its horizon toward many other sectors bringing the innovation to many areas. This technology has shown a great transformation of conventional industry into a much better technological platform with security, persistence, and accuracy features. Decentralization and anonymity also remained the best features of this technology.

Currently, blockchain technologies are booming at an exponential rate and there is still research and investigation that are carried out to ensure the maximum confidence of people toward this technology. Its applications are expanding in various areas of IT, which typically include the sector of IoT and other financial and trading sectors. Instead of having some challenges and issues related to the blockchain network, ultimate advantages can never be ignored. The world is seen to be moving toward this technology to get more optimal solutions. Researchers are putting more effort into making this platform more organized and secure such that any kind of illegal activities could be prevented.

ACKNOWLEDGMENT

This research chapter results from our mutual collaboration of participating actively in all the tasks. We would really like to thank our lecturers for their outstanding guidance and concerns throughout our work, who remained the guiding star for us. Without their engagement and personal interest, this wouldn't have been possible.

We are also very grateful to rest of the university staff members, who have given us environment and space where we can get access to the modern learning recourses whether it is a library or the virtual platform of University of Bedfordshire, Luton, UK. We would also like to thank our rest of the classmates, who have guided us when we have required any help in anything.

REFERENCES

1. "Beyond bitcoin: emerging applications for blockchain technology", NIST, 2018 [Online]. Available: https://www.nist.gov/speech-testimony/beyond-bitcoin-emerging-applications-blockchain-technology. [Accessed: 05 July 2018].
2. E. Zukerman, "Bitcoin reviewed: clever, controversial financial/social experiment", PCWorld, 2018 [Online]. Available: https://www.pcworld.com/article/230594/Bitcoin.html. [Accessed: 02 Jul 2018].
3. Yuan Yong and Wang Fei-Yue, "Blockchain: the state of the art and future trends", Acta Automatica Sinica, J. 2016, 42(4): 481–494.
4. S. Nakamoto, "Bitcoin: a peer-to-peer electronic cash system", Consulted. 2009. https://bitcoin. org/en/bitcoin-paper
5. K. Biswas and V. Muthukkumarasamy, "Securing smart cities using blockchain technology", in 18th IEEE International Conference on High Performance Computing and Communications, 14th IEEE International Conference on Smart City and 2nd IEEE International Conference on Data Science and Systems, HPCC/SmartCity/DSS 2016, December 12–14, 2016, pp. 1392–1393.
6. P. T. S. Liu, "Medical record system using blockchain, big data and tokenization", in 18th International Conference on Information and Communications Security, ICICS 2016, November 29–December 2, 2016, pp. 254–261.
7. Y. Xiao, H. Wang, D. Jin, M. Li, and J. Wei, "Healthcare data gateways: found healthcare intelligence on blockchain with novel privacy risk control", Journal of Medical Systems. 2016, 40: 218.
8. D. Kraft, "Difficulty control for blockchain-based consensus systems", Peer-to-Peer Networking and Applications. 2016, 9: 397–413.
9. M. Vukoli, "The quest for scalable blockchain fabric: proof-of-work vs. BFT replication", in IFIP WG 11.4 International Workshop on Open Problems in Network Security, iNetSec 2015, October 29, 2015–October 29, 2015, 2016, pp. 112–125.
10. F. Idelberger, G. Governatori, R. Riveret, and G. Sartor, Evaluation of logic-based smart contracts for blockchain systems, Springer, Cham, Switzerland, 2016, pp. 167–183.
11. L. Lamport, R. Shostak, and M. Pease, "The Byzantine Generals' Problem", ACM Transactions on Programming Languages & Systems. 1982, 4: 382–401.
12. A. Back, "Hashcash – a denial of service counter-measure", in USENIX Technical Conference, 2002.
13. S. King and S. Nadal, "PPCoin: peer-to-peer crypto-currency with proof-of-stake", 2012.
14. Nxtwiki, "Whitepaper:Nxt", 2015.
15. P. Vasin, "BlackCoin's Proof-of-Stake Protocol v2".
16. https://bitshares.org/
17. https://bitshares.org/technology/delegated-proof-of-stake-consensus/
18. M. Castro and B. Liskov, "Practical Byzantine Fault Tolerance", in Symposium on Operating Systems Design and Implementation, 1999, pp. 173–186.

19. L. Lamport, "The part-time parliament", Acm Transactions on Computer Systems. 1998, 16: 133–169.

20. L. Lamport, "Paxos made simple", Acm Sigact News. 2001, 32, 51–58.

21. D. Ongaro and J. Ousterhout, "In search of an understandable consensus algorithm", Draft of October 2013.

22. Brennon Slattery, "U.S. Senators want to shut down bitcoins, currency of Internet drug trade", Jun 2011. Available: http://www.pcworld.com/article/230084/

23. Jonathan Todd Barker, "Why is bitcoin's value so volatile?", May 2014. Available: http://www.investopedia.com/articles/investing/052014/whybitcoins-value-so-volatile.asp

24. Jeni Tennison, "What is the impact of blockchains on privacy?", Nov 2012. Available: https://theodi.org/blog/impact-of-blockchains-on-privacy

25. N. M. Hamza, R. A. Sarker, D. Essam, K. Deb, and S. M. Elsayed, "A constraint consensus memetic algorithm for solving constrained optimization problems", Engineering Optimization. 2014, 46(11): 1447–1464.

26. J. Zhang, V. S. Sheng, Q. Li, J. Wu, and X. Wu, "Consensus algorithms for biased labeling in crowdsourcing", Information Sciences. 2017, 382: 254–273.

27. Yuan Yong and Wang Fei-Yue, "Blockchain: the state of the art and future trends", Acta Automatica Sinica, J. 2016, 42(4): 481–494.

28. Mei Haitao and Liu Jie, "Industry present situation, existing problems and strategy suggestion of blockchain", Journal of Telecommunications Science. 2016, 32(11): 134–138.

29. S. Nakamoto, "Bitcoin: a peer-to-peer electronic cash system", Journal of Consulted. 2008. https://bitcoin. org/en/bitcoin-paper

30. Melanie Swan and Xiao Feng, Blockchain: New Economy Blueprint and Guide, M. New Star Press, USA. 2016: 1–4.

31. Lin Xiaochi and Hu Yeqianwen, "A summary of blockchain technology", Journal of Financial Market Research. 2016, 4(2): 97–109.

32. Liang Liu, Information security technology research in B2B e-commerce application system, D. North China University of Technology, China, 2013.

33. Kong Gongsheng, "Advances on secure authentication and trusted admission protocols for cloud computing", Journal of Henan University. 2017.

34. Zhang Yi-fan and Dong Xiao-ju, "Visualization analysis and design of DDoS attack", Chinese Journal of Network and Information Security. 2017, 3(2): 53–65.

35. Li Yang, Xin Yonghui, Han Yanni, Li Weiyuan, and Xu Zhen, "A survey of DoS attack in content centric networking", Journal of Cyber Security. 2017, 2(1): 91–108.

36. Lu Rongbo, Analysis and design of proxy signatures and group signatures, Southwest Jiaotong University, China, 2006.

IoT-Based Secure Smart Healthcare Solutions

2

C.M. Naga Sudha
Department of Computer Technology, Anna University–MIT Campus, Chennai, India

K. Gokulakrishnan
Department of Electronics and Communication Engineering, Anna University–Regional Campus Tirunelveli, India

J. Jesu Vedha Nayahi
Department of Computer Science and Engineering, Anna University–Regional Campus, Tirunelveli, India

Contents

DOI: 10.1201/9781003278207-3

2.1 INTRODUCTION

The Internet of Things (IoT) is mainly termed the Internet of Medical Things (IoMT) in the healthcare sector. It is considered as an integration of medical devices and software applications. Healthcare services that are possible in the medical field are known from the symbolic representation of functionalities of the body, as shown in Figure 2.1. Recently, IoMT and IoT have had an enormous set of applications. It is made possible due to the rise in mobile devices designed with near field communication (NFC) to interact with the IT systems. IoMT applications consist of numerous facilities such as medication tracking, remote patients monitoring, and wearable devices to transmit health problems to the respective health professionals. Health data is transmitted efficiently with their enhanced data collection and analysis ability. Healthcare sectors have gained more focus on IoMT technologies through which the medical organizations, innovators, and government bodies are working to reduce loads of healthcare entities.

Internet of Health Things (IoHT) is developed with IoT-based solutions which can form network architecture that can initiate the interaction between the patient and healthcare facilities. Electrocardiography, electroencephalogram, heart rate, diabetes, and other monitoring devices such as biomedical sensors are considered IoHT devices. These biomedical sensors are applied for pulse detection, measuring the airflow during breathing, oxygen level in blood, glucometer (measuring the glucose level), body temperature, and electromyography (measuring the electrical activity of skeletal muscles). Patient data is collected by sensors which are processed through applications. These applications are used by the user terminals like smartphones, smartwatches, computers, or even embedded devices. These terminals are connected to the gateways by short-range communication protocols, namely, 6LoWPAN (IPv6 over Low Power Wireless Personal Area Networks) or Bluetooth Low Energy (BLE) over IEEE 802.15.4 standards. Gateways are connected to the cloud for the services connected with the processing and storage [1, 2]. Patient data can also be stored in electronic health records, which

FIGURE 2.1 IoMT.

will help doctors access the history of patient health details. These can assist all sorts of people, namely pediatric, elderly, and patients with chronic diseases. The health sector has attained rapid development among the IoT-based systems.

The organization of the chapter is as follows: IoT Healthcare System and IoT Healthcare Technologies are described in Sections 2.2 and 2.2.1. IoT healthcare policies of some countries are explained in Section 2.2.2. Heterogeneous IoT is described along with the architecture in Section 2.3. IoHT services and applications are outlined in Section 2.4. IoHT Security is described in Section 2.5. Role of Blockchain in Healthcare is explained in Section 2.6. IoHT Industry Status is described in Section 2.7. Finally, the chapter ends with the open issues in IoHT, which are explained in Section 2.8.

2.2 IoT HEALTHCARE SYSTEMS

In the current healthcare systems, offering low-cost services efficiently is challenging. It is more highlighted when more aged citizens are affected by various diseases, demanding better healthcare recovery mechanisms. Due to the lack of resources in cities and rural areas, it can be tough to provide suitable treatment. Hence, the healthcare system needs changes for the transformation into smart healthcare system. Wearable sensors and devices are integrated with smart healthcare systems designed for smart emergency systems and smart hospitals. Sensor nodes can be installed inside or adjacent to the patient's body. Activity recognition, anomaly detection, behavioral pattern discovery, and decision support are some of the technologies to be integrated with the sensor networks [3, 4].

Intel and Dell have collaborated and launched a smart healthcare system in Saensuk city, Thailand, in January 2016. These corporate companies have initiated providing health services to the citizens. As an initial step, old-aged people who form most of the city population are focused on the project. These patients are provided with Bluetooth-enabled devices involved in collecting and investigating the data regarding their activities such as sleeping movements and walking. The collected data are sent to the central cloud system to contact medical practitioners to provide instant action based on conditions. Data collection plays an important role in smart city development through different tools and techniques. Various sensor devices are employed in sensor networks which help in data collection. These sensors include smart emergency sensors, smart health systems, and sensors for traffic management [5–7].

2.2.1 IoT Healthcare Technologies

IoT-based healthcare solutions are increasing day-by-day and therefore filtering the solutions becomes a tedious task. Core technologies that have the potential for the evolution of IoT-based healthcare solutions are discussed in this section [8–13].

- **Cloud Computing:** Integrating cloud computing into IoT healthcare technologies gives predominant access to shared resources. Services were offered based on the request over the network and operations were executed to meet the needs.

- **Grid Computing:** Introducing grid computing in the healthcare networks helps to improve the computational capability of medical sensor nodes. Grid computing, the backbone of cloud computing, is more accurate than cluster computing.

- **Edge Computing/Fog Computing:** Edge computing helps analyze and streamline the network traffic from the IoT devices. It also plays an important role in implementing real-time local data analysis. Fog computing provides the platform for the devices to operate during critical analysis, eliminating cloud storage processes.

- **Data Streams:** Data streaming is defined as a process where real-time data are processed to extract useful information from it. It means that the continuous stream on unstructured data is processed for analysis into the memory before storing it in the disk.

- **Big Data:** An enormous amount of healthcare data is generated by various medical sensors, which increases the efficiency and relevance of healthcare diagnosis and monitoring methods.

- **Networks:** In the IoT-based healthcare network, short-range such as WBAN, WLAN, WPANs, WSN, 6LoWPAN and long-range communications are included in physical infrastructure. For designing low-power medical sensor devices and communication protocols, the empowerment of ultra-wideband (UWB), BLE, NFC, and RFID technologies were used.

- **Ambient Intelligence:** The application of ambient intelligence is crucial to humans. In a healthcare network, humans are involved in end-users, clients and customers, patients, or health-conscious individuals. The continuous learning of human behavior, execution of any required action triggered by a recognized event was allowed by ambient intelligence. The potentiality of IoT-aided healthcare services can be enhanced by amalgamating autonomous control and human–computer interaction (HCI) technologies into ambient intelligence.

- **Augmented Reality:** In healthcare engineering, augmented reality plays a vital role in IoT. Augmented reality has its applications in the field of surgery and remote monitoring.

- **Wearables:** By adopting wearable medical devices to identify landmarks, patient engagement and population health improvements can be facilitated. The three major interests are connected information, target-oriented healthcare communities, and gamification.

2.2.2 IoT Healthcare Policies

Evidence-based policies and technologies play a vital role in all practical implementations. However, IoT healthcare services are still to be addressed across the world, e-health policies are key goal for many policy initiatives. If someone intends to develop both IoT and healthcare policies, then it means the policies will be based on IoT-based healthcare services. The countries and organizations and their forwarding direction in both IoT and eHealth policies and strategies were discussed in this section.

2.2.2.1 India

In the health sector, to enhance the role of information and communication technology (ICT), India introduced an eHealth policy between 2000 and 2002 to provide comprehensive guidelines in the healthcare field. Recommendations are provided for the country's information technology (IT) infrastructure (2003) and also for the formation of a telemedicine task force (2005). Transforming a digitally empowered society and the country with a knowledge-based economy, various initiatives have been implemented by the Indian government as part of Digital India Program [14]. To develop 100 smart cities, the budget of Rs. 70.6 billion has been allotted by the Indian government. To raise the number of connected devices by over 2.7 billion, to create a $15 billion IoT industry was the ambitious plan by India by 2020. In India's healthcare sector, all these efforts are expected to make great impact [15].

2.2.2.2 Australia

To guide national coordination and collaboration in eHealth, a framework was developed by the Australian health minister in 2008. A strategic framework was developed based on a series of National consultation initiatives including commonwealth, state and territory governments, general practitioners, medical specialists, nursing and allied health, pathology, radiology, pharmacy sectors, health information specialists, health service managers, researchers, scholars, and consumers. In addition to this, the Australian government developed a strategic plan for IoT [16].

2.2.2.3 Japan

To motivate the realization of network access ubiquity, the u-Japan Policy was developed by Japan's Ministry of Internal Affairs and Communications (MIC) in 2004 [17]. For eHealth-friendly policies, some recommendations have been made by the Japanese government, which focused on cost savings and improved clinical outcomes [18].

2.2.2.4 France

For the advancement of the IoT, in 2008 the French government supported the creation of an object-naming service (ONS) root server. Every product is uniquely identified using global standards since they registered with GSI France. Through domestic ONS nodes and portals, the information on these products was enabled. Since the product data are accurate, authentic, and uniform, the customers were convinced. Telemedicine services are widespread at the regional level and stimulate eHealth policy improvement in France. Legislation in 2004 has introduced electronic health records [19]. With the superintendent of solutions for challenges in semantic interoperability and the use of eHealth, the government has worked on the furtherance of IT infrastructure of hospitals. Regarding this, the "Hopitaux 2012" plan and the Law on Hospitals, Patients, Health and Territory (HPST) are worth noting.

2.2.2.5 Sweden

Networking was enabled for all physical objects through the Internet by enhancing IoT. For the headway of IoT, an Object Naming Service (ONS) root server is jointly developed by Global Standards 1(GS 1) Sweden and SE, which SE announced in July 2010. The Swedish "National Strategy provided a detailed set of action areas and statements for eHealth" [20].

2.2.2.6 Germany

In the legislation governing, the core eHealth activities of Germany were expressed in 2003. Germany has a superintendence to become a leader in engineering and manufacturing sector including IoT domain [21]. INDUSTRY 4.0 is the strategic start that helps achieve this goal according to the HighTech Strategy 2020 action plan.

2.2.2.7 Korea

By 2020, domestic market for IoT has achieved the KRW to 30 trillion ($28.9 billion), which was previously planned as 2.3 trillion in 2013. The government established an open IoT ecosystem in May 2014 to develop IoT services and products. Service, platform, network, device, and IT security sectors are parts of an open IoT ecosystem. In 2008, to enhance eHealth's inclusiveness and fair access, Korea has introduced policies. Electronic medical records, ePrescription, and telemedicine were introduced in the healthcare sector, which initiates the driving use of ICT [22].

2.2.2.8 China

In July 2020, China's Ministry of Industry and Information Technology (MIIT) announced that a unified national strategic plan for the IoT would be promoted. To introduce IoT, facilitate R&D, commercialization, creating foundational technologies, network connections and usage would be established by MIIT, which the Chinese government decided. These measures are expected to motivate the development of IoT. China's "eHealth Development Strategy 2003–2010" has attracted the rising investment interest [23].

2.2.2.9 The US

IoT's policy and regulatory implications were discussed by the Federal Trade Commission (FTC) in February 2014. The provision of notice and choice for non-consumer-facing network devices and how devices that are part of the IoT can be ensured to have reasonable data security were the two major areas of IoT that FTC focused on.

2.2.2.10 The EU

A European policy for the IoT was devised by Research and Development (RAND) Europe based on the European Commission's request. From mid and long-term perspectives, policy challenges had been evaluated by a research team addressed by policymakers. In Europe, for stimulating the development of IoT, some recommendations have been made after examining the policy options. To help the IoT, a resolution was proposed by the European Parliament in June 2010. The impacts of this technology on health, privacy, and data protection should be thoroughly assessed, which was recommended by the EU parliament. As part of this resolution, a consumer enjoys the right to opt for a not equipped or connected product. In 2004, the eHealth Action Plan was endorsed by the European Council, to cooperate the area of eHealth, all member states expressed the formal commitment. The European Commission launched a public consultation initiative in April 2014 for input from interested stakeholders on barriers and the issues regarding mHealth in the EU [24].

2.2.2.11 The World Health Organization

For a wide range of public health initiatives, mobile phones are used in both developed and developing countries. In developing countries, an initiative was taken to encourage Mobile Health (mHealth) for tobacco control (WHO, 2011). Text messages (SMS) were mostly used in most eHealth projects in developing countries to increase awareness and communication campaigns, and they focused mainly on HIV, malaria, and MCH. All target countries have been advised to consolidate ICT in their national health information systems and infrastructure by 2015.

2.3 HETEROGENEOUS IoT

Heterogeneous IoT is the predatory area among research fields, impacting every individual's lifestyle. These are implemented in various fields such as security systems, smart cities, vehicular ad-hoc network (VANET), smart homes, manufacturing, and environmental monitoring. It can offer numerous reliable amenities to our lives depending on applications developed. Heterogeneous IoT is designed with the help of mobile networks (3G, 4G, 5G), VANET, WiFi, and wireless sensor networks (WSN). These combinations of architectures assist in achieving the information anytime and anywhere. The overall setup is connected to the cloud servers via satellites or the Internet, which plays a vital role in transmitting the information to the server toward the processing stage. Servers can collect enormous amounts of information to control the smart entities. IoT is termed as a developing paradigm where the various heterogeneous systems are interconnected with four layers namely, application, cloud computing, networking, and sensing layers. Entities are controlled by themselves where they are scalable. Due to the sensing devices and system architectures, heterogeneous IoT is incorporated in almost every application aspect of life. Heterogeneous IoT architecture comprising four layers is described in Figure 2.2 [25].

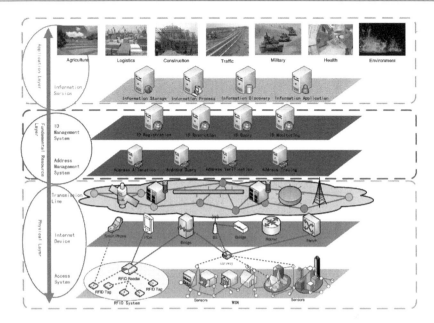

FIGURE 2.2   A heterogeneous IoT architecture.

2.3.1 Application Layer

Heterogeneous IoT can support numerous applications such as VANET, WiFi, and WSN. Mobile users are free to communicate using various applications, namely Whatsapp, Line, Yahoo messenger, WeChat, and Facebook Messenger, which helps monitor emergency traffic situations. Smart devices, cars, or humans connected to the applications will take respective decisions based on traffic information. WiFi can adapt with various protocols and so it is deployed in smart homes, smart healthcare, and smart city systems. WSN helps observe environmental entities such as humidity, temperature, light, smoke, to name a few. Smart appliances are utilized in everyday life, which requires simple and easy interfaces for the applications to be used effectively [26].

2.3.2 Cloud Computing Layer

The Cloud computing layer helps retrieve and execute the information gained from underlying layers. Cloud computing can handle a large amount of information more accurately. It is made possible with the help of storage capacity and also, cloud servers are capable of making decisions based on the information gathered. Additionally, heterogeneous IoT applications take actions based on emergency-aware mechanisms. As there is an increasing growth of data, decision-making through the cloud computing will take more time. Cloud computing has enhanced its heterogeneity power compared to middleware because of prevailing systematic computing capabilities. Different operating systems and a variety of network protocols could be differentiated by middleware to provide high-quality service for several kinds of applications. This will be hard to obtain interoperability because of the scheme used by most common middleware services. Because of the mismatched schemes of the subsystems, the middleware services have shortcomings of memory overhead and time delay constraints. In a specific style, the communication between the heterogeneous networks through cloud server acts as an abstract layer [27].

2.3.3 Networking Layer

Networking layer helps in movement of data between the sender and receiver. Major topologies like tree, star, scale-free, and hybrid for higher data transfer are offered. Through supernodes, sink nodes, and other communication entities, the data is transferred to the cloud server with the help of network structures and also through resourceful network strategies. In heterogeneous IoT, different kinds of protocols for routing have been designed. Data throughput, energy consumption, and malicious attacks were challenges faced by network topologies. In case of a node failure, some self-structured protocols help to improve the strength of network topologies. A high potential of data transfers is required to move a large amount of information to cloud servers in heterogeneous IoT. The network's lifetime in the heterogeneous IoT, hazardous locations, is extended using energy-saving protocols deployed [28].

2.3.4 Sensing Layer

For decision-making, the data from different nodes are collected and given to the cloud servers with the help of various sensors in the sensing layer. A huge number of sensors are located in a specific location to transmit data and thus the topology is formed. Sink, sensor, and management nodes are parts of the conventional network. Retrieving the data from sensor nodes and converting them to a multichip communication style will be performed by the sink node. Management nodes were used to administer the sensor network and observe activities initiated by them. The network structure will be changed if some nodes die or disappear quickly due to energy exhaustion and environmental effects. By choosing the power management and backbone node, unnecessary wireless communication links were subtracted. This helps to ensure the network connectivity and potential network model for data transfer. Several algorithms and mechanisms have been proposed for strengthening the network. Several different sensors in a heterogeneous IoT model exist to handle malicious nodes. Smart sensors are located to improve the privacy of heterogeneous IoT devices, since it lacks privacy. Various fields like industry, agriculture, smart homes, transportation, healthcare, and IoT have started penetrating rapidly from 1999. The purchase of materials, stocks, and auctions uses heterogeneous IoT applications and industrial productions use supply chain management [29, 30].

- IoT devices are used in agriculture to sense the greenhouse temperature, soil conditions, humidity, and other environmental factors.

- IoT devices are used in smart homes to enhance home safety and provide a pleasant living environment.
- To simplify data gathering, its execution, distribution, and travel exploration, intelligent transportation will be useful in vehicular communication.

IoT devices also significantly impact healthcare, varying from primary patient investigation to operation theatre (OT). To enhance wearable smart devices, heterogeneous IoT has been stimulated and a new trend of mobile health has been revealed.

2.4 IoHT SERVICES AND APPLICATIONS

IoT-based healthcare services, including pediatric and older nursing, chronic disorders surveillance, private health, and wellness management, are relevant to different sectors. Applications shall also be split into two groups:

- Single condition
- Clustered condition

An application with a single diagnosis refers to a particular disorder or infirmity, and an application with a clustering treatment encompasses a variety of illnesses or disorders together in their entity.

2.4.1 IoHT Services

IoT has been designed to offer continuous facilities in which each provider has delivered a selection of healthcare strategies. No common definition of IoT facilities exists in the field of healthcare. However, some situations may not critically separate service from a different method. General resources and protocols that could be required for IoT structures require small improvements in the proper operation of these facilities in medical scenarios. These include notification services, resource-sharing services, Internet facilities, heterogeneous computer cross-connection protocols, and large networking protocols. Various forms of IoT healthcare services are discussed as follows [31–33].

2.4.1.1 Ambient assisted living

IoT platform based on artificial intelligence (AI) techniques helps care for aged people and differently abled people. These kinds of integration of techniques are termed ambient assisted living (AAL). The ultimate aim of AAL is to provide an independent life to older adults in their comfortable zone of living. It gives a human-servant-like assisted living which will make them feel happy and comfortable. AAL work on 6LoWPAN, RFID, near-field communication (NFC) which applies for passive communication. As researchers are more eagerly involved in developing smart objects, Keep-in-Touch smart objects have triggered them in multi-dimensions on deploying the application.

2.4.1.2 Adverse drug reaction (ADR)

ADR is caused due to the injury caused by medications provided. Nowadays, more people suffer from the side effects of medications that physicians recommend. ADR helps reduce the reversal reactions of medicines with the help of barcode or NFC-enabled devices. This pharmaceutical intelligent information system helps map medications to the patient's allergy profile and prescribes the respective medicines.

2.4.1.3 Children health information (CHI)

In the present pandemic situation, children's health has to be taken care of in a crucial manner. Therefore, IoT researchers are developing an interactive totem placed in the pediatric ward to offer CHI services and provide guidance on emotional, mental health problems. IoT-based health services are encouraged to acquire nutritional habits for teachers and parents.

2.4.2 IoHT Applications

IoT software should be given more consideration in comparison to IoT facilities. Services are used to create software while consumers and patients access apps directly. Thus, utilities are developer-centered, whereas apps are user-centered. Present on the market today are numerous gadgets, wearables, and other healthcare products in addition to those uses covered in this segment. These products can be seen as IoT inventions that can contribute to different applications in healthcare. Various IoT applications which are developed to serve the medical fields are presented as follows [34–36].

2.4.2.1 Medication management

To solve the non-compliance problems in the medical field, IoT offers solutions such as I2Pack and iMedBox, which can verify the system with the help of field trials. IoT-based medication management packaging method has been developed for delamination materials and controlled through wireless communications such as RFID tags.

2.4.2.2 Wheelchair management

Researchers initiated their focus on developing automated smart wheelchairs which help disabled people. It is developed with wireless body area network (WBAN) technology integrated with various sensors. Medical support system connects peer-to-peer network and IoT in controlling chair vibration and helps detect the wheelchair status. It monitors the individual sitting position in the chair and collects all the data from the surrounding along with the location. It has eventually stated that the standard "things" evolved as connected machines which drive the data.

2.4.2.3 Body temperature monitoring

Body temperature plays an essential role in the healthcare services, such as homeostasis (ability to maintain a stable internal state despite the changes in the world outside) maintenance. IoMT verifies body temperature sensor, which is integrated into TelosB mote. It helps measure the temperature variations, which shows the successful operation of medical-related IoT systems. It includes an RFID module that controls temperature recording and transmission of a module for monitoring body temperature.

2.5 IoHT SECURITY

IoT grows rapidly in the medical field, which can be expected to be a mainstream of IoT acceptance in the next few years and prosper with the latest eHealth IoT products and applications. Medical equipment and software can deal with sensitive private data, such as confidential medical records. Moreover, such intelligent systems can always and everywhere be connected to global communication networks. Consequently, an intruder might threaten the IoT health care domain. It is important to define and evaluate various features of IoT protection and privacy, including safety criteria, flaws, hazard models, and countermeasures from a healthcare perspective to promote the complete deployment of IoT within the healthcare sector [37–40].

2.5.1 Security Requirements

IoT-based healthcare strategies are close to the protection criteria of typical communications situations. Confidentiality means that unauthorized people are unable to obtain patient records. Furthermore, classified communications do not cause eavesdroppers to expose their material. Integrity means that the patient records received are not changed by an enemy during transit. Moreover, the completeness of stored data and material should not be impaired. Authentication allows an IoT health device to guarantee the authenticity of the peer. Availability ensures the sustainability of IoT healthcare systems, either local or global/cloud, even in denial-of-service attacks, to approved parties.

The freshness of data requires freshness and critical freshness of data. Because of the IoT health network, metrics can differ over time when newly created messages. The freshness of data essentially assumes that each data set is new and does not repeat old messages from any adversary. Non-repudiation indicates that a node cannot deny a message sent earlier. Authorization means that registered nodes can only reach network facilities or infrastructure. While interconnected health systems are hacked, the network/device/information should be secured from attacks by a protection scheme. In the case of a failure, a network scheme should always have respective security services. An IoT healthcare network medical system may malfunction or lack resources, while other operating devices can allow a minimum degree of protection [41].

2.5.2 Security Challenges

As Standard protection strategies do not assure IoT security standards, there is a need for innovative countermeasures to comply with current IoT problems. Furthermore, such machines are not designed to carry out costly computing operations. In other words, they are either a sensor or actuators. It is thus a difficult challenge to find a protection solution that minimizes the use of energy and thus maximizes safety efficiency. Most IoT medical devices have no memory on the device. They are enabled by an integrated International Standard Organization (ISO), a device program and an application binary which are enabled.

Consequently, the memory cannot be enough to run complex security protocols. A conventional IoT healthcare network includes portable medical instruments with minimal control of the batteries, such as body temperatures sensors and BP sensors; these instruments save energy when the sensor readings are not registered by switching to power-saving mode. Moreover, if nothing is relevant, they run at a low CPU speed. The energy restriction property of IoT health devices is also difficult to find an energy-conscious protection approach.

Medical instruments are usually not static but mobile through IoT service providers connected to the Internet. For example, wearables can be linked to the Internet utilizing a wearable body temperature sensor or a heart monitor and the user can note their condition. Those consumer wearables are linked to the home network, where the consumer is linked to the office network. Various networks have different configurations and settings for security. The development of a protective algorithm recognizes versatility and poses a significant challenge. The number of IoT devices has steadily risen, which means that more devices are connected to the global communication network. Therefore, it is a difficult challenge to build a highly flexible defense framework without violating safety criteria.

Healthcare devices are typically connected through various wireless networks, including Zigbee, Z-Wave, Bluetooth, Bluetooth Low Energy, WiFi, GSM, WiMax, and 3G/4G. The capabilities of these networks are less suitable for conventional wired safety systems. Therefore, a robust safety protocol is difficult to locate and can accommodate wired and wireless features equally. Consequently, connecting numerous health devices within an IoT health network is complex, from full-length PCs to low-end RFID tags. Such instruments differ in computing, control, memory, and embedded software depending on their capabilities. Therefore, the task is to build a protection framework that can suit even the most straightforward machines. A health computer can enter wherever and everywhere in the IoT health network. It can either gracefully (with a right acknowledgment of the exit) or disgracefully (abruptly) leave a network. The network topology is complex with medical equipment's temporal and spatial entry features. For this cause, it is a challenging task to develop a security model for such a complex network topology [42].

A health system can communicate in a proprietary network protocol with other devices in the local network. IoT systems can also connect via the IP network with IoT service providers. Therefore, security experts can't establish a sound security strategy for multi-protocol communications. Protection protocols must be up-to-date to minimize possible vulnerabilities. Security updates for IoT health devices are also needed.

But it is a daunting challenge to develop a system for the complex implementation of security patches. IoT health equipment's physical stability is an important aspect. An attacker will access computers, extract encryption secrets, change code, or substitute malicious nodes. Tamper-resistant packaging protects against such threats, but in reality it is impossible to enforce. When an attack occurs from a proximal network healthcare system, the attack is more serious. The expanded attack surface makes IoT health sensors and networks vulnerable to security hits.

Furthermore, the malicious or compromised node inside the proximal network is difficult to ascertain.

IoT model continues to evolve, with many other IoT healthcare equipment and facilities planned. In comparison, the attacker can aggressively and deliberately target a health system and network that can use related IoT devices or power supplies like tablets and laptops to enter the network. An intruder will then formulate multiple security vulnerabilities to present potential IoT-medical systems and networks. Some risks are tangible while others can be forecasted and others are impossible to foresee. Different categories of attacks are discussed as follows [43]:

1. **Attacks Based on Information Disruptions:** An attacker can manipulate or analyze in-transit and saved health data to provide incorrect information and delete the integrity of information. The competitor conducts denial-of-service (DoS) attacks that result in the failure or unavailability of communication connections. This method of intrusion jeopardizes the liability of network hardware. An enemy passes patient information found in communications that violate confidentiality and data protection. An enemy receives unwanted access to patient records to generate chaos and confuse innocent organizations through the IoT health network. An enemy forges messages by injecting bogus material to undermine the credibility of messages and deceive innocent citizens. An enemy plays back current signals to jeopardize freshness. This further raises misunderstandings and misleads innocent people.

2. **Attacks Based on Host Properties:** Three types of attacks are initiated based on host assets.
   - Compromise: The reverse entails cheating or stealing the customer's fitness equipment and networks. Critical material, including passwords, encryption keys, and user data, is exposed in this attack.
   - Hardware compromise: An adverse system tamper and will steal firmware, keys, and data from the software on the computer. An attacker can reprogram malicious coded computers.
   - Software compromise: An intruder exploits the program bugs and weaknesses and causes IoT health systems to malfunction or dysfunction (e.g. buffer overload and depletion of resources).

3. **Attacks Based on Network Properties:** The method of attack is in two forms: a particular agreement between protocols and layers and a compromise in standard protocol where an attacker deviates from the standard protocols (application and networking protocols) to compromise compatibility, anonymity, honesty, and authenticity. The various types of vulnerabilities that an

opponent can exploit to initiate malicious activities are defined in any layer of the IETF working group Protection in each layer of the protocol stack should be maintained to enhance the efficiency of the IoT networks in terms of safety, durability, and connectivity under different environmental conditions.

2.6 ROLE OF BLOCKCHAIN IN HEALTHCARE

In recent times, blockchain technology has been widely discussed by researchers and industries, particularly since the onset of Blockchain 2.0 & Blockchain 3.0. This technology is increasingly expanding its reach into almost every major market, including insurance, shipping, drone communication, and even healthcare. The global COVID-19 health crisis is neither clustered nor autonomous. There has been no space for a seclusion of the COVID-19 pandemic and people around the world must be mobilized to solve the epidemic. Distributed ledger technology, such as blockchain, can also be beneficial in dealing with this. Blockchain technology makes it possible for people and institutions worldwide to access a single network that securely enables data exchange. Blockchain is tamper-proof, immune to unwanted alterations, and minimizes the ability to disseminate fake data and false information using consensus algorithms and smart contracts [44]. Digital control and supervision of the patients of COVID-19 are possible by blockchain-based software, thus reducing the workload of certain hospital employees and other health professionals. Some of the essential ways blockchain technologies can help battle COVID-19 are increased testing and reporting, managing the details of the COVID-19 patients, addressing the lockdown implementation prevention of the fake news, and providing a platform for incentive-based volunteer participation.

2.7 IoHT INDUSTRY STATUS

Fresh start-ups, corporations, and multinationals are turning into a gigantic market and improving innovations and technologies. Bittium, certified as the world's most secure mobile phone, offers a solution for the safe transmission of data between sensor devices and cloud providers because protection in all IoHT systems is essential, being a company specializing in designing reliable, stable systems communications and networking solutions. A significant range of new healthcare applications is supported with this unit. The BMI, body surface area, glomerular approximation (eGFR), and the number of scores used in cardiovascular disorders are readily collected. One notable statistic is that 6 million smartphones were sold only in 2016. Most of these contemporary systems use a large range of technical tools, including Bluetooth, GPS, and GIS. Some applications have also used blockchain, a new technology that helps store data as immutable blocks.

Blockchain is a ledger of transactions between two parties that continually expand. This data can be used to validate a party's statements that a transaction has occurred [45].

Thanks to its vast implementations in different fields of life, blockchain has become more and more popular each day. As a result, many businesses and organizations worldwide have begun developing applications that can effectively counteract COVID-19 with blockchain. These implementations fix a key concern, namely the lack of convergence of validated data sources. Experts agree that the capacity of the blockchain to verify data continuously is one of the key benefits of using blockchain-enabled software. This will act as a critical method for the increasingly escalating situation of COVID-19. The two applications based on blockchain, developed to tackle the COVID-19 pandemic, are shown in Figure 2.3 [44].

1. **Civitas:** There exist a lack of technological awareness on the blockchain, which can be increased with the help of social media. A Canadian blockchain-related start-up, a security framework in the form of an app, known as Civitas, has recently been established, enabling local authorities in different countries of the world to handle the effects of COVID-19. This app provides official IDs of citizens with blockchain histories to search whether or not they are allowed to leave their homes. This application also decides the time of day to purchase essential products for individuals experiencing the signs of COVID-19, reducing the chance of infection of others. Civitas also provides a feature of automated telemedicine that permits physicians to keep track of their patient's conditions give them notes on the medication used and monitor the treatment approaches. The software guarantees that data from the company remain confidential and secure, as stated by the company. Blockchain has a drawback of scalability and performance issues which can be eliminated with the help of directed acyclic graph (DAG) [46].

2. **Tracy:** Tracy is an application developed for contact tracing, enabling medical professionals, digital citizens, and government to use the location data privately. This application provides "anxiety-free" movement to the citizens along with data privacy. Medical teams which access the data using personal identifier information (PII) will be restricted to business rules. There is also a data broker service that can hide personal information and helps in focusing the affected users without affecting the privacy data.

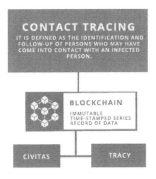

FIGURE 2.3   Applications of blockchain in COVID-19 pandemic.

2.8 OPEN ISSUES ON IoHT

Many scientists have worked on the design and deployment of various IoT health systems and the solution of various problems relating to technology and the development of these systems.

2.8.1 Standardization

Several vendors are manufacturing various goods and equipment in the healthcare setting, and new vendors continue to enter this promising technical race. However, common guidelines and legislation on compliant interfaces and protocols across platforms have not been complied with. This raises concerns about interoperability. Immediate steps are expected to resolve the diversity of applications. For starters, a dedicated community may standardize IoT technology. These include physical (PHY) and media access control (MAC) layers, system interfaces, data storage interfaces, and gateways. Another standardization concern is handling many value-added resources such as electronic health reports. This system is accessible in various ways, including access management and authentication. Various MHO and IoT researchers should work together to form IoT Technologies Working Groups to normalize IoT-Based Health Systems (IoT) and to form current standardization such as the IETF, Internet Protocol for Smart Objects, and the European Telecommunications Standards Organization (ETSI) [47].

2.8.2 IoT Healthcare Platforms

Since IoT-based healthcare hardware infrastructure is more complex than standard IoT devices and needs a more stringent real-time operating system, a tailored programming interface with runtime libraries is required. To create an effective architecture, a service-oriented approach (SOA) may be used to allow multiple application package interfaces (APIs) for services. In addition to a specialist database, libraries and relevant applications need to be developed to effectively use such papers, protocols, classes, message models, and other valuable resources for healthcare development software developers and designers. In addition, a certain kind of library focused on disease might be useful [48].

2.8.3 Cost Analysis

Investigators might consider IoT-based health systems as a cheap technology, but no empirical research has provided evidence for the authors' awareness. A standard IoThNet cost analysis can be helpful in this regard.

2.8.4 Application Development

Creating an app on the Android platform takes four simple steps: set-up, creation, debugging, testing, and publishing. Identical approaches normally accompany other networks. The presence of an accredited agency or group of medical experts is usually required to guarantee a product of reasonable quality in the production of the healthcare software. Furthermore, daily healthcare application upgrades are vital based on recent advancements in medical research.

2.8.5 Technology Transition

By including IoT methods in current network settings, healthcare institutions will modernize their latest equipment and sensors in the entire healthcare sector with intelligent services. Therefore, a smooth transition to an IoT-based setup from the legacy system is an essential task. In other words, incorporating current techniques has to be backward compatible and scalable.

2.8.6 The Low-Power Protocol

There are several instruments in IoT health settings, such as sleep, reception, delivery, and composition. These systems appear to be heterogeneous. Furthermore, each connectivity layer faces an external power constraint problem as far as service availability is concerned. For instance, it is difficult to find a suitable application discovery protocol that needs less power while providing MAC layer service availability.

2.8.7 Network Type

The IoT health network can have one of three essentially separate types, namely data operation and patient-centering structures, as far as its design strategy is concerned. In the data-centric method, it is normally possible to divide the health structure into items based on the reported health records. The healthcare framework is distributed by combining the features they would offer within a service-centered system. In the patient-centered system, programs for rehabilitation are separated by the presence of patients and their families. In this relation, it becomes accessible to address the question of what network type is ideal for IoT-based healthcare solutions [49].

2.8.8 Scalability

IoT health networks, software, services, and back-end systems should be versatile and clinical activities become more complicated due to the increasing demand growth among both individuals and healthcare organizations with the inclusion of numerous technologies.

2.8.9 New Diseases and Disorders

Smartphones are known as an IoT medical system at the frontier. While many health-care software and new technologies are introduced every day, the trend was limited to certain disease categories. R&D initiatives for new disease types and illnesses are crucial and it has long been a vital challenge to develop the methods for early diagnosis of uncommon diseases [50].

2.8.10 The Business Model

IoT is also not stable since the approach requires a range of different criteria such as new operating policies, updated service technologies, dispersed target clients, and revamped frameworks. Furthermore, physicians and nurses typically discourage modern techno-logical learning and use. This is why a new business model is desperately needed.

2.8.11 The Quality of Service (QoS)

Time-sensitive health systems need QoS assurances with respect to critical metrics, such as reliability, safety, and service standards. The quantitative analysis of each of these parameters can be helpful in this respect within the IoThNet system. Furthermore, device availability and robustness are critical to ensuring QoS, since a device catastro-phe can endanger lives in medical circumstances. An interesting problem is the viability of Plan B in the event of a device breakdown.

2.8.12 Data Protection

It is important to protect documented health data from unauthorized access by multiple sensors and devices. With respect to health data sharing with approved users, organiza-tions, and applications, strict protocols and technological security measures should be defined. It is an open challenge to develop an optimum collective algorithm to prevent dif-ferent attacks, threats, or vulnerabilities between security, detection, and response services.

2.9 CONCLUSION

In the current pandemic situations, people have become more concern about their health. Critical situations are well-planned and handled with technological advancements such as IoT, AI, and blockchain which helps in balancing the contact-less environments. Hence, IoT healthcare systems, technologies, and policies are explained in Section 2.2. Heterogeneous IoT layers are described in Section 2.3. IoHT services and applications developed for the benefits of digital citizens are defined in Section 2.3. However, along with the technological developments, security measures must be integrated proactively. To handle the security issues, blockchain has made revolutionary changes. Thus, the role of blockchain and IoHT security challenges are depicted in Sections 2.5 and 2.6. Industrialists have begun to show their higher interest in investing a significant amount in developing their products to serve the people in pandemic situations. Therefore, IoHT industry status is described in Section 2.7. Finally, the open issues in IoHT are briefly described, which helps the researchers focus on. Thus, overall, this chapter helps gain knowledge about the smart techniques that prevails in healthcare sectors.

REFERENCES

1. Deloitte Centre for Health Solutions, Medtech and the Internet of Medical Things. [Online], Jul. 2018. Available: https://www2.deloitte.com/content/dam/Deloitte/global/Documents/LifeSciences-Health-Care/gx-lshcmedtech-iomt-brochure.pdf
2. J.J.P.C. Rodrigues, D.B.D.R. Segundo, H.A. Junqueira, M.H. Sabino, R.M. Prince, J. Al-Muhtadi, V. Hugo, C. De Albuquerque, "Enabling technologies for the Internet of health things", *IEEE Access*, vol. 6, pp. 13129–13141, 2018.
3. A.M. Khairuddin, K.N.F.K. Azir, and P.E. Kan, "Limitations and future of electrocardiography devices: a review and the perspective from the Internet of Things". *International Conference on Research and Innovation in Information Systems*, pp. 1–7, 2017.
4. S. Deshkar, R.A. Thanseeh, and V.G. Menon, "A review on IoT based m-Health systems for diabetes". *International Journal of Computer Science and Telecommunications*, vol. 8, pp. 13–18, 2017.
5. M.W. Woo, J.H. Lee, and K.H. Park, "A reliable IoT system for Personal Healthcare Devices". *Future Generation Computer Systems*, vol. 78, pp. 326–640, 2018.
6. F. Firouzi, A.M. Rahmani, K. Mankodiya, M. Badaroglu, G.V. Merrett, P. Wong, and B. Farahani, "Internet-of-Things and big data for smarter healthcare: From device to architecture, applications and analytics". *Future Generation Computer Systems*, vol. 78, pp. 583–586, 2018.
7. *Enterprise Innovation, Saensuk Smart City Launches Smart Healthcare Pilot*. Accessed: Feb. 22, 2018. [Online]. Available: http://www.dell.com/learn/lt/en/ltcorp1/press-releases/2016-07-26-saensuk-smart-city-pilots-_rst- healthcare-iot-project-with-dell-intel
8. C.G. Loiselle and S. Ahmed, "Is connected health contributing to a healthier population?", *Journal of Medical Internet Research*, vol. 19(11), p. e386, 2017.
9. I. Olaronke and O. Oluwaseun, "Big data in healthcare: prospects, challenges and resolutions", *Future Technologies Conference*, IEEE, San Francisco, CA, pp. 1152–1157, 2016.
10. Y.I.N. Yuehong, Y. Zeng, X. Chen, and Y. Fan, "The internet of things in healthcare: an overview", *Journal of Industrial Information Integration*, vol. 1, pp. 3–13, 2016.
11. S.H. Kim and K. Chung, "Emergency situation monitoring service using context motion tracking of chronic disease patients". *Cluster Computing*, vol. 18(2), pp. 747–759, 2015.
12. I. Zagan, V.G. Gaitan, A.I. Petrariu, and A. Brezulianu, "Healthcare IoT m-green CARDIO remote cardiac monitoring system – concept, theory of operation and implementation", *Advances in Electrical and Computer Engineering Journal*, vol. 17(2), pp. 23–31, 2017.
13. H.A.G. Elsayed, M.A. Galal, and L. Syed, "HeartCare+: a smart heart care mobile application for Framingham-based early risk prediction of hard coronary heart diseases in Middle East". *Mobile Information Systems*, p. 11, 2017. https://doi.org/10.1155/2017/9369532

14. *IoT Policy Document.* [Online]. Available: https://www.meity.gov.in/sites/upload_files/dit/files/Draft-IoT-Policy%20%281%29.pdf, accessed Dec. 27, 2014.

15. *Government Aims to Make $15 Billion Internet of Things Industry in India by 2020.* [Online]. Available: http://articles.economictimes.indiatimes.com/2014-1026/news/55446641_1_iot-100-smart-cities-draft-policy-document, accessed Dec. 27, 2014.

16. *The National e-Health Strategy.* [Online]. Available: http://www.health.gov.au/internet/main/publishing.nsf/Content/NationalCEhealthCStrategy, accessed Dec. 27, 2014.

17. *The Internet of Things in Japan.* [Online]. Available: http://www.huawei.com/en/about-huawei/publications/winwin-magazine/hw-110837.htm, accessed Dec. 27, 2014.

18. M. Akiyama and R. Nagai, "Information technology in health care: E-health for Japanese health services", A report of the CSIS global health policy center, The Center for Strategic and International Studies and the Health and Global Policy Institute, Mar. 2012.

19. M. Akiyama and R. Nagai, "Information technology in health care: e-health for Japanese health services", [Online]. Available: https://csis-website-prod.s3.amazonaws.com/s3fs-public/legacy_files/files/publication/120327_Akiyama_JapaneseHealthCare_web.pdf, accessed Dec. 27, 2014.

20. J. Artmann and G.S. Empirica, "Dumortier 'e-health strategies - country brief: France,'" ICT for Health Unit, DG Information Society and Media, European Commission, Oct. 2010.

21. *France Country Brief Strategy.* [Online]. Available: https://www.meity.gov.in/sites/upload_files/dit/files/Draft-IoT-Policy%20%281%29.pdf, accessed Dec. 27, 2014.

22. *Internet of Things Needs Government Support.* [Online]. Available: http://www.informationweek.com/government/leadership/internet-of-things-needsgovernment-support/a/d-id/1316455, accessed Dec. 27, 2014.

23. K.A. Stroetmann, J. Artmann, and V.N. Stroetmann, "e-health strategies – European countries on their journey towards national e-health infrastructures", Information Society, European Commission, Jan. 2011. [Online]. Available: http://ehealth-strategies.eu/report/eHealth_Strategies_Final_Report_Web.pdf, accessed Dec. 27, 2014.

24. *Building Foundations for e-Health: Republic of Korea.* [Online]. Available: http://www.who.int/goe/data/country_report/kor.pdf, accessed Dec. 27, 2014.

25. *Advancing the 'Internet of Things'_Digital Economy Strategy Submission to Industry Canada.* [Online]. Available: https://www.ic.gc.ca/eic/site/028.nsf/eng/00307.html, accessed Dec. 27, 2014.

26. *Examining Europe's Policy Options to Foster Development of the Internet of Things.* [Online]. Available: http://www.prgs.edu/content/rand/randeurope/research/projects/internet-of-things, accessed Dec. 27, 2014.

27. S.S. Reka and T. Dragicevic, "Future effectual role of energy delivery: a comprehensive review of internet of things and smart grid". *Renewable and Sustainable Energy Reviews*, vol. 91, pp. 90–108, 2018.

28. Mohammad Saeid Mahdavinejad, Mohammadreza Rezvan, Mohammadamin Barekatain, Peyman Adibi, Payam Barnaghi, and Amit P. Sheth, "Machine learning for internet of things data analysis: a survey". *Digital Communications and Networks*, vol. 4(3), pp. 161–175, 2018.

29. O. Elijah, T.A. Rahman, I. Orikumhi, C.Y. Leow, and M.N. Hindia, "An overview of internet of things (IoT) and data analytics in agriculture: benefits and challenges". *IEEE Internet of Things Journal*, vol. 5(5), pp. 3758–3773, 2018.

30. Parvaneh Asghari, Amir Masoud Rahmani, and Hamid Haj Seyyed Javadi, "Internet of things applications: a systematic review". *Computer Networks*, vol. 148, pp. 241–261, 2019.

31. *AMD Telemedicine. Telemedicine Defined.* [Online]. Available: https://amdtelemedicine.com/telemedicine-defined, accessed Apr. 20, 2020.

32. M. Shah and A. Tosto, "Industry voices – how Rush University Medical Center's virtual investments became central to its COVID-19 response", *FierceHealthcare*, Apr.

2020. [Online]. Available: https://www._ercehealthcare.com/hospitals-healthsystems/industryvoic%es-how-rush-university-system-for-health-s-virtual

33. A. Chakraborty, "Assam: Telemedicine, video monitoring for COVID-19 home quarantined people in Dhemaji", *Northeast Now*, Apr. 2020. [Online]. Available: https://nenow.in/north-east-news/assam/assam-telemedicine-video-monitoring-for-covid-19-home-quarantined-people-in-dhemaji.html

34. M. Pourhomayoun, N. Alshurafa, F. Dabiri, E. Ardestani, A. Samiee, H. Ghasemzadeh, and M. Sarrafzadeh, "Why do we need a remote health monitoring system? A study on predictive analytics for heart failure patients". *11th International Conference on Body Area Networks*, Turin, Italy, 2017.

35. W. Naude, "Artificial intelligence against covid-19: an early review", *Medium*, Apr. 2020. [Online]. Available: https://towardsdatascience.com/arti_cial-intelligence-against-covid-19%-an-early-review-92a8360edaba

36. T. Alladi, V. Chamola, N. Sahu, and M. Guizani, "Applications of blockchain in unmanned aerial vehicles: a review", *Vehicular Communications*, vol. 23, pp. 1–25, Jun. 2020.

37. J. Redfern, "Smart health and innovation: facilitating health-related behaviour change". *Proceedings of the Nutrition Society*, vol. 76(3), pp. 328–332, 2017.

38. J.Z. Zhang, Y.K. Li, L.Y. Cao, and Y. Zhang, "Research on the construction of smart hospitals at home and abroad". *Global Health Journal*, vol. 38(12), pp. 64–66, 2018.

39. K. Li, J. Wang, T. Li, F.X. Dou, K.L. He, "Application of internet of things in supplies logistics of intelligent hospital". *Chinese Medical Equipment*, vol. 15(11), pp. 172–176, 2018.

40. A. Belle, S.-Y. Ji, W. Chen, T. Huynh, and K. Najarian, "Rule based computer aided decision making for traumatic brain injuries," in *Machine Learning in Healthcare Informatics*, vol. 56, pp. 229–259, Springer, Berlin, Germany, 2014.

41. A.A. Monrat, O. Schelén, and K. Andersson, "A survey of blockchain from the perspectives of applications, challenges, and opportunities", *IEEE Access*, vol. 7, pp. 117134–117151, 2019.

42. S. Sayeed and H. Marco-Gisbert, "Assessing blockchain consensus and security mechanisms against the 51% attack". *Applied Sciences*, vol. 9(9), p. 1788, 2019.

43. I.C. Lin and T.C. Liao, "A survey of blockchain security issues and challenges". *International Journal of Network Security*, vol. 19(5), pp. 653–659, 2017.

44. Vinay Chamola, Vikas Hassija, Vatsal Gupta, and Mohsen Guizani, "A comprehensive review of the COVID-19 pandemic and the role of IoT, Drones, AI, Blockchain, and 5G in managing its impact. *IEEE Access*, vol. 8, pp. 90225–90265, 2020.

45. Z. Zheng, S. Xie, H. Dai, X. Chen, and H. Wang, "An overview of blockchain technology: architecture, consensus, and future trends", Proceedings of the IEEE International Congress on Big Data (BigData Congress), IEEE, 2017, pp. 557–564.

46. M.C. Lacity, "Addressing key challenges to making enterprise blockchain applications a reality". *MIS Quart Executive*, vol. 17, pp. 201–222, 2018.

47. Christiana Aristidou, Evdokia Marcou, Christiana Aristidou, and Evdokia Marcou, "Blockchain standards and government applications". *Journal of ICT Standardization*, vol. 7(3), pp. 287–312, Sep. 2019.

48. A. Kosba, A. Miller, E. Shi, Z. Wen, and C. Papamanthou, "Hawk: the blockchain model of cryptography and privacy-preserving smart contracts", Proceedings of 2016 IEEE Symposium on Security and Privacy (IEEE, New York, 2016), pp. 839–858.

49. M. Gagnon and G. Stephen, "A pragmatic solution to a major interoperability problem: using blockchain for the nationwide patient index". *Blockchain in Healthcare Today*, 2018. https://doi.org/10.30953/bhty.v1.28

50. V. Chauhan, S. Galwankar, B. Arquilla, M. Garg, S. Di Somma, A. El-Menyar, V. Krishnan, J. Gerber, R. Holland, and S.P. Stawicki, "Novel coronavirus (COVID- 19): leveraging telemedicine to optimize care while minimizing exposures and viral transmission", *Journal of Emergencies, Trauma, Shock*, vol. 13(1), p. 20, 2020.

Blockchain for Security Engineering in Embedded and Cyber-Physical Systems

Blockchain and Cyber-Physical System for Security Engineering in the Smart Industry

3

Javaid Ahmad Malik and Muhammad Saleem

National College of Business Administration and Economics
Rahim Yar Khan, Punjab, Pakistan

Contents

DOI: 10.1201/9781003278207-6

3.1 INTRODUCTION

Manufacturing is of paramount importance in this modern age, where preserving the various stages is a significant issue. Thanks to the Fourth Industrial Revolution, we are entering a new age of invention and progress. New dangers and difficulties are introduced as a result. And in today's manufacturing cyber world, this could be most apparent.

Blockchain and cyber-physical systems have been adopted to secure the documents so that security can be further enhanced and hacking from one system to another can be prevented, in this chapter, during each transaction, as the entire transaction takes place electronically. In the meantime, blockchain and cyber-physical systems have been adopted.

Cryptography and distributed systems are primarily the basis of blockchain technology. Blockchains are public registries to accumulate all transactions in the block list. If several blocks continue to be added, they form like a chain. Encryption techniques are known to obscure content so that only the intended users have access to it. However, specific groups of people must be provided with certain information and it creates a further risk of data being operated. Blockchains are tackling the problem (Velmurugadass, Dhanasekaran et al. 2021).

When information is gathered and restructured, any changes that have been made are documented and proved. It is then encoded to prevent further variations. These modifications are then modernized to the main documents. This is a tiresome procedure and every change takes place, the data is well-preserved in a novel chunk. It is noteworthy that the first variety is well linked to the newest version (Li, Zhang et al. 2021).

Blockchain replicates a database system by assimilating data recreated diagonally in the network (Sadeq, Kabir et al. 2021). This means that the record has several positions and documents are public and easy to verify. Data corruption is futile because there is no centralized version. Changing records is boring, assembling it easier to pinpoint if nobody tries to do so. Therefore, almost everyone can see the variations, but only the newest block can be altered. Therefore, a blockchain could be regarded as a data piece with the following properties:

- Continuously updated. This allows operators to access and adapt data at all times.
- It is a disseminated system that stores replicated copies of the data throughout the network. Almost every copy is updated to one record in real time.
- It has proved data. When data is changed, users must verify it using encryption techniques.
- Data are secure because encryption algorithms and distributed structures do not permit data and security systems to be manipulated.

Blockchains are classified as unauthorized blockchains and blockchains allowed. Unauthorized blockchains are accessible and can be linked and left by any pair by a book worm or author. They are distributed in addition, users can read the data. Limited readers and authors are authorized by blockchains allowed. They are run through a dominant entity, which chooses who can write or read (Bera, Das et al. 2021).

3.1.1 Need for Blockchain Security

Technology from blockchain provides a way to segment information and to certify transparency. This feature is useful in the procedural field and is further used. The parties concerned are responsible for ensuring that their information is incorrect and can't be rehabilitated. There are a few explanations why blockchain is in many areas favorite (Shuaib, Alam et al. 2021, Verma 2021).

- Blockchain technology is accessible to prevent other users from modifying it. It guarantees transparency. Registered data into a blockchain is problematic to change, making it a generally secure technology. A blockchain does not challenge transactions by pair to pair (Maity, Tolooie et al. 2021).
- Transaction settlements are faster for blockchain technology than traditional banks that rely on work time and rules. The location in different portions of the world more underwrites to the postponement. But blockchain doesn't have such limitations, so transaction settlements can be slightly faster (Dicuonzo, Donofrio et al. 2021).
- It promotes decentralization because the central data hub is not available. This consents specific communications to be genuine. When data is added to dissimilar servers, a trivial quantity of data is exaggerated even if adversaries find data.
- As third parties are no longer participating in transactions, users and developers are taking the inventiveness and thus creating user-controlled networks (Khan, Arshad et al. 2021).
- Blockchain removes human fault because it records and protects data against alteration. The accuracy of records is guaranteed from node to node. This inevitably leads to accountability, improved goods, and therefore transparency. This also simplifies various other management practices (Schönle, Wallis et al. 2021).
- In case of detection of anomalies, you can continually trace the origin of the point, making it easy to start investigating the actions required. This provides quality assurance (Liang, Xiao et al. 2021).
- Intelligent and sophisticated contracts with blockchain technology can easily be legalized, signed, and obligatory.
- Blockchain technology removes electoral fraud and thus makes voting clear (Baudier, Kondrateva et al. 2021).
- For stock exchanges, the reliability of cryptocurrency is envisaged.
- The energy supply container is followed precisely.

- Blockchain technology promotes global transactions between peers. Transactions in cryptocurrency are fast, secure, and cheap.
- The technology of blockchain leads to data rationality. It maintains data integrity and can also average increase to changes in data. Even if data is broken for a company, it cannot be utilized, thus maintaining the balance between security and management.
- Used for authenticating devices is blockchain technology. They could soon replace passwords to eliminate human intervention. It does not encourage central architecture.
- Meanwhile, each transaction is digitally printed and contracted, no repudiation is highlighted. Even with the new iteration of the system, previous records are deposited in the ancient time's log. This results in traceability.

3.1.2 Challenges Faced by Blockchain Technology

Blockchain is one of the latest technical developments. Industries from various fields such as finance, healthcare, cloud storage etc. have adopted them. Despite the supremacy of blockchain technology in technology, it has multiple concerns. A few challenges facing blockchain technology are as follows:

- **Scalability or Network Size.** Scalability is a challenge with every block of storage data and the development of new blocks of transactions. If there is no robust network support for a blockchain, several system problems can arise. Blockchain storage or blockchain redesign can be useful in dealing with scalability issues (Singh and Vardhan 2021).
- **Privacy Leakage.** Blockchain networks do not guarantee the confidentiality of transactions. Bitcoin transactions may disclose personal user information. Despite routers and IP addresses translators, IP addresses can be tracked down to use pseudonyms. Privacy is one way of addressing confidentiality matters (Wu, Dai et al. 2021).
- **Selfish Mining.** Selfish mining principles to uncertainty blocking. It depends on little dangerous power to venerate the system. The mining blocks are kept free of broadcasting and only when certain requirements are met, the public can access the private sector. Therefore, egoistic miners can use private chains without worrying about losing their competition and earning more (Li, Wang et al. 2021).
- **Initial Cost.** Initial blockchain installation is costly, with software costs and skilled personnel expertise included. This also contributes to enormous demand and low **supply** (Gopalakrishnan, Hall et al. 2021).
- **Integration with the Legacy System.** Moving to a blockchain system can either rebuild the **entire** system or fuse with blockchain technology the existing system. It could take time, money, and skills (Gopalakrishnan, Hall et al. 2021). Eradicating the legacy systems cannot be easy, so it would be a viable solution to change a current strategy that enables blockchain technology.

- **Energy Consumption.** The validation of blockchain transactions requires the processing of **complex** checks and mathematical algorithms for network safety. Computers devour a lot of control and energy (Jamil, Iqbal et al. 2021).
- **Public Perception.** Many people don't know because blockchain technology is new. Many think it's synonymous with bitcoins. People must be aware of it **before** the technique is used in several fields.
- **Privacy and Security.** Initially, blockchains were published. However, blockchains are allowed to protect and restrict access to data. This requires much planning and practice (Wu, Dai et al. 2021).
- **Complexity.** Blockchain knowledge relies on novel vocabulary, including multiple jargons. The **phrases** must be familiar to people associated with blockchain technology work (Frolov 2021).
- **Human Error.** Blockchain data may not be reliable; therefore, events must be accurately recorded.
- **Politics.** Several public discrepancies have occurred among communities since Bitcoin protocols **can** digitize governance models. Blockchain forking reports have been reported that update the blockchain protocol.

3.1.3 The Future of Blockchain Technology

Technologies like blockchain can reduce cyber risks, which are a significant problem. Furthermore, blockchain technology in various industries has been used for specific advantages. More and more organizations adopt blockchain technology and hopefully, blockchain based seems to be the future of the internet. Because cryptocurrencies are growing and financial institutions rely on block chaining methods, global banking may change. See how this innovation will influence the future in this section (Hasankhani, Hakimi et al. 2021).

- **Blockchain Testing.** The performance of blockchain can be proven false to entice users. Understanding which blockchain complies with business requirements is important to oblige blockchain testing. Two phases support this. Blockchains are tested in the standardization phase based on certain validation criteria. The testing stage shows that blockchains are tested for various criteria (Ahmad, Saad et al. 2021).
- **Big Data Analytics.** When combined with blockchains, big data can lead to data administration and analysis. Data management ensures that data is saved and secured during data mining transactions.
- **Blockchain Miscellaneous Applications**. Traditional organizations could adopt blockchains to improve the functioning of their systems. Blockchains could implement the concept of an intelligent contract (Alam 2021).
- **Crime-Block Chaining Technology (Software)**. This can track criminals. It seems much more inexpensive than the present methods.
- **Banking Sectors.** Technology from blockchain could cut substructure costs, cross-border expenses, and trading safety. Central banks might be substituted with blockchains shortly.

- **Industries.** Blockchains can start creating and distorting new opportunities for the industry. The transactions between two parties are rapid and efficient without any third-party interference.
- **Governments.** Cryptocurrencies can influence finance in many countries.
- The human authentication factor can be eliminated.

In recent years, the smart manufacturing movement has advanced toward blockchain technology, physical and cyber capabilities to gain advantages. It is frequently observed by way of Industry 4.0, a term which originates from the German government scheme to inspire the fourth Output to create an easy decision-making process with the thought of cyber-physical schemes, apparatus and procedures in smart factories. The intelligent leverage in the manufacturing process is correlated with advanced large-data speed, volume, and variety (Borowski 2021).

In recent years, the growth and desirability of blockchain technology, particularly in the financial sector, have attracted attention (Shahbazi and Byun 2021). The use of big data techniques grows analytical strength and helps to predict. However, this capacity is based on contractors and installation approaches in most industries and has several features and speeds, i.e., their needs. The common ground between several productions can, therefore, assistance in clarifying and advancing specific industries' proficiencies.

Most regular blockchain applications are based on benefit transfer and distribute data over networks based on smart agreements ideal for companies and industries. Industry 4.0 focuses primarily on qualifying the relation among different production units, installations, retailers, etc. to support further the manufacturing industries centered on the overall value chain. This process automates and optimizes operations, improves flexibility, security, reduces costs, productivity, and profits.

However, industry 4.0 has many compensations and challenges in the manufacturing sector that stand in the way of advantages. Connectivity sums up most of the challenges of exchanging information between machines, etc. Figure 3.1 displays the process summary. This state takes into account the transaction between the producer

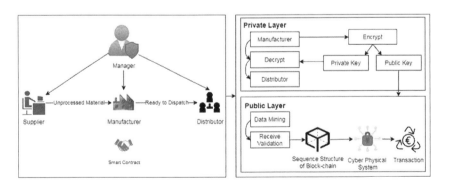

FIGURE 3.1 Outline of the proposed system.

and the supplier. There are two main layers for carrying out the producer's transactions in the proposed blockchain: public likewise private layers. In the first stage, the manager contacts the supplier, manufacturer and distributor to manage and monitor the manufacturing process to lower the failure rate. Intelligent manufacturing contracts have defined rules. Each layer contains the data kept in the blockchain. The private one mentioned in the product distribution process of the manufacturer. The producer initially decrypts and distributes the data supplied in the private layer. The dataset is also encoded in two main sections: private and public. The private key is linked to the decoded folder and the public key. The public mentioned on the transaction unit of this process. Before the transaction, a cyber-physical system was integrated to control and stop hacking. The first step is to manage and justify the payment data set in the data mining process. The dataset is then saved to the blockchain codified form and the payment is validated.

The positive aspects of this chapter are:

- Effective monitoring of the environment centered on IoT sensors.
- Reduce the expectancy of blockchain decisions.
- Securing distributed and transparent blockchain transactions.
- Use of intelligent contracts to improve the production network.
- Predict founded on manufacturing system error diagnosing.
- Apply large data tools to reduce mass production data.

3.2 RELATED WORK

Blockchain has been recognized to encourage transformation and creativity in current business theories and approaches. This technology has attracted a growing interest in management and processes from academia and industry. Although management research in the blockchain is getting stronger, this field offers a discontinuous summary of the present scope of knowledge study (Tandon, Kaur et al. 2021).

For global trade-related services, effective port supply chains and management are essential. The present port logistics programs are extremely centralized and offer limited opportunities for cooperation between different stakeholders. Furthermore, current systems do not ensure the traceability, transparency, security of information, and immutability of saved and exchanged data through different operational processes. As a result, the port terminal's productivity is adversely affected. Blockchain technology is emerging that offers auditors traceability, openness, and ability through unchanging data on trustworthy, intermediate, or trusted transactions (Ahmad, Hasan et al. 2021).

Blockchains, a disruptive technology with many applications in modern supply chain transactions, have not adequately reflected the theory. Researchers and managers must understand where and when blockchains are expected and investigated (Durach, Blesik et al. 2021).

In the advancement of decentralized applications, blockchain was very interested. A typical application class uses blockchain to manage company-wide business processes and assets. However, developers cannot develop such apps with no vulnerability, not least as the code deployed cannot be changed and anyone with network access can retrieve it (Lu, Binh Tran et al. 2021).

Blockchain is still growing and comparatively untapped. From the perspective of big data, this research assessed the need for blockchain throughout the supply management industry 4.0. The research method used for this study is a mixture of action research with case studies. In two industry case studies that have conducted and tested the constructed architectural design in a global logistical environment, the action research method was applied in particular (Sundarakani, Ajaykumar et al. 2021).

Blockchain technologies have become increasingly prominent in recent years, with many experts quoting potential technology claims in different aspects of industry, market, agency, or government. There has been an unbelievable number of successes in the short history of blockchain in how blockchain can be used and how multiple industries may be affected. The sheer scale and diversity of these issues can avoid tackling the potential and intricacy of blockchain, especially in terms of its purpose and strength and conditioning for a particular task (Berdik, Otoum et al. 2021).

As a solution to key financial challenges with a more effective and resilient recording approach, distributed ledger technology (DLT) is growing rapidly. Its success is mainly determined by the ability to transfer secure data over a peer-to-peer system in large numbers. Greater adoption raised concerns about its ability to expand and operate as a usable system in the real world. Optimizing the block size of the blockchain network is a big problem, as scalability bottlenecks prevent higher output and minimize latency. Increased block size can increase the transaction rate and make the system achieve its maximum transaction clearing capacity. The small block size is more effective associated with the greater block size, but the build/creation time of a block is too small. An effective blockchain app requires an optimal block size to achieve reasonable performance (Singh and Vardhan 2021).

The exponential increase in the number of smart policies and the information coming from these devices requires effective and stable access control, ensuring user and data privacy. Most conventional significant management engineering firms trusted on third parties, including a critical generation registration center and key management. The trust of a third party affects itself. It contributes to a centralized architecture and this article, therefore, addressed the problem by developing a distributed IoT architecture based on blockchain that uses Hash Chain to cryptographically secure management. The proposed architecture benefits from key features of blockchain such as openness, inflexibility, traceability, and fault tolerance to data security in IoT and thus provide a secure communications environment (Panda, Jena et al. 2021).

Blockchain technology becomes ever more attractive for the next generation, as it is particularly appropriate for the information age. The Internet of Things (IoT) can also use blockchain technology. The progress of IoT technology in various areas has resulted in significant progress in distributed systems. Blockchain design recognizes a decentralized network traffic storage and sharing data management system. This chapter describes the blockchain notion and important factors to analyze potential security attacks in detail and introduces solutions for attacks such as countermeasures (Singh, Hosen et al. 2021).

The recent increase in cyber-attacks, which focus on critical systems such as industry, medical, and energy ecosystems, raised strong concerns about safer alternatives. Although most of the recent industrial infrastructure depends on AI maintenance, predictions are based on malicious nodes certainly lead to life and capital loss. Of course, an inadequate data protection mechanism can easily keep challenging network quality and protection. The faults of conventional cloud or trust-based technology have led us to establish a different and efficient Industry 4.0 system based on the blockchain. After expanding blockchain throughout the consortium, the demonstrable framework removes the longstanding certificate authority, reduces data analysis delays, and improves economic performance. However, Industry 4.0's distributed safety model includes a cooperative trust rather than a particular country that essentially accepts the cost and threat of a single failure point. The multi-signature method of the suggested scheme completes multi-party authentication and confirms its usefulness for a collaborative cyber-physical system in real time (Rahman, Khalil et al. 2021).

As technology evolves quickly, i.e., from wired to wireless, human and device/machine communication has moved to a new level. Some new technologies/concepts have been developed in today's daily life. The Internet of Things, as well as cyber-physical systems, is one of them. The Internet includes integrating "Things" (things and machinery) to the Internet in general and eventually (also known as the connected Internet). In contrast, computing, networking, and physical processing are integrated by cyber-physical systems (CPS) (Nair, Kumari et al. 2021).

In advancing organizations, Industrial IoT sends each action of its entities to the next level for tracking and managing. However, several confidential issues and personal concerns about the interdependence, implementation, and communication between connected devices also called IoT devices. Although using sensing devices in the industry helps and decreases environmental efforts by improving quality and production costs. Several attackers may encounter various attacks by hacking different sensors/objects/devices (Rathee, Balasaraswathi et al. 2021).

In recent years, smart production, the fundamental idea of the 4th Industrial Revolution (Industry 4.0), is growing globally which is important. The development of smart technology has been motivated by recent developments in multiple information technology and technologies of production such as the Internet of Things (IoT), large-data analysis, artificial intelligentsia (AI), cloud computing, digital twin and cyber-physical systems (My 2021). It is very important to detect anomalies (or errors) in smart manufacturing in Industry 4.0 because failures usually do not immediately stop the system and may jeopardize all production processes. Thus, an online diagnostic approach based on Petri's prototype of a particular computer or part of a smart factory system is proposed to determine failure by saving a sequence of observational occurrences and updating the status of the observable event after every new occurrence to verify whether two sets of inadequacies have been met (Paiva, de Freitas et al. 2021). Table 3.1 illustrates related studies of blockchain technology.

TABLE 3.1   Related studies of blockchain technology

AUTHOR	TITLE	THEORETICAL APPROACHES	TECHNOLOGICAL APPROACHES
(Sicato, Cha et al. 2021)	Deep Learning Adoption Blockchain Secure Framework for Cyber-Physical System	Risk reduction approaches	Deep learning and blockchain techniques
(Snehi and Bhandari 2021)	Vulnerability retrospection of security solutions for software-defined Cyber-Physical System against DDoS and IoT-DDoS attacks	Software-defined Anything (SDx) paradigm has offered effective solution approaches to catastrophic IoT-based DDoS attacks	Software-defined Cyber-Physical System and recommends amalgamation of Fog Computing
(Li, Chen et al. 2021)	A blockchain- and IoT- based smart product-service system for the sustainability of prefabricated housing construction	Building Information Modeling and smart construction	Blockchain, IoT and Cyber-Physical System
(Gati, Yang et al. 2021)	Differentially private data fusion and deep learning Framework for Cyber-Physical-Social Systems: State-of-the-art and perspectives	Technological advancement in CPSSs requires the modifications of previous techniques to suit their dynamics	Data Fusion, Deep Learning and CPS
(Andronie, Lăzăroiu et al. 2021)	Sustainable Cyber-Physical Production Systems in Big Data-Driven Smart Urban Economy: A Systematic Literature Review	Technological and operations management features of cyber-physical systems constitute the components of data-driven sustainable smart manufacturing	Internet of Things sensing networks and deep learning-assisted smart process planning
(Madaan, Bhushan et al. 2021)	Blockchain-Based Cyberthreat Mitigation Systems for Smart Vehicles and Industrial Automation	Smart vehicles and ongoing advancement from motorized industries	Blockchain technology

(Continued)

TABLE 3.1 (*Continued*) Related studies of blockchain technology

AUTHOR	TITLE	THEORETICAL APPROACHES	TECHNOLOGICAL APPROACHES
(Prajapati and Reddy 2021)	Online Voting System Using Blockchain	e-Voting and Security	Blockchain technology
(Dehghani, Ghiasi et al. 2021)	Blockchain-Based Securing of Data Exchange in a Power Transmission System	Power transmission system	Blockchain technology and false data injection attack (FDIA) is launched on the information
(Gati, Yang et al. 2021)	Differentially private data fusion and deep learning Framework for Cyber-Physical-Social Systems: State-of-the-art and perspectives Considering Congestion Management and Social Welfare	Technological advancement in CPSSs requires the modifications of previous techniques to suit their dynamics	Data Fusion, Deep Learning, and CPS exchanged between independent system operation (ISO) and under-operating agents
(Lone and Naaz 2021)	Applicability of Blockchain smart contracts in securing Internet and IoT: A systematic literature review	Identify and analyze peer-reviewed literature that seeks to use blockchain smart contracts for securing Internet	Blockchain technology
(Shuaib, Alam et al. 2021)	Self-sovereign identity for healthcare using blockchain	The critical factor of the user record, privacy, and security	Blockchain technology
(Smetana, Aganovic et al. 2021)	Food Supply Chains as Cyber-Physical Systems: A Path for More Sustainable Personalized Nutrition	Securing Food Supply Chains	Cyber-Physical System and Machine Learning
(Egala, Pradhan et al. 2021)	Fortified-Chain: A Blockchain-Based Framework for Security and Privacy Assured Internet of Medical Things with Effective Access Control Vehicles in the Battlefield	Patient Security and privacy	Selective Ring based Access Control (SRAC) mechanism and blockchain technology

(*Continued*)

TABLE 3.1   *(Continued)* Related studies of blockchain technology

AUTHOR	TITLE	THEORETICAL APPROACHES	TECHNOLOGICAL APPROACHES
(Spathoulas, Negka et al. 2021)	Can Blockchain Technology Enhance Security and Privacy in the Internet of Things?	Security and privacy of transmission through the internet	Blockchain technology

3.3 METHODOLOGICAL APPROACHES

Figure 3.2 shows that the cyber-physical system is located at the blockchain layer to be more secure from hacking.

3.3.1 Smart Manufacturing Quality Control Design and Architecture

This segment discusses the system's comprehensive design. The system architecture based on the quality control blockchain is shown in Figure 3.2. The system proposed includes four major strands: an IoT sensor layer, a distributed leader layer, an intelligent contract layer, and an organization layer with different functions. The information leaflet quality, assets, logistical support, and transactions are safely distributed by blockchain

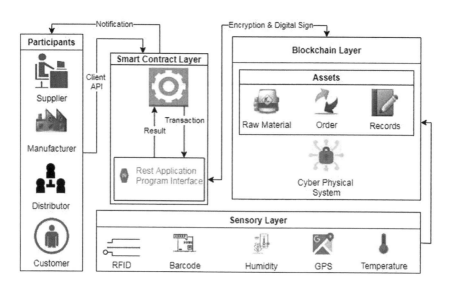

FIGURE 3.2   System architecture diagram.

technology and cyber-physical system. The smart agreement gives information, privacy, and automation to the system presented and the IoT sensor extracts data in real time.

The first layer, the sensor layer, customs GPS to track the logistics and the location of the products. RFID provides information on transactions, quality, and assets. Because of the in-height cost of RFID, bar codes can use procedures if the values of precision and data are low. In addition, related information can be collected by other sensors, such as temperature, humidity etc. The second layer is the blockchain layer containing four key elements: transactions, resources, logistics, and quality data. Each supply chain company retains the supplier, producer, logistics manager, retailer, and operator of the major bank copies of this information. The blockchain layer also contains CPS for more secure sensitive data. This data is used for quality monitoring and system efficiency. The third layer is the global market layer used to improve the supply chain performance by data collection/sharing. Digital identities are being used to control the privacy access authority. The possible explanation for this is that competing companies in the same supply chain must maintain confidentiality for specific information. Finally, various business activities in the business logic are covered. It can also monitor and control the quality and support agreements via blockchain.

3.3.2 Quality Control in Real Time

A lot of corporations also plant worldwide to enhance blockchain technology. When their data sets are shared within the plant and abroad, machinery, networks, attendees, parts, products, and logistics companies face security concerns. The best place for blockchain in any industry is for manufacturers to identify their needs and problems correctly. The manufacturer can choose the best choice and solve the problem of blockchain technology by providing challenges, possibilities, and industry understanding. In every production stage, from the collection of raw materials to the delivery of the final product, limpidity and confidence in blockchain technology are significant. Strengthening the supply chain aimed at improved unambiguity, observing material causes, managing business characteristics, asset tracking, quality assurance, and adopting standards are key points. Figure 3.3 shows real-time data monitoring using a blockchain system during the production process. Evidence of data quality and processing of artifact quality is assessed based on intelligent contracts, and feedback from this procedure is sent to the provider, constructors, etc. Different suppliers can afford smart contracts with digital characteristics. Each section has its own digital identity with a particular. In addition, a manufacturer cannot read this information, which is to evade see-through the information to other providers. However, constructors are intelligent to monitor the earnings based on the rules of smart contracts.

3.3.3 Digital Identity

The personal footprint plays a vital role in measurement structure security in connected devices. A user may need to profile him/her on numerous websites and use his/her data to use the online services. This data is stored and made available without the operator's

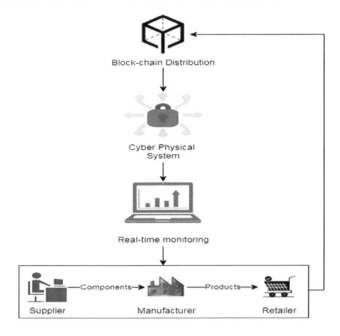

FIGURE 3.3   Real-time controlling as well as quality monitoring.

knowledge to third parties. Each user could have a distinct digital ID using these IDs by using the decentralized blockchain service for online activities and can process with advanced detection techniques. This method allows user data to be saved in the approval network and accessed by the user. Figure 3.4 shows the disseminated digital identity ledger blockchain. Data collected from the distributed ledger are centered on digital personality and access control of logistics machinists, providers, vendors, factory companies, and financial institutions.

3.3.4 Contract Automation and Logistics Planning

Suppliers access blockchain data and intelligent contracts to customer feedback and brand analysis to improve their production. Data from IoT sensors are used to detect and train the transport of a product for environmental information temperature, humidity, etc. The usefulness of intelligent contracts in the transport system is the smart transport of the product. The manufacturers and suppliers have access to transport information. The logistics plans are determined based on an intelligent contract's product position and volume. The digital identity also supports the system of logistics suppliers' confidentiality and struggle. Figure 3.5 shows the mechanization of the contract in the distributed ledger blockchain. The supplier, logistics manager, producer, and retailer can access the execution of the contract. The contracts are also uploaded to the distributed directory. The uploaded agreements are the input data for automated business goes and the system decided to pursue this process to improve safety and rules.

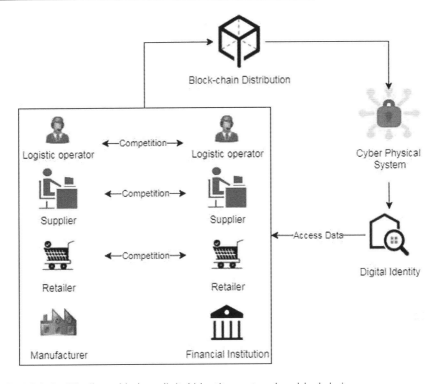

FIGURE 3.4   Distributed ledger digital identity centered on blockchain.

3.3.5 Blockchain Transaction

The procedure of execution is the transaction procedure in the industrial industry, which is clarified in this section. The user's aptitude to communicate to the blockchain structure is predicated on his registered ID as a front-end application. The administrator is responsible for registering users to permit definite employers to carry out the right transactions. A transaction suggestion requires user login data and demand for transaction predicated on listed documents. The transactions part the nodes following the completion of the procedure. There are two kinds of nodes: endorsers and committers. The endorser peers shall execute and validate the request message and reject it. The committer couples initially allow the transaction and write it into the block of the ledger. A supporter is a specific form of contractor used for smart contracts. In addition, the endorser is functional to extract a smart contract for the selected transaction before upgrading the leader to the proposed transaction in its simulated environment. The simulated endorser is an RW set. The RW set contains the applicable data before the deal and carries out the transaction in a virtual atmosphere. In the next phase, the contracted transaction is added to this solution based on the RW set and the customer returns the transaction to the manager. It has been updated with the RW set to arrange the dataset for a block at this stage. The data are compared with real transaction information, generated by nodes, and after matching, the contract is written into the ledger.

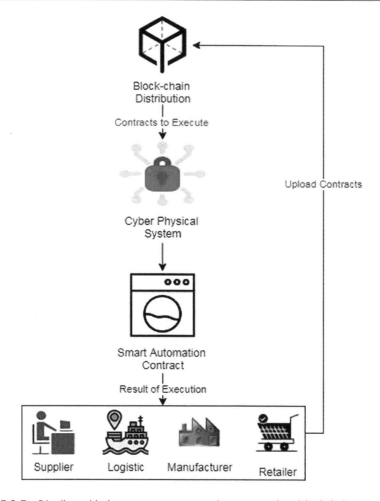

FIGURE 3.5   Distributed ledger contract automation centered on blockchain.

Finally, the update of the ledger is based on the data supplied. Finally, the committer server sends a state validation notification to the client. The REST API is used for the client-blockchain network process.

3.4 ISSUES AND CHALLENGES

- Blockchain slowdown when there are many users on the network.
- Some solution consumes too much energy.
- Blockchain implementation is a costly process and does not offer interoperability.

- It is hard to integrate into the legacy system.
- It still has a long way to go before it matures and gets standardized.

3.5 CONCLUSION

This study assesses multi-stage quality control-based blockchain solutions—data validation based on classification output performance. The main objective and novelty of the presented system by implementing an integrated blockchain and cyber-physical system is to improve smart production processes and environmental quality, secure the transmission, and generate excellent results. This system provides a safe environment for manufacturers and users to enhance business environments with wider reassurance. We plan to improve the network size to test and accurately validate the system's performance for more complicated production environments as part of the future.

REFERENCES

Ahmad, A., et al. (2021). Performance evaluation of consensus protocols in blockchain-based audit systems. 2021 International Conference on Information Networking (ICOIN), IEEE.

Ahmad, R. W., et al. (2021). "Blockchain applications and architectures for port operations and logistics management". Research in Transportation Business & Management (41): 1–17.

Alam, S. (2021). "A blockchain-based framework for secure educational credentials". Turkish Journal of Computer and Mathematics Education (TURCOMAT) 12(10): 5157–5167.

Andronie, M., et al. (2021). "Sustainable cyber-physical production systems in big data-driven smart urban economy: A systematic literature review". Sustainability 13(2): 751.

Baudier, P., et al. (2021). "Peace engineering: The contribution of blockchain systems to the e-voting process". Technological Forecasting and Social Change 162: 120397.

Bera, B., et al. (2021). "Private blockchain-based access control mechanism for unauthorized UAV detection and mitigation in Internet of Drones environment". Computer Communications 166: 91–109.

Berdik, D., et al. (2021). "A survey on blockchain for information systems management and security". Information Processing & Management 58(1): 102397.

Borowski, P. F. (2021). "Digitization, digital twins, blockchain, and industry 4.0 as elements of management process in enterprises in the energy sector". Energies 14(7): 1885.

Dehghani, M., et al. (2021). "Blockchain-based securing of data exchange in a power transmission system considering congestion management and social welfare". Sustainability 13(1): 90.

Dicuonzo, G., et al. (2021). "Blockchain technology: Opportunities and challenges for small and large banks during COVID-19". International Journal of Innovation and Technology Management 18(4): 1–25.

Durach, C. F., et al. (2021). "Blockchain applications in supply chain transactions". Journal of Business Logistics 42(1): 7–24.

Egala, B. S., et al. (2021). "Fortified-chain: A blockchain based framework for security and privacy assured internet of medical things with effective access control". IEEE Internet of Things Journal 8(14): 11717–11731.

Frolov, D. (2021). "Blockchain and institutional complexity: An extended institutional approach". Journal of Institutional Economics 17(1): 21–36.

Gati, N. J., et al. (2021). "Differentially private data fusion and deep learning framework for cyber- physical-social systems: State-of-the-art and perspectives". Information Fusion 76: 298–314.

Ghimire, B., et al. (2021). "Sharding-enabled blockchain for software-defined internet of unmanned vehicles in the battlefield". IEEE Network 35(1): 101–107.

Gopalakrishnan, P. K., et al. (2021). "Cost analysis and optimization of blockchain-based solid waste management traceability system". Waste Management 120: 594–607.

Hasankhani, A., et al. (2021). "Blockchain technology in the future smart grids: A comprehensive review and frameworks". International Journal of Electrical Power & Energy Systems 129: 106811.

Jamil, F., et al. (2021). "Peer-to-peer energy trading mechanism based on block-chain and machine learning for sustainable electrical power supply in smart grid". IEEE Access 9: 39193–39217.

Khan, K. M., et al. (2021). "Empirical analysis of transaction malleability within block-chain-based e-Voting". Computers & Security 100: 102081.

Li, C. Z., et al. (2021). "A blockchain- and IoT-based smart product-service system for the sustainability of prefabricated housing construction". Journal of Cleaner Production 286: 125391.

Li, C., et al. (2021). "Light weight block chain consensus mechanism and storage optimization for resource - constrained IoT devices". Information Processing & Management 58(4): 102602.

Li, T., et al. (2021). "Semi-selfish mining based on hidden Markov decision process". International Journal of Intelligent Systems 36(7): 3596–3612.

Liang, W., et al. (2021). "Data fusion approach for collaborative anomaly intrusion detection in blockchain-based systems". IEEE Internet of Things Journal. DOI: 10.1109/JIOT.2021.3053842

Lone, A. H. and R. Naaz (2021). "Applicability of Blockchain smart contracts in securing Internet and IoT: A systematic literature review". Computer Science Review 39: 100360.

Lu, Q., et al. (2021). "Integrated model-driven engineering of blockchain applications for business processes and asset management". Software: Practice and Experience 51(5): 1059–1079.

Madaan, G., et al. (2021). Blockchain-based cyber threat mitigation systems for smart vehicles and industrial automation. Multimedia Technologies in the Internet of Things Environment, Springer: 13–32.

Maity, M., et al. (2021). "Stochastic batch dispersion model to optimize traceability and enhance transparency using Blockchain". Computers & Industrial Engineering 154: 107134.

My, C. A. (2021). "The role of big data analytics and AI in smart manufacturing: An overview". Research in Intelligent and Computing in Engineering: 911–921.

Nair, M. M., et al. (2021). Internet of Things, cyber physical system, and data analytics: Open questions, future perspectives, and research areas. Proceedings of the Second International Conference on Information Management and Machine Intelligence, Springer.

Paiva, P. R., et al. (2021). "Online fault diagnosis for smart machines embedded in Industry 4.0 manufacturing systems: A labeled Petri net-based approach". IFAC Journal of Systems and Control 16: 100146.

Panda, S. S., et al. (2021). "Authentication and key management in distributed IoT using block-chain technology". IEEE Internet of Things Journal 8(16): 12947–12954.

Prajapati, A. and V. Reddy (2021). Online voting system using blockchain. Communication Software and Networks, Springer: 665–672.

Rahman, Z., et al. (2021). "Blockchain-based security framework for a critical industry 4.0 cyber-physical system". IEEE Communications Magazine 59(5): 128–134.

Rathee, G., et al. (2021). "A secure IoT sensors communication in industry 4.0 using blockchain technology". Journal of Ambient Intelligence and Humanized Computing 12(1): 533–545.

Sadeq, M. J., et al. (2021). Integration of blockchain and remote database access protocol-based database. Proceedings of Fifth International Congress on Information and Communication Technology, Springer.

Schönle, D., et al. (2021). Industry use cases on blockchain technology. Industry Use Cases on Blockchain Technology Applications in IoT and the Financial Sector, IGI Global: 248–276.

Shahbazi, Z. and Y.-C. Byun (2021). "Smart manufacturing real-time analysis based on blockchain and machine learning approaches". Applied Sciences 11(8): 3535.

Shuaib, M., et al. (2021). Blockchain-based initiatives in social security sector. The International Conference on ICT for Digital, Smart, and Sustainable Development, ICIDSSD 2020, February 27–28, New Delhi, India.

Shuaib, M., et al. (2021). "Self-sovereign identity for healthcare using blockchain". Materials Today: Proceedings (in press).

Sicato, J. C. S., et al. (2021). Deep learning adoption blockchain secure framework for cyber physical system. Advanced Multimedia and Ubiquitous Engineering, Springer: 195–200.

Singh, N. and M. Vardhan (2021). Multi-objective optimization of block size based on CPU power and network bandwidth for blockchain applications. Proceedings of the Fourth International Conference on Microelectronics, Computing and Communication Systems, Springer.

Singh, S., et al. (2021). "Blockchain security attacks, challenges, and solutions for the future distributed IoT network". IEEE Access 9: 13938–13959.

Smetana, S., et al. (2021). "Food supply chains as cyber-physical systems: A path for more sustainable personalized nutrition". Food Engineering Reviews 13(1): 92–103.

Snehi, M. and A. Bhandari (2021). "Vulnerability retrospection of security solutions for software-defined Cyber–Physical System against DDoS and IoT-DDoS attacks". Computer Science Review 40: 100371.

Spathoulas, G., et al. (2021). Can blockchain technology enhance security and privacy in the Internet of Things? Advances in Core Computer Science-Based Technologies, Springer: 199–228.

Sundarakani, B., et al. (2021). "Big data driven supply chain design and applications for blockchain: An action research using case study approach". Omega 102: 102452.

Tandon, A., et al. (2021). "Blockchain applications in management: A bibliometric analysis and literature review". Technological Forecasting and Social Change 166: 120649.

Velmurugadass, P., et al. (2021). "Enhancing blockchain security in cloud computing with IoT environment using ECIES and cryptography hash algorithm". Materials Today: Proceedings 37: 2653–2659.

Verma, M. (2021). "Modeling identity management system based on block chain technology". Journal homepage: www.ijrpr.com ISSN 2582: 7421.

Wu, Y., et al. (2021). "Blockchain-based privacy preservation for 5g-enabled drone communications". IEEE Network 35(1): 50–56.

Applications of Blockchain Technology and Related Security Threats

4

A Comparative Study

Amer Kareem and Rejwan Bin Sulaiman

School of Computer Science and Technology,
University of Bedfordshire, Luton, UK

Contents

DOI: 10.1201/9781003278207-7

4.1 INTRODUCTION

Blockchain technology is one of the emerging technologies in an IT world and without any doubt, it has altered the financial infrastructure to a greater extent. Bitcoin is composed of a backbone of certain cryptographical instances, referred to as the blockchain [1]. At some stage, Bitcoin has been banned in certain countries, i.e., Russia, European states, and other countries, because of the lack of centralized infrastructure and also sudden changes in the value of bitcoins itself. But as far as the security aspects of this technology are concerned, it has been adopted by a wide range of public and people have developed their confidence towards this revolutionary technology [2–4].

Blockchain technology emerges as an outstanding way of giving the opportunity of data storage so that it can manage the data and transmit the data over the platform in a decentralized manner without the involvement of any third-party firm or related organization. This technology has brought a big revolution in all private and public sectors. However, while looking at its base it has started from cryptocurrency and over the period of time it has contributed to a more significant extent in various credit assets. Even now, it has grown up in an information system and other sectors of data transmission. Confidentiality, reliability, authenticity, and availability are always a big concern about this technology.

Blockchain is one of the technologies spreading very quickly, and many firms and organizations are getting familiar with the ultimate advantages of its applications shortly. However, while considering all the positive aspects of this technology, security limitations and threats could make this infrastructure invulnerable to attacks [5]. Over time the ultimate possible weaknesses are getting exposed and the experts and researchers are working to put all their efforts into ensuring the integrity of this technology. Delays in the data transmission and the finite size of the blockchain have been in a serious consideration and possible solutions are implemented to reduce the risk caused by them [6–8].

4.2 BENEFITS INVOLVED IN SECURITY OF BLOCKCHAIN

The ultimate backbone of this technology for the users is to rely on the database, which is deprived of any physical medium like banks or corporations. Figure 4.1 gives the technical infrastructure of blockchain technology.

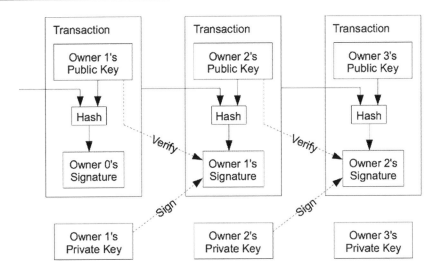

FIGURE 4.1   Blockchain system.

As shown in Figure 4.1, a number of blocks are responsible for generating data and providing the storage place. All the blocks are connected in a consecutive order to form the centralized data model. As shown, all the endpoint nodes of the users are involved in the authentication and management process of the data. And in case of addition of any new block required authentication for over half of the total available users, and the process of centralized synchronization goes overall user's platform once the new block is added. Afterward, when the process of centralized synchronization is established, the system won't allow making any alterations or formatting of the data [1].

According to all the technical aspects of the database of the blockchain, point to point network strategy and other cryptographic measures, it ensures the best possible security solution to the users in terms of the overall operation of the system as well as it keeps in consideration the bandwidth utilized in the distributed database strategy [9]. In terms of security point of view, blockchain technology has brought tremendous advantages, among which some are as follows.

4.2.1 Strategy of Antitamper

One of the great things about blockchain technology is that it is tamperproof, which doesn't allow any alteration of the data. This is achieved by the structure of data used in blockchain and building up that data. Figure 4.2 demonstrates the real operation behind the mechanism of its antitamper strategy.

As elaborated in Figure 4.2, whenever any transaction is added to the combined form of blockchain topology in its centralized data infrastructure, at the same instance, another timestamp will be noticed as well [10, 11]. And interestingly, any alteration of data performed earlier will no longer be allowed. And in any case of addition of

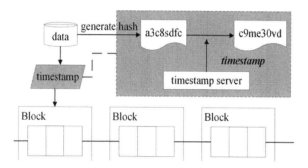

FIGURE 4.2   Antitamper operation of the blockchain.

transaction, it must be decided mutually by agreement method. In simple, the acceptance of the number of users are required to write the data in the block format and usually, this number goes up to 50 percent. In the case of the data monitoring process, the over networking nodes are required to consider possessing strong processing power for its operation.

4.2.2 Recovery Procedures

Blockchain technology utilizes specific protocols that are open source and involved in the monitoring of the data. Secondly, it synchronizes the storage data overall end-user platform. This strategy is quite different than the one used in a conventional database system, where it provides storage and monitoring of the data in one or multiple locations. In contrast, in blockchain topology, all the users have complete information about the data and they keep all the possible records of the generated data. However, in this case, redundancy is one of the factors that can be an issue to a certain level, but on the other hand integrity of the overall network is enhanced and due to this random attack will no longer create massive damage to the overall network system of the blockchain [12, 13].

4.2.3 Confidentiality

Blockchain ensures the maximum protection to the data by considering the privacy factor by utilizing the asymmetric method of data encryption and this method is quite more secure than others as it lets the users create their private key [14–16]. And the public is distributed across the network, which is used for user identification. The exciting thing about this terminology is the hash value that is not concerned with the actual user identity, thus ensuring the user's confidentiality and privacy. The scope of this strategy can be monitored because the user's private key cannot be known by anyone else, and it is impossible to generate the private key while using the public key. Figure 4.3 illustrates the confidentiality in the blockchain.

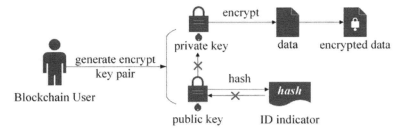

FIGURE 4.3 Confidentiality in the blockchain.

4.3 BLOCKCHAIN APPLICATIONS INVOLVED IN CYBERSECURITY

As blockchain technology was pursued while considering the Bitcoin evolution, at the root level, the blockchain system is quite transparent, open-source, and allows equal distribution. Relying on blockchain technology is that it uses complex cryptographic algorithms that ensure maximum protection and doesn't involve any conventional medium in the middle of its operation. Due to its excellent security insurance, it has become popular not just only in the cryptocurrency sector. Still, it has also gained huge importance in managing assets and credits. Over time, it evolves in various other sectors that typically involve finance, banking, engineering, medical, etc. The importance of its application is getting common day by day.

The taking can determine the scope of this technology in consideration of the financial sector where blockchain provides the best possible cleaning and other payment solutions without any alteration in the normal conventional system. No doubt this technology has played a significant role while increasing the ultimate efficiency of the business operation. Similarly, in the medical sector, this technology is being used to electronic medical data records over the various hospitals and clinics. It also provides a solution to various information database management. The same trend can be observed in the energy sector and others. The advancements in the security field have led to improvement and significant innovations in the building process of blockchains. Ultimately, this can be used as the best possible solution for the major privacy and other issues involved in cybersecurity [17]. There are a number of blockchain applications that are in use. Among them, some are as follows.

4.3.1 Domain Name System Security

The major function of the domain name system is to issue the name of the servers based on the IP address and vice versa. This strategy follows the hierarchical design and the primary operation is managed over the centralized DNS-based server. Due to this adoption, several attacks based initially on the servers could be possible. The most considerable ones are hijacking DNS servers, another DDoS attack, etc. While considering the scenario above, several studies are available based on the blockchain DNS. This constitutes building the domain name system while considering the blockchain used in Bitcoin technology [17, 18]. The overall secure communication is achieved by mapping the DNS with the hash. It could give the user flexibility to use this system by performing tasks that typically include registration, data transfer, and data checksum over the system. In this case, the node is always responsible for providing the storage place to the two generated keys by the asymmetric method, i.e. private and public keys. Other than that, it also records the domain names. This situation which combines the domain name system with the blockchain technology results in better encryption in the working of the blockchain system; this also results in providing a better security solution as this strategy makes the system decentralized and there is no longer any central place that could provide any favorable place for the attacker, as the storage of data has no any central unit to be a target. Based on the blockchain topology, which is built upon the DNS system, every single node of the system acts as the DNS server. As a result, there will be no threat of getting any attacks like Hijacking attacks and other related sniffing attacks.

4.3.2 Signatures with No Key Strategy

The advancement in the computer industry, which typically includes the massive development in quantum computers, can cause the breaking down of the conventional system of asymmetric algorithm standards. While considering the environment, where it is required to deal with a significant amount of data at a time, this results in the problem of publication of the key and the alteration and other updating issues. While considering this strategy, the researcher has come up with a solution to cope with these issues and threats by introducing the topology of keyless signature infrastructure (KSI) [19–22]. This keyless system takes the full benefits of considering the timestamp that can be used in blockchain technology. So, while looking at the operation of this keyless infrastructure, it utilizes and stores the available state of the data, the overall system, and the value of the hash. Afterward, the KSI system will add consecutive monitoring of the hash values while considering the timestamp. This results in adding more security in terms of any unauthorized access or any other type of attack to the OS and on various applications. So, this type of monitoring system is not required to perform the maintenance of the keys and the revocation process. This helps the KSI secure a large amount of data at a time. From the implementation point of view, it has various applications that are being used in a number of areas that typically include the nuclear sector and commonly in flood prevention systems that are widely adopted in the United Kingdom.

4.3.3 Security for the Storage of Data

For a long time, it's been pervasive about the number of incidents that have happened in the past due to the leaking of data to unauthorized access in the central database that provides the data storage facility. This didn't happen in the small corporation. It has affected certain organizations at the national level, which typically includes the area of finance, medicine, and so on. The loss of privacy in these areas could cause significant destruction as it deals with the most sensitive part. One of the solutions that have been proposed is the use of blockchain technology which can be utilized to secure and the management of the hash value, which typically includes the data of users identity, medical history, and another appointment scheduled in the medical sector [23–25]. With the use of the multi-signature procedure, there is the possibility of enhancing the security factor, which can restrict certain access by creating an access list/rules. Rules can only let the users make any changes or updates when the blockchain networking system grants permission to access. Implementing this strategy has greatly affected the medical industry by providing better healthcare to the people by keeping and managing the record of all the doctors, staff, and patients efficiently. This terminology is not just limited to the medical sector. Still, it has also explored its application in other areas as well i.e. certification of IoT devices [26, 27], decentralization of the data used in the cloud [28], and most importantly, in secure transmission process of data [29], as the use of blockchain technology greatly improves all these sectors.

4.4 SECURITY VULNERABILITIES IN BLOCKCHAIN TECHNOLOGY

The recent emergence of this blockchain technology has resulted in research work based on its advantages and many other valuable and secure parameters. After carefully analyzing various applications of blockchain technology, it will be clear that this technology is still at its beginning stage and still requires several amendments and alterations to implement this technology on a broader scale and applications. Undoubtedly, blockchain technology is an outstanding way of providing the best optimization in various sectors. However, security risks and other vulnerabilities are still part of the system. Despite its decentralization feature, it has already created specific issues that require serious attention. Following are some of the possible risks involved in blockchain technology.

4.4.1 Practical Limitations

Many technical points restrict blockchain technology from being a fully reliable component for data management. One of the aspects that must be considered is the limited capacity of the blocks involved in the blockchain. Because of this, many applications don't allow this technology to be implemented. At the early stage, each block capacity was given the value of 1 MB to prohibit attacks, especially the one based on DDoS attacks. And there always be an argument between the size of the blocks i.e. smaller or bigger. Although the big blocks can result in giving more storage capacity to accommodate more records and data, however on the other side, overall management and operation of these nodes of blockchain are interrupted. While the smaller blocks give a more reliable data management solution without the involvement of any organization, however, where it requires dealing with the big data, smaller blockchain cannot accommodate enough storage space for the data records.

The operation of blockchain technology involves a distributed system to store records and data. While in the blockchain operation, the system keeps the copy of each data at all the user's end, which is involved in the process, it can be noticed that the attacker will get several ways to access the records, which can be pretty destructive. However, at the same time, it is giving more exposure to the attacker to access the data in various ways. The worth thing to consider about the blockchain terminology is that it doesn't allow any user to alter or change records or data. However, even because of these certain parameters, an attacker can still find its way to attack the system, which typically includes data mining methods and other various ways, resulting in retrieving the sensitive data, which typically includes data about the network infrastructure, user personal information, etc.

Another major issue about blockchain technology is the risk of corporative attack, which assumes that most of the nodes involved in blockchain technology work smoothly and securely. However, suppose one or multiple nodes are applied together to operate 51% of the computing process of the overall blockchain infrastructure. In that case, they can combine altogether and cause an attack on the system, resulting in the alteration of the various contents available in the blocks. Other than that, it may cause severe attacks, which can cause massive destruction on a broader scale. Like DDoS attack is one of the common to be considered.

4.4.2 Threats Involved in Cryptography

The whole structure of blockchain technology relies on cryptographic standards and methods. In contrast, in this cryptography strategy, specific issues associated with blockchain technology are not resolved, mainly including the problems related to the management of the private key. The current scenario of various blockchain applications utilizes the private key to check the owner's identification while performing payment, etc. The significant risk involved in this strategy is the private key used by the user. The point to be considered is that the user is the only owner and knows its key without any third-party organization, i.e., bank. So, in this case, the user is the only one who can take care of its private key. The issue will arise if the user loses its key. This can result in a destructive situation for the user as it will not be able to get access to its various assets based on the blockchain without knowing its private key.

As blockchain technology is implemented on a broader scale, it creates specific vulnerabilities and weaknesses, usually based on cryptographic algorithms. The point to consider is that blockchain uses a complex algorithm, i.e., RSA, etc., to carry out its cryptographic operation. However, specific security weaknesses can be added during the implementation or maybe afterward, creating a backdoor for the attackers, even possibly to the algorithm itself. And this adoption of vulnerability in the system can cause severe destruction to the overall blockchain infrastructure or some of its applications.

Due to the emergence of quantum computing, it is causing the probability to crack the algorithms that are involved in asymmetric cryptography.

4.4.3 Issues with the Open-Source Strategy of Blockchain

Blockchain technology is involved in most of the applications associated with the upper layer, and it manages and operates various applications and its association with the users. To understand this strategy, it can analyze its application used in multiple sectors, i.e., medical records, finance, and other telecommunication sectors where the data is generated and stored and transmitted over the blockchain system. Due to the open-source nature of the blockchain system, it gives favorable environments to the attacker and hacker to exploit the various vulnerabilities of the system, which ultimately results in massive destruction in terms of data privacy and access.

4.4.4 Management of Blockchains in Terms of Security

In the case of blockchain systems, it is quite clear that it uses the distributed data strategy to store data, so to achieve that, there involves the continuous flow of data quite frequently to keep the whole system in operation as the blockchain structure consists of the storage of the copy of data at every user's side. And at the time when any transaction is made to a block, it will simultaneously update all the copies of data at the user's end. So, the users based on the wider geographical regions use this blockchain system. The quick processing of data results in improving the management of records and data transmission.

Another thing about the security of the blockchain is the consideration of anonymity technique which may cause problems towards the attack. According to the blockchain operation for the other users, they compute a hash value from the public key generated by a certain user. But the key thing to consider is the feature of securing the privacy of the users where it is impossible to keep track of the real identity of the users according to the rules and regulations of cybersecurity.

4.5 CONCLUSION

Due to the advancements in blockchain technology, individuals and organizations have high hopes for this technology. Its applications have been adopted in various areas, and even it has emerged into ICT. Besides that, due to its unique infrastructure, it is also being used in the finance sector. However, along with these advancements, many associated issues are considered a priority by the researchers and the experts.

Undoubtedly, this technology has brought a great revolution. Its applications are continuously expanding, and the advancements are at the pace. It is emerging itself into the already existing technology and developing a better infrastructure for the business operation. And at the same time, it is also challenging in the field of network security. This chapter has explored comparative research on blockchain technology and related issues while opening the future doors of considering those issues and coming up with the best possible solutions for introducing standards and other parameters so that its application could be adopted on a broader scale.

REFERENCES

1. N. Satoshi, "Bitcoin: A peer-to-peer electronic cash system," Consulted, 2008, pp: 1–9.
2. G. Varriale, "Bitcoin: How to regulate a virtual currency," International Financial Law Review, 2013, 32(6), pp: 43–45.
3. D. Swartz N., "Bursting the Bitcoin bubble: The case to regulate digital currency as a security or commodity," Tulane Journal of Technology and Intellectual Property, 2014, 17, pp: 319–335.
4. N. Wenker, "Online currencies, real-world chaos: The struggle to regulate the rise bitcoin," Texas Review of Law and Politics, 2014, 19, pp: 145–184.
5. M. Swan, "Blockchain: Blueprint for a New Economy," O'Reilly Media, Inc., 2015.
6. Bitcoinwiki, 2015, https://en.bitcoin.it
7. A.M. Antonopoulos, "Mastering Bitcoin: Unlocking Digital Cryptocurrencies," O'Reilly Media, Inc., 2014.
8. Double-spending, https://en.bitcoin.it/wiki/Double-spending
9. J. Yli-Huumo, D. Ko, S. Choi, S. Park, K. Smolander, "Where is current research on blockchain technology? - A systematic review," PLoS ONE, 2016, 11(10), pp: 1–27.
10. D. Tapscott, A. Tapscott, "Blockchain Revolution: How the Technology behind Bitcoin is Changing Money, Business, and the World," Portfolio Publisher, 2016.
11. B. Gipp, N. Meuschke, A. Gernandt, "Decentralized Trusted Timestamping Using the Crypto Currency Bitcoin," Proceedings of the iConference 2015, Newport Beach, CA, Mar. 24–27, 2015.
12. G. Paul, P. Sarkar, S. Mukherjee, "Towards a More Democratic Mining in Bitcoins." In: Prakash A, Shyamasundar R, editors. Information Systems Security. vol. 8880 of Lecture Notes in Computer Science. Springer International Publishing, 2014, pp: 185–203.
13. L. Wang, Y. Liu, "Exploring Miner Evolution in Bitcoin Network." In: Mirkovic J, Liu Y, editors. Passive and Active Measurement. vol. 8995 of Lecture Notes in Computer Science. Springer International Publishing, 2015, pp: 290–302.
14. G. Zyskind, O. Nathan, "Decentralizing privacy: Using blockchain to protect personal data," Security and Privacy Workshops (SPW), IEEE, 2015, pp: 180–184.
15. Ahmed Kosba, "Hawk: The Blockchain Model of Cryptography and Privacy-Preserving Smart Contracts," Security and Privacy (SP), 2016 IEEE Symposium on Security and Privacy (SP). IEEE, 2016, pp: 839–858.
16. Amer Kareem, Rejwan Bin Sulaiman, Muhammad Umer Farooq, "Algorithms and Security Concern in Blockchain Technology: A Brief Review" (August 19, 2018). Available at SSRN: https://ssrn.com/abstract=3234933 or http://dx.doi.org/10.2139/ssrn.3234933
17. H. Weihong, A. Meng, Sh. Lin, X. Jiagui, L. Yang, "Review of blockchain-based DNS alternatives," Chinese Journal of Network and Information Security, 2017, 3(3), pp: 71–77.

18. M. Ali, J. Nelson, R. Shea, M. Freedman, "Blockstack: Design and Implementation of a Global Naming System with Blockchains," USENIX Annual Technical Conference (USENIX ATC '16). Denver, CO, 2016, 25(2), pp: 181–194.

19. K. Deepak Tosh, "Security Implications of Blockchain Cloud with Analysis of Block Withholding Attack," Proceedings of the 17th IEEE/ACM International Symposium on Cluster, Cloud and Grid Computing. IEEE Press, 2017, pp: 458–467.

20. Xueping Liang, "Provchain: A Blockchain-Based Data Provenance Architecture in Cloud Environment with Enhanced Privacy and Availability," Proceedings of the 17th IEEE/ACM International Symposium on Cluster, Cloud and Grid Computing. IEEE Press, 2017, pp: 468–477.

21. Christopher Jämthagen, Martin Hell, "Blockchain-Based Publishing Layer for the Keyless Signing Infrastructure," Ubiquitous Intelligence & Computing, Advanced and Trusted Computing, Scalable Computing and Communications, Cloud and Big Data Computing, Internet of People, and Smart World Congress (UIC/ATC/ScalCom/CBDCom/IoP/SmartWorld), 2016 Intl IEEE Conferences. IEEE, 2016, pp: 374–381.

22. Nitesh Emmadi, Harika Narumanchi, "Reinforcing Immutability of Permissioned Blockchains with Keyless Signatures' Infrastructure," Proceedings of the 18th International Conference on Distributed Computing and Networking. ACM, 2017 (46), pp: 1–6.

23. Asaph Azaria, "Medrec: Using blockchain for medical data access and permission management," International Conference on Open and Big Data (OBD). IEEE, 2016, pp: 25–30.

24. Xiao Yue, "Healthcare data gateways: Found healthcare intelligence on blockchain with novel privacy risk control," Journal of Medical Systems, 2016, 40(10), pp: 1–8.

25. Ariel Ekblaw, "A Case Study for Blockchain in Healthcare: 'MedRec' Prototype for Electronic Health Records and Medical Research Data," Proceedings of IEEE Open & Big Data Conference, 2016, pp: 1–13.

26. Konstantinos Christidis, Michael Devetsikiotis, "Blockchains and smart contracts for the internet of things," IEEE Access, 2016, 4, pp: 2292–2303.

27. Yu Zhang, Jiangtao Wen, "The IoT electric business model: Using blockchain technology for the internet of things," Peer-to-Peer Networking and Applications, 2017, 10, pp: 983–994.

28. Wilkinson, S., Lowry, J., & Boshevski, T. (2014). Metadisk a blockchain-based decentralized file storage application. *Storj Labs Inc., Technical Report, hal*, 1–11. https://www.diplomatie.gouv.fr/IMG/pdf/sante_mondiale_en_web_cle4c7677-1.pdf, 2014

29. Rejwan Bin Sulaiman, Ranjana Lakshmi Patel, "Statistical In-depth Security Analysis for Vehicle to Everything Communication Over 5g Network" (December 24, 2021). Available at SSRN: https://ssrn.com/abstract=3509351 or http://dx.doi.org/10.2139/ssrn.3509351

Smart Applications of Big Data and Blockchain

Challenges and Solutions

5

Swathi Lakkineni
University of the Cumberlands, Williamsburg, Kentucky

Lo'ai Tawalbeh
Texas A&M University, College Station, Texas

Contents

DOI: 10.1201/9781003278207-8

5.1 SMART APPLICATIONS OF BIG DATA AND BLOCKCHAIN: CHALLENGES AND SOLUTIONS

Internet of Things (IoT) slowly raised from consumer usage to usage in the manufacturing process. Because of IoT's benefits in the manufacturing process, industry owners are fostered to implement them. Although the generated data from Manufacturing Internet of Things (MIoT) adds value to the industrial process, there are challenges encountered in analyzing the collected and stored data. Also, the uncertain nature of big data further affects the results of big data analytics and uncovers different kinds of challenges. Computational intelligence techniques are discussed that can help to overcome the challenges of uncertainty.

Integrating big data with Business Intelligence leverages the vast amounts of information that gets accumulated. As a part of the exploration of this fact, two case studies have been considered. The application of Business Intelligence transformed companies and earned profits.

Bitcoin is one of the applications of blockchain. But it is not accepted everywhere. A case study is explained about Switzerland, where Bitcoin was legalized, and another few countries where Bitcoin was not legalized. In addition to that, advantages and disadvantages of Bitcoin were also studied. Cybersecurity is another area where blockchain is applied.

Cybersecurity can be improved in different areas like IoT, networking, etc., by using blockchain. Gaps in blockchain and various attacks that happened with blockchain were also discussed.

Finally, a few use cases of blockchain in cybersecurity are discussed, which organizations can leverage.

There are five different concepts where blockchain and big data can be applied. It starts with discussing the application of big data and blockchain in e-governance. The advantages and challenges are discussed. The second one is about healthcare, and the third is about personal big data management, where a prototype is discussed to overcome the challenges of blockchain when storing big data. Fourth is about the importance of big data and blockchain in cryptocurrency. The last concept discussed is the application of big data and blockchain in fog-enabled IoT devices.

5.2 BENEFITS AND CHALLENGES OF BIG DATA ANALYTICS FOR MANUFACTURING INTERNET OF THINGS

Manufacturing has relied on data for a long time. Improve efficiency, performance and production, and minimize waste have all been attributed to the employment of this technology. Since Industry 4.0 and the Internet of Things (IoT) came into existence, the quantity of data available has expanded tremendously. Big data analytics are being used by manufacturers to do two critical tasks: the ability to effectively manage and utilize the massive volumes of data that their firm generates is essential for enhancing productivity and making better business decisions.

5.2.1 Benefits

By applying big data to the Manufacturing of the Internet of Things provides us with many advantages. Some of its benefits are discussed here.

5.2.1.1 Improving factory operations and production

Through predictive analysis of manufacturing data, predicting the customer demand, and then keeping machinery and raw materials ready for manufacturing is possible (Dai et al., 2020). For example, manufacturing of down coats can be made ready, forecasting a cold wave. Due to this, factory operations and machinery are best utilized.

5.2.1.2 Reducing machine downtime

Sensors deployed all over the assembly line collect data related to the machines' status (Dai et al., 2020). By analyzing the root cause of a machine failure, steps can be taken to avoid failures to reduce machine downtime. It also helps to detect if any machines are overloaded to balance the load among other machines.

5.2.1.3 Improving product quality

By analyzing manufacturing data, it is possible to identify defective goods and eliminate the root cause to improve product quality (Dai et al., 2020). Further, by analyzing marketing data and customer requirements, the product design can be enhanced.

5.2.1.4 Enhancing supply chain efficiency

The inventory supply can be arranged based on analyzed supplier data (Dai et al., 2020).

A lot of data gets generated from an increasing number of sensors, RFID, and tags, which on analysis can help reduce holding time of supplies and meet the customer demand.

5.2.1.5 Monitoring manufacturing process

IoT-based sensors combined with big data processing proved to be sufficient to monitor and detect faults in the manufacturing process (Syafrudin et al., 2018). The data generated by IoT devices is enormous that without a big data processing capability, it is hard to analyze and retrieve useful information. Fault detection is essential in the manufacturing process to ensure that everything is running fine. By applying DBSCAN to the collected data, outliers can be removed. The Random Forest method is further used to predict the faults in the manufacturing process.

5.2.1.6 Reduction in energy consumption and energy costs

Data collected through IoT sensors in the energy-intensive manufacturing process is further analyzed by big data technologies to identify wastages in energy (Zhang et al., n.d.). Thus, identified waste can be eliminated, which also reduces energy consumption and energy costs.

5.2.1.7 Reduction of scrap rate

Every manufactured product goes through a series of tests to determine whether the product meets the desired standard (Lade et al., 2017). Suppose if it does not, then the product is scrapped. By analyzing the data generated during the manufacturing process, it is possible to reduce the scrap rate.

5.2.2 Challenges

Many challenges are encountered when applying big data analytics to MIoT data. Dai et al. (2020) classified the challenges into three groups. They are challenges in data acquisition, data preprocessing and storage, and finally, generating data analytics.

5.2.2.1 Data acquisition

Data acquisition deals with collecting data from different sources and representing and transmitting it (Dai et al., 2020). As data comes in heterogeneous forms representing the vast data in a standard format is not easy. Similarly, transferring enormous volumes of data to a storage system is also challenging as it requires high bandwidth and industrial wireless sensor networks have to be highly efficient.

5.2.2.2 Data preprocessing and storage

The collected data should be integrated and cleaned to perform analytics (Dai et al., 2020). Below are some of the challenges encountered in this phase.

5.2.2.2.1 Data integration
Data collected from multiple sources in multiple formats is challenging to integrate (Yu et al., 2020). The data can be in many forms, structured, unstructured, and semi-structured data (H.-N. Dai et al., 2020).

5.2.2.2.2 Redundancy reduction
Data collected from different devices might have temporal and spatial redundancy that might affect the analytics (H.-N. Dai et al., 2020). Therefore, eliminating data redundancy is not easy.

5.2.2.2.3 Data cleaning and data compression
Due to defects in the machinery or sensor errors, the collected data might have noise and errors (Dai et al., 2020). Therefore, it is crucial to clean the data before performing the analytics to be accurate. But the volume of data generated through manufacturing IoT devices is vast. Therefore, efficient schemes have to be designed to compress the data and then clean the data for analytics purposes. Further discussed are the challenges in data storage.

5.2.2.2.4 Reliability and persistence of data storage
One of the big data analytics requirements is the reliability and persistence of the data (Dai et al., 2020). It is challenging to meet the requirement because storing tremendous amounts of data also has a cost associated with it.

5.2.2.2.5 Scalability
As data generated by various machines, sensors are in huge number, the storage to save the data is always expanding (Yu et al., 2020). In addition to the storage, the tools and

techniques applied to the big data should also be scalable. For example, machine learning techniques, open-source tools should also be scalable.

5.2.2.2.6 Efficiency
There is a prodigious number of queries that access the data concurrently (Dai et al., 2020). Therefore, the data storage should be efficient, reliable, and persistent in supporting the analytics.

5.2.2.3 Data analytics

After collecting data, preprocessing, and storing, the last phase is to generate data analytics, which further presents the below challenges.

5.2.2.3.1 Data temporal and spatial correlation
The data from conventional data warehouses are different from the MIoT data. MIoT data is spatially and temporally correlated (Dai et al., 2020). Extracting valuable information from such data is challenging.

5.2.2.3.2 Efficient data mining schemes
The conventional data mining schemes may not apply to MIoT data because of its volume and nature (Dai et al., 2020). Efficient data mining schemes have to be designed to manage the tremendous volume and uncertainty of MIoT data.

5.2.2.3.3 Privacy and security
It is also essential to take care of the data's privacy and security while generating analytics (Dai et al., 2020). The conventional schemes cannot be applied to MIoT data due to its volume, heterogeneous structure, and spatio-temporal correlations.

Although multiple challenges are encountered while generating the analytics, the benefits add value to the industrial process. Next comes big data's challenges, primarily due to uncertainty. Computational intelligence techniques that help mitigate the challenges are discussed further.

5.3 UNCERTAINTY CHALLENGES AND COMPUTATIONAL INTELLIGENCE TECHNIQUES

There are a separate set of challenges encountered in big data analytics due to uncertainty.

5.3.1 Uncertainty Challenges

Uncertainty is a condition that represents unknown or imperfect information (Hariri et al., 2019). Each of the "V" that represents big data introduces many sources that bring uncertainty to the data. Because of the uncertainty, lot of challenges are introduced. When dealing with big data, security is also considered another challenge (Iqbal et al., 2020). Below discussed are some of the challenges introduced by each "V".

5.3.1.1 Volume

It is impossible to specify a specific limit to big data size (Hariri et al., 2019). Generally, data that is exabyte (EB) or zettabyte (ZB) is considered big data. But challenges exist for smaller data sets too. For example, Walmart collects 2.5PB of customer data every hour.

Continuous storage of this data presents scalability and uncertainty problems because the data storage technologies may not handle infinite amounts of data. Data Analysis techniques are designed mostly for smaller data sets and may fail when applied to extensive data.

5.3.1.2 Variety

Variety refers to different forms of data like structured, semi-structured, and unstructured data (Hariri et al., 2019). Structured data refers to a relational form of data and is very easy to analyze. Unstructured data, for example, refers to images and videos which is challenging to analyze, and to analyze semi-structured data, the data has to be separated from the tags. Uncertainty is introduced when converting unstructured data to structured data.

5.3.1.3 Velocity

It refers to the speed at which a vast volume of data arrives (Hariri et al., 2019). The processing speed of the big data must match the incoming rate of the data. The velocity presents itself as a challenge because it is crucial. For example, IoT devices continuously generate data. When used in healthcare, if the processing speed does not match with the incoming rate of the data, then delay in sending the results to the clinicians might injure the patient.

5.3.1.4 Veracity

Veracity refers to the quality of data and is categorized as good, bad, and undefined (Hariri et al., 2019). Low quality of data adds unnecessary processing costs. Due to that accuracy and trust of big data analytics is hard to achieve. For example, when performing analytics to mitigate disease, any ambiguities in the data might affect the data analytics process's accuracy.

5.3.1.5 Value

The value represents the usefulness of the analyzed data in making decisions (Hariri et al., 2019). The prior V's deal with the challenge of representing big data. Companies like Facebook, Amazon, and Google leverage the analytics and use them to make decisions.

For example, Amazon collects the user data and analyzes it, thereby sending product recommendations to its customer, thus increasing sales. Similarly, Google uses the location services data to improvise google maps services. Facebook analyzes users' activities to send target advertisements and also friend recommendations. Computational intelligence techniques can be applied to mitigate the challenges.

5.3.2 Computational Intelligence Techniques

Computational intelligence (CI) consists of nature-inspired algorithms designed to imitate human information processing and reasoning to deal with complex and uncertain data (Iqbal et al., 2020). CI is also a subclass of Machine Learning approaches. To handle the growing class of real problems, fuzzy logic (FL), evolutionary algorithms (EA), and artificial neural networks (ANN) form a triad of core CI techniques. Further discussed are each one in detail.

5.3.2.1 Fuzzy logic

Fuzzy logic uses linguistic quantifiers, which are fuzzy sets, and provides an approximate reasoning approach, qualitative modeling data, and adaptive control (Iqbal et al., 2020).

Linguistic quantifiers are also used to represent the uncertain real world, user and data defined concepts, and human interpretable fuzzy rules. Thus, represented data is further used for decision-making purposes. Due to big data's nature, collecting from different sources has many uncertainties, noise, and outliers. Fuzzy logic systems are capable of handling uncertainties. For example, creating models to predict the users' emotions has to deal with a lot of ambiguous data.

In addition to dealing with uncertainty, fuzzy logic systems can deliver results in a reasonable amount of time (Iqbal et al., 2020). Fuzzy logic is used to analyze big data generated by social networks to analyze public opinion. The experiments that were conducted to analyze Twitter data resulted in a high prediction rate and good performance. Similarly, fuzzy logic-based matching algorithms and MapReduction helped in clinical decision support. Further discussed are Evolutionary Algorithms that deal with another type of challenge.

5.3.2.2 Evolutionary algorithms

As mentioned earlier, one of the challenges of big data is its high dimensionality and sparseness due to high volume and variety (Iqbal et al., 2020). Evolutionary algorithms are another CI technique applied to explore the search space and meet high dimensionality. They are also used in machine learning problems utilized in big data analysis, such as clustering, feature selection, etc. EAs discover an optimal solution to a complex problem by imitating the evolutionary process and slowly developing the solutions (Hariri et al., 2019). For example, using a parallel genetic algorithm for medical image processing using the Hadoop system brings effective results. Artificial neural networks also play a vital role.

5.3.2.3 Artificial neural networks

Artificial neural networks are based on the parallel processing and information representation of neurons like animals and the human brain (Iqbal et al., 2020). They help to perform feature extraction and learning from experimental data. Feature extraction is essential as it helps to identify critical input parameters that affect the output. Therefore in big data analytics, it is vital to determine spatial co-relations between input variables at a given instant. At the same time, it is also essential to determine temporal co-relations between input parameters that change over time.

Feature learning methods are based on supervised approaches such as deep neural networks, convolutional neural networks, and recurrent neural networks (Iqbal et al., 2020). There are also unsupervised techniques such as deep belief networks. Deep learning approaches leverage supervised and unsupervised training. They are based on the principle of artificial neural networks with multiple hidden layers. First, unsupervised (bottom-up) training is used to produce a higher-level representation of sensory data. It can be further used for training classifiers (top-down) based on a standard supervised training algorithm.

Three types of computational intelligence techniques, such as fuzzy logic, evolutionary algorithms, and artificial neural networks, are designed based on human interpretation and reasoning. Therefore, they seem to overcome the challenges that occur due to uncertainty. The next part discusses the integration of big data with Business Intelligence.

5.4 INTEGRATION OF BIG DATA WITH BUSINESS INTELLIGENCE

Integrating big data with Business Intelligence leverages the vast amounts of information that gets accumulated. As a part of the exploration of this fact, two case studies have been considered. One is Bikers Haven Restaurant, where migration happened from a manual way of storing data as receipts to a Business Intelligence system. The second one is ChangQing Drilling Company, whose information systems were scattered, and data is distributed in different locations. The application of Business Intelligence transformed these two companies and earned profits. The case studies are elaborated further.

5.4.1 Bikers Haven Restaurant Case Study

Bikers Haven has become a popular restaurant in Tagaytay and Amadeo to serve authentic dishes to its customers (Alday & Rosas, 2019). But its success was affected due to its inefficient way of managing the data and manually storing the data. The way Bikers Haven does business is the manual way. That means all the transactions are done physically without retaining the data using technologies like data warehouse.

Decision-making regarding sales is based upon assumption and not based upon data. Some of the existing problems are reasons for inefficient data management.

5.4.1.1 Problem

The existing system problems can be classified into three types (Alday & Rosas, 2019).

One is data storage. The data is currently stored in different locations physically and is not accessible to everyone. The second is data retrieval. Due to the way the information is stored, the retrieval of data is time-consuming. And the last one is data management. There is no way to use the data and get useful information out of it, resulting in the data's wastage.

5.4.1.2 Solution

Researchers proposed few solutions to avoid the wastage of the data and efficiently use it (Alday & Rosas, 2019). For data storage problems, an efficient design for a big data solution is needed. For the data retrieval problem, a data warehousing solution is necessary so that business owners can access it from anywhere. And to solve the data management problem, data mining resources and tools are needed. In addition to the mentioned solutions, efficient forecasting methods are required to solve the Business Intelligence problem so that data can be used efficiently and effectively.

5.4.1.3 Methodology

As part of this research, a Web Design-based platform is used for data storage purposes where employees can track the data from the business into the system (Alday & Rosas, 2019). For business owners to retrieve the data from anywhere, a mobile platform is connected to the web design. GSuite's sheets and Microsoft's Excel is used to address the data management problems. Finally, Google Analytics is used to address Business Intelligence problems aligned with Rapid Miner for complexity and technological forecasting.

The usage of Google sheets made it easy for the employees to input the data (Alday & Rosas, 2019). Data owners were also able to view the data from anywhere, anytime, thus providing transparency. The usage of a web-design platform and connectivity to mobile devices enabled employees and data owners to view data on any device from any location. Security has to be implemented for data access based on the business owner's requirements.

5.4.1.4 Results

Through the employee's contribution and collecting logs of data, results are gathered (Alday & Rosas, 2019). Thus, gathered core information would be transitioned and cleaned for further migration to a Data warehouse. Thus, migrated data can be used for forecasting as data grows big. Forecasting the data helped the data owners visualize peaks in the sales. They were able to visualize sales hourly. The data owners were able to identify the periods when sales are low and can then decide upon replenishing the supply. They could also develop ideas to boost sales during the downtime, like introducing combos, etc. With the help of this prototype, the owners of the restaurant were able to survive the competition.

5.4.2 ChangQing Drilling Company Case Study

ChangQing Drilling Company has information systems built as per the need and are scattered (Xiang & Fang, 2017). The data is distributed among servers and in different databases such as SQLServer, Oracle, MYSQL, Microsoft Access, and Microsoft Excel. If the information is gathered, cleaned, and analyzed, it could help decide new drilling projects. For this reason, the first step is to integrate the distributed and heterogeneous data in a data warehouse.

5.4.2.1 Data integration

A data integration tool called kettle management is used along with extract-transform-load (ETL) to construct a data warehouse (Xiang & Fang, 2017). There are three modules in the construction of the drilling data warehouse. The metadata management module drives the entire ETL process and plays a significant role in the overall data process. The ETL management module is the core of the ETL process and handles extraction, transformation, and loading of the data from source to the target database. The task management module records configuration information.

5.4.2.2 Implementation of Business Intelligence

Once the data warehouse is ready, it needs to be integrated with online analytical processing (OLAP) and data mining techniques to generate data visualization reports (Xiang & Fang, 2017). Through data visualization, the company was able to view data related to the drilling speed. The company was also able to identify critical factors that can enhance the drilling speed. By improving the drilling speed, the company was able to enhance its return on investment.

5.4.3 Discussion

The idea behind the prototype used in Bikers Haven Restaurant was good, but the selection of tools might be better. GSuites have incompatibilities in the automation of input that further connects to the data warehouse (Alday & Rosas, 2019). The whole prototype combines the employee input data with data warehouse, data mining, and Business Intelligence. Before data goes into the data warehouse, it has to be extracted, transformed, and loaded, and the whole process is called the ETL process (El Bousty et al., 2018). The researchers did not mention the tool they used for the ETL process. It is one of the significant steps in integration.

Identifying patterns through data mining also needs efficient algorithms that were not mentioned by Alday and Rosas (2019) in their paper. There might be a scope of improvement at that point. However, Google Analytics and Rapid Miner provided required analytics to the business owner to improve the restaurant business.

Improvement in the return of investments was experienced by ChangQing Drilling Company after using the Business Intelligence (Xiang & Fang, 2017). In this case study, the implementation of a Data warehouse was one of the challenges because of the existing data's distributed nature in different databases. However, the data warehouse implementation was handled efficiently. Another good thing that was done in the ChangQing Drilling case study was improving data retrieval speed.

With the help of materialized squares and constructing the OLAP index structure, the data is retrieved faster from the data warehouse (Xiang & Fang, 2017). The data visualizations were also valuable as the factors that influence the drilling speed can be identified. It is important because by taking care of the influential factors, the drilling speed can be enhanced. The only thing that is not specified here is the selection of a data mining algorithm. The visualizations result from the application of a data mining algorithm, and they show an increase in the return of investments to the company. Data warehouse, OLAP, data mining, and visualization tools are the essential components that can help to integrate big data with Business Intelligence. Thus, the case studies prove that big data can be integrated with Business Intelligence, and no separate system is again needed. Besides integrating big data with Business Intelligence, it is also possible to combine big data with blockchain. Bitcoin is a well-known application of blockchain.

5.5 BITCOIN ADOPTION AND REJECTION

Bitcoin is not accepted everywhere in the world. A case study is explained about Switzerland, where Bitcoin was legalized, and another few countries where Bitcoin was not legalized. For example, Bangladesh, Vietnam etc. are some of the countries where Bitcoin was not legalized.

5.5.1 Bitcoin Adoption

Zug's canton was the first public institution to accept Bitcoins as a payment mechanism in 2016 (Kondova, 2018). The finance minister of Switzerland, Mr. Johann Schneider-Ammann, wanted the country to be a cryptocurrency leader. He also praised Canton of Zug as a model of making Switzerland a crypto nation. Many blockchain companies all over the world were attracted to the Canton of Zug. It is also the foundation of another cryptocurrency called Ethereum. Although the value of Bitcoin was on the rise for some time, it slowly declined.

In 2018 due to the investors' theft that has stolen cryptocurrency, the Bitcoin value decreased (Kondova, 2018). However, with the support of the police and politicians, Zug of Canton got its image back. Last year, there was an announcement that the tax payments for Feb 2021 could be accepted as Bitcoin payments (Zug/db, n.d.).

In 2016, Canton of Zug accepted payments for government services (Kondova, 2018).

But it was only up to $220. The Bitcoin payment amount for taxes now has a limit of 111,226.20$, which is CHF 100K. With this move, the Switzerland government encourages the citizens to get used to Bitcoin payments. Additionally, Zermatt in Switzerland will also accept tax payments in unlimited Bitcoin amounts starting this year. Italy, too, has started accepting a limited amount of Bitcoins for tax payments. Although Switzerland embraced Bitcoins, some other countries rejected them.

5.5.2 Bitcoin Rejection

Despite many advantages of Bitcoin, like decentralization, security, speed, there is also a negative side of Bitcoin due to which some governments did not encourage Bitcoins in their countries (Sahoo, 2017). For example, Mt. Gox (Magic: The Gathering Online eXchange) has suffered from fraud due to hackers getting access to the user's credentials (Sahoo, 2017). Before that, Mt. Gox used to be an online exchange for cryptocurrencies where users can buy and sell their Bitcoins. But after the fraud hit the exchange, it was closed. Similarly, Silk Road is another example.

Silk Road is a website that is exclusively designed for illegal activities (Sahoo, 2017). Its activities started in 2011. Money transactions for illicit activities such as drugs, malicious software, weapons, etc., were done in a cryptocurrency called Bitcoin. These transactions were quickly done as the parties involved are unknown to each other. In 2013, FBI captured Ross William Ulbricht, the creator of the Silk Road, and after that, the website was shutdown. FBI ceased a lot of money in this process where a large amount came from Ross William Ulbricht's computer. Thus, generated Bitcoins between 2011 and 2012 were further exchanged with Bitcoin exchanges.

Due to these fraudulent activities, the trust in cryptocurrencies has decreased (Sahoo, 2017). Many governments did not legalize Bitcoins or any form of cryptocurrency because of fraudulent activities. Below mentioned are some of the countries which restrict the use of Bitcoins.

5.5.2.1 Bangladesh

In 2014, Bangladesh Central Bank altogether banned the usage of cryptocurrency (Sahoo, 2017). It also mentioned that if anyone caught using virtual currency will be punished under the 2012 ACT for being involved in unapproved money laundering activities.

5.5.2.2 Bolivia

Bolivia, which is located in Central South America, banned cryptocurrency and made usage of any virtual currency illegal (Sahoo, 2017). The money that is approved by a central authority is only considered legitimate.

5.5.2.3 Russia

Russia also banned cryptocurrency usage, but it did not ban blockchain as it can enhance many online services (Sahoo, 2017).

5.5.2.4 Vietnam

Vietnam's government did not legalize Bitcoins and announced individuals and financial institutions not to use Bitcoins (Sahoo, 2017). It also mentioned that usage of cryptocurrency would increase money laundering activities.

5.5.3 Advantages and Disadvantages

There are both advantages and disadvantages of Bitcoin that made some countries accept while others still reject them.

5.5.3.1 Advantages

Further discussed are the advantages followed by the disadvantages of a Bitcoin.

5.5.3.1.1 Personal data protection

If the retailer or another partner's transaction is hacked and a hacker gets access to the financial and personal information, other users' personal information is still confidential (Dumitrescu, 2017). Until the private key is safe, the hackers will not gain access to the other Bitcoin users' data.

5.5.3.1.2 Lower transaction fee

The processing fee of a transaction is much lesser with Bitcoin than with a credit card (Dumitrescu, 2017). For a $100 fee, a merchant pays a $3.37 transaction fee, and when the same amount is processed using Bitcoin, it would only cost a $0.61 transaction fee. Therefore, some countries like China, Ethiopia, and Denmark would like to use blockchain technology to improvise their public services.

5.5.3.1.3 Protection through speed of transfer

Transfers through Bitcoin are much faster than the banking system (Dumitrescu, 2017). It takes 10 minutes to a maximum of 30 minutes to confirm a Bitcoin payment, whereas banks might take several days. Due to that, merchant can have his payment even before delivering the goods. Once a transaction is done, it cannot be reversed unless both parties agree upon that. Due to the speed of transfer in Bitcoin payments, merchants are protected from chargeback fraud.

5.5.3.1.4 Immunity to inflation

Bitcoin is immune to inflation. Its monetary inflation decreased from 2010 to 2017 as the Bitcoins were increased (Dumitrescu, 2017). The inflation is expected to decrease until the maximum limit of 21 million Bitcoins is reached. It is predicted to happen in 2060. Therefore, all these advantages made some countries like the USA and the UK allow Bitcoin currency.

5.5.3.2 Disadvantages

In addition to the previously discussed example, further discussed are the disadvantages.

5.5.3.2.1 Lack of solid anonymity

The flooding protocols used in Bitcoin technology do not guarantee a hundred percent anonymity (Dumitrescu, 2017). Therefore, every fifth user considers leaving the Bitcoin network.

5.5.3.2.2 Prone to scams

Every Bitcoin user will have his private key (Dumitrescu, 2017). If he/she loses that private key, then they will lose their Bitcoin amount. Many fraudsters scammed innocent cyber customers. Between 2011 and 2014, there were 10 million dollars that were scammed from Bitcoin deposits. Such scams include Mining Investment Scam, where customers pay for mining equipment but never received one. Similarly, exchange scams that promise higher rate but never deliver the money.

5.5.3.2.3 Trust

It might take some time for people to accept Bitcoin as everyone is used to regular payment systems like cash and credit cards (Dumitrescu, 2017). Older people are especially hesitant to invest in this new technology and be frightened about the virtual wallet. Some younger generations might be coming forward to experiment with the latest technology but may not be entirely investing in Bitcoin currency. Because of the Bitcoin's advantages and disadvantages, some countries accept Bitcoin, but some reject Bitcoins. But blockchain technology is not limited to Bitcoin. The benefits of blockchain technology are leveraged into several other areas like cybersecurity.

5.6 BLOCKCHAIN IN CYBERSECURITY

Cybersecurity can be improved in different areas like IoT, networking, etc., by using blockchain. A few use cases of blockchain in cybersecurity are discussed, which organizations can leverage.

5.6.1 Improving Cybersecurity through Blockchain

The current techniques that are available in cybersecurity offer a centralized storage system to authorize access (Taylor et al., 2020). However, blockchain uses distributed ledger technology that gives it additional power of not getting compromised quickly. Below are some of the areas where blockchain can be applied from a cybersecurity perspective.

5.6.1.1 IoT devices

Blockchains can be used to track data and malicious activity on the IoT devices connected to the network (Taylor et al., 2020). In addition to that, firmware deployment can also happen securely on IoT devices through peer-to-peer propagation. It also ensures device identification, authentication, and continuous, secure data transfer.

5.6.1.2 Data storage and sharing

Blockchain uses hashing techniques to ensure that data stored anywhere, including the cloud, is not tampered with and is secured (Taylor et al., 2020). Since blockchains are decentralized networks and have client-side encryption, changes to the data must be approved through consensus and shared across the network.

5.6.1.3 Network security

Software-defined networks security can be improved by authenticating stored data in a distributed and robust manner (Taylor et al., 2020). Public and private blockchains can be used to handle secure communication between the nodes in the network.

5.6.1.4 Navigation and utility of the World Wide Web

Wireless connection points can be validated by storing and monitoring the ledger's access control data (Taylor et al., 2020). Also, the DNS record information can be stored that helps in safely navigating on the webpages. Furthermore, blockchain has some direct applications in cybersecurity.

5.6.2 Application of Blockchain in Cybersecurity

Blockchain achieves trust among the users by applying cryptographic and mathematical algorithms and does not depend on any third party (Dai et al., 2017). The characteristics of blockchain technology like authenticity, transparency, and immutability made it applicable to various other sectors. For example, it is applied in financial sector, medical, IoT, education, and cybersecurity. Further discussed are some of the cybersecurity problems addressed by blockchain.

5.6.2.1 Secure domain name service

The centralized domain name service (DNS) is susceptible to attacks as the core functions of resolving the domain name etc., are located in a centralized location (Dai et al., 2017). A map can be established between DNS and hash using blockchain. Users can register, transmit, and revise domain names. Each block represents the public, private key of domain owners and resolved domain name. Since the information is distributed across the nodes, there is no centralized location to attack. Unlike a centralized DNS system, even if a node is attacked, there is no harm to other nodes in the network.

5.6.2.2 Keyless signature infrastructure

Authentication schemes that rely on keys suffer from the problem of key distribution, key updation, and key revocation (Dai et al., 2017). Recent research in blockchain resolves this problem by using key signature infrastructure (KSI). Each node in blockchain stores the state of the data, network, and hash. KSI will constantly monitor the hash value with a timestamp. Any change in the data changes the hash value and helps to detect unauthorized access. By using a timestamp-based monitoring system, there is no need to distribute, maintain, or revoke keys. KSI-based security protection systems have been applied in nuclear power systems and flood-control systems in England.

5.6.2.3 Secured storage

Information regarding finances and medical is usually stored in a centralized location, and unauthorized access to the information brings various problems to the organizations and the users (Dai et al., 2017). By using the hash value concept of blockchain, the data can be stored efficiently. Apart from the areas discussed, there are other IoT equipment certification areas, cloud data desensitization, and secure data transmission. Though there are advantages of using blockchain in cybersecurity, there are gaps identified.

5.6.3 Gaps and Resolutions of Security Issues in Blockchain

The frauds that happened in a cryptocurrency network are increasing (Al-Dherasi & Annor-Antwi, 2019). The increase in fraud each year is slowing down the cryptocurrency market. Weak security systems and lack of government regulations are blamed for it. Another gap is the increase of quantum power. An increase in quantum power will make hackers break the key used for encryption in the blockchain. It is, therefore, feared to be a cybersecurity threat.

Similarly, one more gap identified is inexperienced users in the blockchain networks (Al-Dherasi & Annor-Antwi, 2019). Users who are unaware of safe practices in the blockchain are prone to get attacked by scammers. Thereby they provide insecure access to the blockchain network. Further discussed are three solutions to handle the security gaps identified in the blockchain.

5.6.3.1 Quantum computing

The gap related to Quantum Computing can be overcome by using a key with a higher number of bits (Al-Dherasi & Annor-Antwi, 2019). The reason is that quantum computers can crack keys with a lower number of bits quickly. Therefore, it is better to offer packages with 64 bit, 128 bit, and 256-bit cryptography so that users can choose depending on their requirements.

5.6.3.2 Dealing with inexperienced users

Proper training has to be provided for inexperienced users not to give away their keys to the scammers (Al-Dherasi & Annor-Antwi, 2019). Similarly, it is better to add two or three layers of authentication for verification purposes. Another solution is to track transactions using network features, alerting users, and confirm access to their systems.

5.6.3.3 User anonymity

The user identity in the blockchain network is hidden. Due to this, scammers and hackers are taking advantage of it (Al-Dherasi & Annor-Antwi, 2019). When a public key gets flagged, there should be a possibility to track the user's identity. The tracing also should be enabled to government agencies that deal with cybersecurity. This feature would create fear among scammers, so the probability of fraud might be reduced. Although blockchain has many features to improve cybersecurity, some attacks happened in the blockchain.

5.6.4 Cyber Security Attacks in Blockchain

According to Misra (2019), some attacks happened in public blockchains. Even though the decentralized nature of blockchain offered security, there are loopholes that hackers and scammers targeted. Below mentioned are some of those attacks.

5.6.4.1 DAO attack

A vulnerability called reentrancy vulnerability was exploited in decentralized autonomous organization smart contracts (Mishra, 2019). The attacker deployed withdraw function code into the contract, and that function executed every time the contract executed, allowing the hackers to steal six million US dollars.

5.6.4.2 Liveness attack

Bitcoin and Etheruem networks were hacked by a Liveness attack where the attacker prevents confirmation of a transaction (Mishra, 2019). It is done in three phases where a group of miners collide and store a transaction in a private block. The attacker will then propose a transaction to create a separate chain with more loyal miners. Thus, another transaction is again selected, ensuring denial of validation for selected transactions.

5.6.4.3 Eclipse attack

The attacker takes control of all the incoming and outgoing requests of a node and isolates it with the blockchain network (Mishra, 2019). Then, the attacker utilizes the computational power of that node. The eclipse attack gives way to attacks like selfish mining and engineering block races etc.

5.6.4.4 Distributed denial of service attack

In this kind of attack, the attacker generates malicious transactions with a higher transaction fee, and miners will pick that transaction and waste their computational power on it (Mishra, 2019). It, in turn, makes valid transactions to be waited to be validated by miners.

Organizations should deploy private blockchains with limited accessibility to overcome these kinds of attacks. Next discussed are the use cases of blockchain in cybersecurity.

5.6.5 Use Cases of Blockchain in Cybersecurity

Despite attacks, there is a lot of scope of applying blockchain in organizations where there is limited accessibility. Below discussed are some of the use cases.

5.6.5.1 Blockchain email

Phishing attacks are prevalent and can lure employees in clicking a button and download malicious code (Vance & Vance, 2019). A blockchain-based email system will have a record of each transaction and can enhance the chance of non-repudiation. Besides, modifying the blockchain-based email system was proven tamper-resistant.

5.6.5.2 Endpoint security

Endpoint security can no longer depend on the centralized protection method (Vance & Vance, 2019). Employees of an organization try to access the company's resources from any electronic device. Therefore, blockchain's distributed nature gives more security and protects a company's assets.

5.6.5.3 Privacy

Organizations that want to keep the customer's data, like personally identifiable information, safe can use blockchain technology and can ensure that the data is secure (Vance & Vance, 2019).

5.6.5.4 Smart contracts

Blockchain-based smart contract system provides encryption when sharing information in a distributed manner. It was not possible before without blockchain technology (Vance & Vance, 2019). Having discussed big data and blockchain's applications, the final section of this paper discusses combining big data and blockchain in various concepts.

5.7 INTEGRATION OF BIG DATA AND BLOCKCHAIN

Five different concepts are explored where blockchain and big data can be applied together. They are using big data and blockchain in e-governance, healthcare, personal big data management, cryptocurrency, and blockchain in fog-enabled IoT devices.

5.7.1 Big Data and Blockchain in e-Governance

Hou (2017) elucidated about "Guangdong Province Big Data Comprehensive Experimental Area" where Chancheng district was the first to implement blockchain technology for China's e-governance. It collaborated with a software company called 21ViaNet China Inc. to build a blockchain-based system for e-governance. Citizens can then find a one-stop solution to obtain government services securely.

5.7.1.1 Advantages

Further discussed are some of the advantages of applying blockchain for e-governance (Hou, 2017).

5.7.1.1.1 Enhancement in quality
The quality of government services can be enhanced (Hou, 2017). Documents like certificates, property papers, and public and personal records can be obtained on one platform. Each document can be provided with a digital identity. Since blockchain has immutability, all the documents stored in the blockchain are free from tampering. It would also help the government process the requests faster because the government will rely on individual credit rather than considering various other conditions.

5.7.1.1.2 Ease of access
The storage of citizens' records is not centralized (Hou, 2017). For example, identity records and permanent registered records are stored separately. Similarly, educational and employment records are preserved at the respective institutions. Due to that, citizens should go to multiple places to collect documents necessary for any public service. With blockchain's help, each citizen is given a digital identity that can help them access all their information in one place.

5.7.1.1.3 Strengthening trust
Once citizens' documents are managed by blockchain technology, there is transparency between the government and the public since any transaction to their data is visible (Hou, 2017). It also helps respective governments to manage better and govern.

5.7.1.2 Framework for secured e-governance

Although there are advantages of blockchain-based e-governance systems, there are a few challenges like scalability, flexibility, and security (Assiri et al., 2020). A framework was proposed so that the e-governance system is protected from internal and external attacks. The framework uses a combination of firewalls and intrusion monitoring systems to avoid suspicious traffic from entering the network.

The framework is comprised of different layers. One end of the framework represents users on the internet and is denoted as an untrusted network (Assiri et al., 2020). The other end is semi-trusted, where the connection has to be made to other user systems to serve the requests made by customers or citizens in an untrusted network. It is called a semi-trusted network. The zone between untrusted and semi-trusted networks is called DMZ (de militarized zone). There is another layer called secure intranet that contains various apps related to government services.

Placing the blockchain between secure intranet and DMZ results in a high level of confidentiality, trust, privacy, and access control (Assiri et al., 2020). This framework was proposed for Saudi Arabia. The proposed framework supports three kinds of access very securely. They are consumer to government (C2G), government to business (G2B), and government to government (G2G). Since the blockchain technology sits between DMZ and secure intranet, all three access types are done securely.

5.7.2 Big Data and Blockchain in Healthcare

Many sectors like banking and retail used big data (Bhuiyan et al., 2018). Healthcare is also one of the industries that can leverage big data. The data that gets generated every day is increasing. Healthcare data generated by healthcare devices, providers' computer systems, and wearable devices can be structured and unstructured. The data, when transformed into big data, can help in clinical decision-making purposes. Traditionally, doctors used to depend on their judgment in providing treatment. With big data, decision-making takes into consideration of the best available information. However, there are concerns regarding the privacy and security of big data in healthcare.

Blockchain is considered a solution for privacy and security. There are different types of blockchains, such as public, private, and hybrid (Bhuiyan et al., 2018). For healthcare purposes, a patient can choose a private or hybrid blockchain where he/she can decide whom to give access to their medical information. For example, to the healthcare provider, family, etc. In this way, the patient will have complete control over his/her health information. Otherwise, if a patient goes to four different providers, then he/she will have his medical information at four different places and cannot control any modification to his medical information.

In the case of blockchain, to add information, it needs the approval of at least half of the blockchain participants (Bhuiyan et al., 2018). The blockchain proposed for healthcare data consists of three layers. The first layer is the interface to the blockchain and is called the application layer. The second layer is the private blockchain that consists of nodes and an essential authoring entity responsible for generating public and private keys. The third layer is the encrypted database layer, where all the protected health information is saved.

When a health record gets created, it would be encrypted and stored in the database (Bhuiyan et al., 2018). Every time a new record is inserted, a pointer is made in the blockchain along with the creator information. The patient would also get notified. The patient can access his health records from anywhere in the world. He/she can control whom to give access to their health records.

5.7.3 Personal Big Data Management Using Blockchain

The data collected by companies and organizations is growing day by day and leads to big data (Chen et al., 2019). Such data must be efficiently stored and secured to avoid data leakage and data tampering. Traditionally all the data is stored in a centralized system and is more prone to attacks. The distributed ledger technology, consensus mechanism, and encryption technology of blockchain provide an efficient and secured way to store data. However, blockchain has limited storage space that makes storing big data a challenge.

The two ways to solve this problem are either to increase the memory inside each block from 1 MB (Chen et al., 2019). It would further expand as blockchain starts to synchronize and bloat the whole system. Another way is to reduce the block's size, which would increase the speed, but the storage problem still exists. The solution to this problem is to store the data represented in each block into a database. A prototype is built based on the idea that can resolve the capacity problem of the blockchain.

The prototype is developed based on Hyperledger Fabric blockchain (Chen et al., 2019). It is an open-source blockchain structure that has a throughput of 2000 transactions per second. More than 250 companies use it, including IT companies like IBM, Intel, Accenture, etc. The prototype runs on Ubuntu virtual machine, an Intel processor with 8 GB RAM and MYSQL Ver 14.14 simulation central database. With this, the personal data is ready to be stored.

The idea is to store only the personal data's core information into the blockchain and create a hash of the remaining data using SHA 256 (Chen et al., 2019). Core information refers to a person's first name, last name, date of birth, etc. Each block in the blockchain will then contain core information and the hash value of the remaining data. The hash value is further stored in the database. A comparison is performed with the hash value present in the blockchain with the hash value present in the database. If the hashes do not match, then the data has tampered, and if matched, then the information is reliable. In this way, the blockchain's performance does not go down, and the storage problem also gets resolved.

The performance difference is seen more when the data size grows (Chen et al., 2019). If all the personal data is stored in the blockchain, the performance is very slow. If only the core data is stored and the rest is stored in the database increased the performance. Only core data is stored without storing additional information; then, the performance was even better. But the problem with the last approach is that not all the data is stored, and similarly, in the first approach, where all the information is in blockchain, the performance was very slow. Therefore, the prototype not only ensures security through hashing but also improvises performance.

5.7.4 Big Data, Blockchain, and Cryptocurrency

Blockchain is the technology behind cryptocurrency (Hassani et al., 2018). The distributed ledger technology, immutability, and consensus protocol make blockchain ideal for cryptocurrency. In google trend analysis, the top searches were related to blockchain and cryptocurrency. Although blockchain is ideal for cryptocurrency, preserving the anonymity attracted cybercriminals that hacked blockchains. The other problem with the blockchain is the performance. Verification of a new transaction requires an acknowledgment from more than 50 percent of the participating nodes. All the processing requires high computational power and storage space.

Two technologies can be used to overcome the limitations (Hassani et al., 2018). One is TANGLE based on IOTA protocol and does not need a transaction fee, and is much faster in the machine to machine micropayments. The other is Hashgraph that uses gossip for consensus. The first one may not be widespread in use because there is no transaction fee, and miners might be discouraged. The second one is a patented technology and cannot be validated in a public setting. Apart from its limitations, blockchain has extensive applications in different sectors like banking, healthcare, IoT, AI, cryptocurrency, etc.

The nature of cryptocurrency makes it ideal for big data analytics (Hassani et al., 2018). As new transactions keep adding to the blockchain to generate cryptocurrency, the data keeps on increasing. Thus, generated data in a blockchain is structural and accurate and is ideal for big data analytics. Two main areas where big data and cryptocurrency interact are security and privacy, analysis and prediction. Research in the area of improving safety and privacy is progressing. Due to that, the application of blockchain in various sectors like banking and healthcare is also increasing. The same is repeating for analysis and prediction as well.

5.7.5 Big Data and Blockchain in Fog-Enabled IoT Applications

A device connected to the internet with processing and storage power is called an IoT device (Tariq et al., 2019). IoT devices collect a lot of information, including personal data. Hence, there comes a need to store and protect the information efficiently. Cisco expects to be 500 billion devices connected to the internet by 2025, and the data thus generated is enormous. Companies depend on cloud computing that provides an on-demand solution to processing and storage requirements. However, there are few limitations like low latency, insufficient bandwidth, mobility support, and location unawareness. Fog computing emerged to overcome the problems.

Unlike cloud computing, fog computing puts storage, computation, control, and management on the network side rather than creating channels to store in a centralized location (Tariq et al., 2019). However, there are still privacy and security concerns in fog computing.

There is no standard architecture for fog computing. The proposed architecture has three distinct layers: the core network and service layer, datacenter layer, and the device layer.

The core layer is responsible for providing functionalities to the end-user (Tariq et al., 2019). It comprises of devices such as routers, bridges, and switches, etc. They are also called fog nodes and can be deployed anywhere in the network. Datacenter layer is responsible for scalability, flexibility, computation, and resource sharing. The device layer refers to mobile IoT devices such as smart mobiles and fixed IoT devices such as sensors and RFID tags. As mentioned earlier, security and privacy are of significant concern.

Blockchain technology can be applied to address privacy and security concerns (Tariq et al., 2019). The immutability, decentralization, and security make it ideal for fog-enabled IoT devices. Another essential feature of blockchain is smart contracts. They define rules based on which authentication is carried out. Thus, privacy is preserved. Smart contracts are also able to sense malicious actions and breached blockchains reject updates. Besides, a unique GUID is provided along with a symmetric key pair for each IoT device connected to the blockchain network. However, there are also challenges in blockchain as the data starts to grow bigger. Therefore, further research is needed to overcome the challenges of blockchain. Using a database to handle enormous amounts of data and linking blockchain might overcome the difficulties of storing big data in a blockchain.

5.8 CONCLUSION

This chapter discussed the challenges and benefits of big data. The advantages of integrating big data with Business Intelligence are studied with the help of case studies. It also discussed Bitcoin and the application of blockchain in cybersecurity. Finally, it combined big data with blockchain and examined five different concepts to use blockchain for storing big data.

Although the solutions presented are feasible, there is still a lot of scope for research.

REFERENCES

Alday, R. P., & Rosas, M. F. (2019). Business Intelligence Solution for Bikers Haven Restaurant. *2019 IEEE 10th Annual Ubiquitous Computing, Electronics Mobile Communication Conference (UEMCON)*, 1204–1210. https://doi.org/10.1109/UEMCON47517.2019.8992956

Al-Dherasi, A. A. M., & Annor-Antwi, A. (2019). Dependence on Blockchain technology for future cybersecurity advancement: A systematic analysis. International Journal of Computer Applications, 117(23), 31–38.

Assiri, H., Nanda, P., & Mohanty, M. (2020). *Secure e-Governance Using Blockchain*. EasyChair Preprint no. 4252.

Bhuiyan, M. Z. A., Zaman, A., Wang, T., Wang, G., Tao, H., & Hassan, M. M. (2018). Blockchain and Big Data to Transform the Healthcare. *Proceedings of the International Conference on Data Processing and Applications - ICDPA 2018*, 62–68. https://doi.org/10.1145/3224207.3224220

Chen, J., Lv, Z., & Song, H. (2019). Design of personnel big data management system based on Blockchain. *Future Generation Computer Systems*, *101*, 1122–1129. https://doi.org/10.1016/j.future.2019.07.037

Dai, F., Shi, Y., Meng, N., Wei, L., & Ye, Z. (2017). From Bitcoin to Cybersecurity: A Comparative Study of Blockchain Application and Security Issues. *2017 4th International Conference on Systems and Informatics (ICSAI)*, 975–979. https://doi.org/10.1109/ICSAI.2017.8248427

Dai, H.-N., Wang, H., Xu, G., Wan, J., & Imran, M. (2020). Big data analytics for manufacturing internet of things: Opportunities, challenges and enabling technologies. *Enterprise Information Systems*, *14*(9–10), 1279–1303. https://doi.org/10.1080/17517575.2019.1633689

Dumitrescu, G. C. (2017). Bitcoin – A brief analysis of the advantages and disadvantages. *Global Economic Observer*, 5(2), 9.

El Bousty, H., Krit, S., Elasikri, M., Dani, H., Karimi, K., Bendaoud, K., & Kabrane, M. (2018). Investigating Business Intelligence in the Era of Big Data: Concepts, Benefits and Challenges. *Proceedings of the Fourth International Conference on Engineering & MIS 2018 - ICEMIS '18*, 1–9. https://doi.org/10.1145/3234698.3234723

Hariri, R. H., Fredericks, E. M., & Bowers, K. M. (2019). Uncertainty in big data analytics: Survey, opportunities, and challenges. *Journal of Big Data*, 6(1), 44. https://doi.org/10.1186/s40537-019-0206-3

Hassani, H., Huang, X., & Silva, E. (2018). Big-crypto: Big data, blockchain and cryptocurrency. *Big Data and Cognitive Computing*, 2(4), 34. https://doi.org/10.3390/bdcc2040034

Hou, H. (2017). The Application of Blockchain Technology in E-Government in China. *2017 26th International Conference on Computer Communication and Networks (ICCCN)*, 1–4. https://doi.org/10.1109/ICCCN.2017.8038519

Iqbal, R., Doctor, F., More, B., Mahmud, S., & Yousuf, U. (2020). Big data analytics: Computational intelligence techniques and application areas. *Technological Forecasting and Social Change*, 153, 119253. https://doi.org/10.1016/j.techfore.2018.03.024

Kondova, G. (2018). The "Crypto Nation" Switzerland 2018. CARF Luzern 2018. Controlling, Accounting, Risiko, Finanzen. Konferenzband, CARF Luzern 2018, 362.

Lade, P., Ghosh, R., Llc, R. B., & Srinivasan, S. (2017). Manufacturing analytics and industrial Internet of Things. *IEEE Intelligent Systems*, 32(3), 74–79.

Mishra, V. K. (2019). Cyber security in blockchain based system. *Scholastic Seed*, 1(1), 3.

Sahoo, P. K. (2017). Bitcoin as digital money: Its growth and future sustainability. *Theoretical and Applied Economics*, XXIV, 53–64.

Syafrudin, M., Alfian, G., Fitriyani, N., & Rhee, J. (2018). Performance analysis of IoT-based sensor, big data processing, and machine learning model for real-time monitoring system in automotive manufacturing. *Sensors*, 18(9), 2946. https://doi.org/10.3390/s18092946

Tariq, N., Asim, M., Al-Obeidat, F., Zubair Farooqi, M., Baker, T., Hammoudeh, M., & Ghafir, I. (2019). The security of big data in fog-enabled IoT applications including blockchain: A survey. *Sensors*, 19(8), 1788. https://doi.org/10.3390/s19081788

Taylor, P. J., Dargahi, T., Dehghantanha, A., Parizi, R. M., & Choo, K.-K. R. (2020). A systematic literature review of blockchain cyber security. *Digital Communications and Networks*, 6(2), 147–156. https://doi.org/10.1016/j.dcan.2019.01.005

Vance, T. R., & Vance, A. (2019). Cybersecurity in the Blockchain Era: A Survey on Examining Critical Infrastructure Protection with Blockchain-Based Technology. *2019 IEEE International Scientific-Practical Conference Problems of Infocommunications, Science and Technology (PIC S&T)*, 107–112. https://doi.org/10.1109/PICST47496.2019.9061242

Xiang, G., & Fang, W. (2017). The Research of Data Integration and Business Intelligent Based on Drilling Big Data. *Proceedings of the 9th International Conference on Information Management and Engineering - ICIME 2017*, 64–68. https://doi.org/10.1145/3149572.3149603

Yu, W., Dillon, T., Mostafa, F., Rahayu, W., & Liu, Y. (2020). A global manufacturing big data ecosystem for fault detection in predictive maintenance. *IEEE Transactions on Industrial Informatics*, 16(1), 183–192. https://doi.org/10.1109/TII.2019.2915846

Zhang, Y., Ma, S., Yang, H., Lv, J., & Liu, Y. (n.d.). A big data driven analytical framework for energy-intensive manufacturing industries. *Journal of Cleaner Production*, 197, 57–72.

Zug/db, C. (n.d.). *"Crypto Valley" Canton to Accept Bitcoin for Tax Payments*. SWI Swissinfo. Ch. Retrieved February 6, 2021, from https://www.swissinfo.ch/eng/-crypto-valley–canton-to-accept-bitcoin-for-tax-payments/46010364

Cybersecurity-Based Blockchain for Cyber-Physical Systems

6

Yassine Maleh
University Sultan Moulay Slimane, Beni-Mellal, Morocco

Ahmed A. Abd El-Latif
Menoufia University, Al Minufiyah, Egypt

Saad Motahhir
Sidi Mohamed Ben Abdellah University, Fes, Morocco

Contents

DOI: 10.1201/9781003278207-9

6.1 INTRODUCTION

The term "blockchain" gained widespread recognition in 2009 with the launch of the cryptocurrency Bitcoin, and only lately have the potential for blockchain use in other fields been considered. Blockchain is a term that refers to a method of storing and processing data in computer networks via a chain of blocks. It does not relate to any particular type of data (Melanie, 2015). Each block in the chain can contain arbitrary data, including production processes, which allows describing the possibilities of using this technology in production systems (Porru et al., 2017).

The growth of cyber-physical systems (CPSs) and the industrial Internet of Things (IoT) necessitate the resolution of several data interchange and processing issues, including storage, access, security, and so on. Furthermore, there is a contemporary trend toward developing distributed systems rather than centralized ones. One of the essential characteristics of the IoT is its nodes' autonomy and capacity to interact with one another (Teslya & Ryabchikov, 2017). This is a service-based interaction in which specialized nodes deliver services to other nodes in the network. Some blockchain implementations use a smart contract mechanism to enable such interaction.

A smart contract is a self-executing script stored with other data in the blockchain. Each smart contract has its algorithm written in a specific programming language and automatically conducts any activities without the involvement of other parties. A smart contract monitors the fulfillment of specified circumstances and, using the given algorithm, takes choices based on them. Because every network member may sign a contract, this mode of engagement extends to IoT nodes. This technique creates a dependable environment for transferring network nodes and makes services visible and uniform. Furthermore, because all contracts are already maintained in blockchain, there is no need to construct a separate service registry (Christidis & Devetsikiotis, 2016).

Blockchain technology is highly general; many of its applications are now employed in various domains of human activity (Daza et al., 2017). To effectively use all of the benefits of blockchain technology for developing CPS and the Industrial IoT, it is required to design the ideal blockchain network topology based on the tasks to be done and select the most relevant tools (software and hardware).

A CPS results from integrating computation with physical processes. On the other hand, some argue that it is a system that combines environmental elements with the computational part. Data acquired from the environment and actions correspond to the environmental aspects. From the moment there is a translation of data from the environment into the digital world, it is the responsibility of computing to handle this data. CPSs monitor and control the physical world, with the possibility of having sensor networks, as well as associated actuators (Monostori, 2014). Thus, this type of systems depends on the synergy between physical and computational components. On the other hand, and unlike traditional embedded systems, the CPSs emphasize a holistic view of the system, i.e., it is seen as a whole, and not only as several isolated modules. Figure 6.1 shows a basic architecture of a CPS.

CPSs have applications in a wide variety of areas, including high-reliability medical and life-support systems and devices, traffic control and safety, advanced automotive systems, process control, energy conservation, environmental control, aviation, instrumentation, distributed robotics (telepresence, telemedicine), defense systems, manufacturing, smart structures, and control of critical infrastructures (e.g., power grids, water resources, and communication systems) (Maleh et al., 2019).

So, after a detailed consideration of the concepts of "industrial internet of things" and "cyber-physical production systems", we can go directly to implementing blockchain technology in their structure.

There are two types of blockchain networks: global and private. The first is the most advanced and is typically employed to tackle global challenges. Global peer-to-peer networks are extremely stable due to many members, but they are inappropriate for

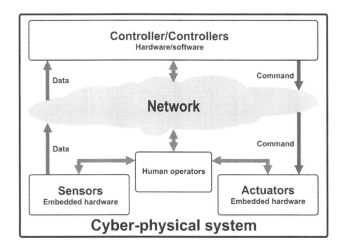

FIGURE 6.1   Cyber-physical system architecture.

building corporate networks comparable to the industrial networks mentioned above. The fundamental drawback is that all data exchange activities are rigidly bound to the cryptocurrency utilized in one or more global blockchains. Changes in exchange prices in the cryptocurrency market are nearly hard to foresee, making the cost of ownership of the planned CPS challenging to estimate. As a result, the architecture now under construction will be built on a private blockchain. The following blockchain functionalities should be implemented in the CPS:

- Organizing a single information space for inter-machine interaction within the CPS
- Ensuring the cybersecurity of the CPS
- Ensuring easy scaling and restructuring of the CPS
- Provision of redundancy of equipment and communication channels
- Organization of a single data storage facility
- Implementation of "digital twins" technology through the use of smart contracts
- Ensuring performance of common tasks for the CPS through the use of smart contracts

Blockchain technology was primarily used to protect storage systems, smart contracts, financial transactions, and notaries. Other applications, like healthcare, supply chain, transportation, and cybersecurity, swiftly recognized its benefits, as the sector realized it could increase its efficiency by implementing blockchain. This has resulted in an active field of inquiry, with researchers and scientists currently looking at various uses for this technology. Among the most commonly mentioned uses are healthcare, transportation, and cybersecurity. This paper's main contributions are as follows:

- Provide a detailed and in-depth analysis of the applications in CPS systems where blockchain is implemented.
- Identify the various challenges and limitations of blockchain applications.

This chapter is organized as follows: Section 2 introduces the core concepts of blockchain technology. Blockchain applications in CPS systems including healthcare, transportation, and cybersecurity are discussed in Section 3. Section 4 discusses the limits of the blockchain and offers suggestions for the future. Section 5 concludes this work.

6.2 BLOCKCHAIN TECHNOLOGY

It all started on November 1, 2008, when an anonymous article titled "Bitcoin: A Peer-to-Peer Electronic Cash System", signed by the pseudonym Satoshi Nakamoto, was published. It described the theoretical foundations for creating a new generation of electronic currency: decentralized, transparent, and independent of central banks and regulators (Nakamoto, 2008). However, it was not widespread and in the first months it was discussed in academic circles – among cryptographers, mathematicians, and programmers. Bitcoin, the world's first blockchain, which is the embodiment of the concept of this article, was launched on January 3, 2009 and has been successfully functioning for almost 10 years. Several thousand blockchains have emerged during this time, replicating Bitcoin with minor variations and bearing little resemblance to its progenitor. Satoshi Nakamoto's identity is still unknown, as he stepped away from Bitcoin development in 2010 and has never revealed his name or even the country where he lives. Researchers and journalists have put forward many theories about Satoshi, but none have been confirmed. There have also been many imposters who have claimed to be Satoshi Nakamoto, but not one of them has been able to provide sufficient evidence to back up their claims. To date, the public is likely to accept only one way to confirm Satoshi's identity: ownership of bitcoins he mined in 2009–2010. Satoshi is credited with more than a million bitcoins, which have never come to fruition except for a few test transactions sent to prove the blockchain is working. In particular, Satoshi sent the first-ever 10 BTC blockchain transaction to the famous cryptographer Harold (Hal) Finney, who was actively involved in the discussion of the theoretical foundations of Bitcoin. However, while all the glory of creating Bitcoin as the world's first workable blockchain undoubtedly belongs to Satoshi Nakamoto, the blockchain did not emerge as an isolated discovery that appeared out of nowhere, from nowhere. In fact, blockchain is the result of the synthesis of several trends in information and financial technology, united by the insights of Satoshi Nakamoto, whoever he may be. Among the technologies and solutions from which Bitcoin and blockchain emerged are commonly cited:

1. BitGold, a virtual monetary system created in theory by cryptographer Nick Szabo back in 1998, more than 10 years before Bitcoin appeared. BitGold was never put into practice, but its concept is almost identical to Bitcoin in some aspects of a decentralized payment network. Nick Szabo has been repeatedly "put on a pedestal" by declaring that he is Satoshi Nakamoto, but Szabo himself denies it. He is also the author of the term "smart contract". The smart contract was realized with cryptocurrencies and will be met many times in this book.

2. Proof-of-Work method, created by cryptographer Adam Beck in 2003 to protect against spam in the e-mail service HashCash. In the HashCash system, a user had to perform a certain amount of computation on their computer to send an email. This spared the system from mass mailings, most often commercial or malicious spam. The Proof-of-Work method was used in the Bitcoin blockchain to confirm transactions while ensuring the issuance of new coins. Figure 6.2 shows the illustration of transaction records of blockchain.

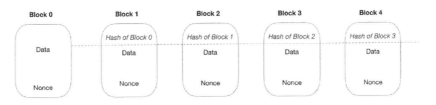

FIGURE 6.2 Transaction records of blockchain.

3. Public key cryptography emerged in the last century to ensure the security of electronic communications, including financial transactions. Bitcoin uses elliptic curve cryptography (ECDSA), sends transactions, and creates addresses using a classical pair of private and public keys. Like any other blockchain token, owning bitcoins is analogous to owning the private key needed to send it to another network participant.

4. Using a specific algorithm, hacking technology, i.e. obtaining a unique "fingerprint" of the original character set. It is theoretically impossible to get the same hash for two different character sets (so-called collision) or the original character set from the hash. The Bitcoin blockchain uses the widely used hashing standard SHA2-256, while other blockchains often use other hashing algorithms. The hash tree is used to form a block header, and calculating a hash of the required complexity is a computational task that must be performed to create a new block and generate bitcoins (mining).

5. BitTorrent technology of a peer-to-peer distributed file storage and transmission network. The block distribution method in the Bitcoin network is much the same as the distribution of files using torrents. In addition, peer-to-peer (P2P) file exchanges do not have a single control center, except for the source content and torrent files.

The blockchain industry becomes more mature every year, and many new projects are created with the identified exploitation problems of pioneers such as Bitcoin and Ethereum in mind. In addition to the term "blockchain", the phrase "distributed ledger" is also often used. There is some conceptual difference between the two, because a distributed ledger is a broader concept. We can even say that blockchain is a particular case of a distributed ledger. Government and corporate projects often create distributed registries with a hierarchical rather than peer-to-peer structure, where some nodes have a higher level of authority and can influence the entire network and make decisions without the support of the majority.

6.2.1 Blockchain Categories

We distinguish the decentralized public approach and the centralized private approach. The concept of blockchain appeared thanks to the emergence of crypto-currencies and Bitcoin.

To maintain transaction security and integrity, various cryptographic techniques are employed. Cryptography is used to validate transactions and produce new money in the Bitcoin electronic currency system, peer-to-peer or decentralized. There will be no need for a trusted third party using the protocol's decentralized fiduciary mechanism. Decentralization dictates that anybody can contribute to the code's development (although an entry fee must be obtained). If a transaction has been approved, it is added to the Bitcoin blockchain; otherwise, it is removed. Currently, Bitcoin is the most popular public blockchain system on the internet. Bitcoins are created in exchange for processing each transaction, according to the software source code. Users (miners) use their computing power to verify, save, and guarantee transactions and burn them into the blockchain. This work done by miners is called Proof of Work (PoW) and consists of solving algorithmic problems that are part of the Bitcoin protocol. Once the transaction is validated, it is time-stamped, added to the blockchain, and visible to the recipient and all network members. The blockchain described above and used to generate Bitcoins is a public blockchain.

A blockchain is considered private if the consensus principle is validated by a small and specified number of participants instead of a public blockchain. The ability to participate in transactions and the verification tasks are both determined by an organization. There is a private network with a predetermined number of nodes, such as a blockchain of location, described in the literature. A cryptography-based technique isn't required in a private blockchain. There are no miners, no proof-of-work, and monetary rewards on a private blockchain. These are the primary differences between public and private data storage and transmission systems (public key infrastructure). Thus, a blockchain of any sort is a low-cost, decentralized, and fully secure storage and data transmission mechanism.

Currently, private blockchain applications may be divided into three broad categories:

Applications for asset transfer (monetary use, but not only: securities, votes, industrial patents, connected objects, diploma security, stocks, bonds, etc.).

Applications of blockchain as a registry: Assets and products will be easier to find as a consequence. In a smart contract, the terms and conditions of a contract are automatically implemented by autonomous programs without the need for human interaction.

The choice of the consensus protocol is a crucial element of blockchains. Behind the technical dimension of this question lies a strong issue of security. However, this classification into a public, permissioned, and private blockchain are reductive, given the many characteristics that can be played on (Zhang & Lee, 2020). Table 6.1 shows two examples of classifications. In practice, these classifications are always imperfect. With the open-source software used in blockchains, creating many variants and playing with multiple parameters is possible, depending on the intended use. Some of these parameters are technical, while others relate to the system's governance.

6.2.2 Blockchain Explanation

Classic blockchain is much like existing electronic payment systems (EPS) and interbank financial messaging networks (such as SWIFT). Still, it has a number of differences in how it is communicated and managed. Blockchain nodes, called wallets, are analogous to bank accounts, just as a Bitcoin address is analogous to a customer's bank account number or SWIFT bank identifier (Chang et al., 2020). A blockchain wallet is an instance of blockchain access and transaction software. The wallet can run on almost any electronic device with an operating system, including a server, PC, laptop, or smartphone. A blockchain wallet has similarities to online banking, which provides access to money in a bank account. Still, the blockchain user has sole and complete control over their money and can independently start any number of wallets without providing

TABLE 6.1   Different types of blockchains

TYPE OF BLOCKCHAIN	NAME	THE REGISTER RECORD	REALIZATION OF A TRANSACTION	VALIDATION	EXAMPLE
Public	Blockchain without permission	Open to everyone	Anyone	Anyone, as long as they make a significant investment in computing power (proof of work) or in holding cryptocurrency (proof of stake)	Bitcoin, Ethereum
	Blockchain public permission	Restricted to authorized participants	Participants authorized	All or part of the authorized participants	Banks operating a shared registry
Private	Consortium	Restricted to authorized participants	Authorized participants	All or part of the authorized participants	Banks operating a shared registry
	Permitted private (enterprise blockchain)	Totally private or limited to a set of authorized nodes	Limited to the network operator	Limited to the operator of the network	Internal bank register shared between subsidiaries

personal information or documents to any organization. At the same time, the user is solely responsible for all actions with the wallet, and all technical and legal problems he will have to solve. The blockchain circulates virtual units of account, which can be used as money or perform certain technical functions. These units have the same name: bitcoin (Bitcoin, BTC, from "bit", a minimal unit of information, and coin, a coin) in the Bitcoin system. Because bitcoin was conceived as the electronic equivalent of gold, cryptocurrency monetary units are commonly referred to as coins. At the same time, the broader term "token", long used in IT systems and games, is now used for nonfinancial blockchains. As blockchain systems became more complex and tiered networks emerged, more or less established terminology emerged:

- Units of account that circulate directly on the blockchain are still called coins.
- Derivative units transmitted within the transactions of the main blockchain, that is, using it as a transport medium, are called tokens.
- In generalizations, tokens can be all virtual units of account circulating in the blockchain, regardless of the levels at which they are applied.

Each wallet has one or many identifiers, to which coins (tokens) can be sent. Each address is unique and the probability of creating two identical addresses in different wallets is almost zero. The movement of coins (tokens) between wallets in a blockchain is certified by a user's unique private key, which he uses to make a cryptographic signature of the transaction, thus certifying his authority as a wallet owner. A wallet's private key is the only proof of token ownership, and anyone who receives a copy of that key will have the same power in the blockchain as the owner of the original wallet. Therefore, the security of private keys requires the highest level of security possible. Hacking into the Bitcoin network from the outside is now virtually out of the question, as its reliability has been confirmed by many years of operation. However, individual hacking wallets or centralized services that handle cryptocurrencies and tokens cannot be ruled out. A wallet can also be lost after a hardware failure or natural disaster. The wallet or private keys can be stored in any number of copies, as long as you manage to keep them secure. If all wallet copies are lost, all bitcoins associated with it will forever remain immovable in the blockchain, since the private key is the only guarantor of their transferability. Therefore, the node owner (wallet) must be fully responsible for the safety of its assets.

To transfer coins (tokens) in a blockchain, so-called transactions are made – debits from one address and credits to another in financial blockchains or the transfer of information messages with different content in other types of blockchains. Each transaction is a financial message composed according to the established rules and signed with the sender's cryptographic key. The transaction contains the amount of coins (tokens) to be transferred, the sender's signature and the recipient's address based on his public key. To use the coins transmitted in a transaction, a private key must be paired with the public key specified in the transaction. Once transmitted to the network, the transaction must be validated, written into a blockchain block, and distributed to all nodes in the Bitcoin peer-to-peer network. The block contains a header for transmitting technical information and a list of transactions in which user data – payment or any other transaction – is transmitted. A blockchain consists of blocks connected in series. The previous block's hash is supplied in each new block's header. In this way, an unbreakable chain is formed. It can only be broken or changed by recalculating all block headers and reassembling the chain from the break point. This requires using computational resources equivalent to or greater than those expended in assembling the original chain. This means that the long-term security of a classic blockchain depends on total computational power. The most trusted blockchains are those that require a resource expenditure that is incomparable to the benefit gained.

6.2.3 Benefits of Blockchain

The blockchain, a distributed ledger technology, became known after bitcoin appeared in 2009 (Nakamoto, 2008). At first, the cryptocurrency was worthless, until it was used to pay for the first purchase – two Papa John's pizzas. It was blockchain technology that allowed the seller to transfer the money. How does it work? Every transaction on the blockchain network, such as a transfer of funds from one person to another, is translated as a block and added to the chain of other blocks in the chain. Such transfers are secure because they are effectively an encrypted message that only the recipient can open and use the contents. All transactions are undisputed and recorded in a blockchain that resembles a large ledger. With a blockchain, participants in a process store information about transactions and transactions between them. This data is visible to all of them and cannot be deleted or changed retroactively. This technology property opens up great opportunities for businesses and consumers: many processes can be simplified, paperwork and intermediaries can be eliminated, and all transactions can be controlled in real time. Companies can significantly reduce business costs, and their customers can get the final product at a lower price. Perhaps the only drawback of the technology to date is the small number of parties connected to it. In a blockchain network, all parties, including the manufacturer and often even the customs authorities, must be involved to maximize the efficiency of the commercial cycle, from the production of the product to its delivery to the customer.

The benefits of the blockchain include: eliminating the need for transactions, transparency, and immutability via the shared register and the fact that transactions cannot be deleted or altered, as well as the high quality of the blockchain's data due to its completeness, consistency, date, and wide availability. The use of a common transaction register reduces the likelihood of data loss or unavailability due to any malfunction. There are various new concepts governed by the blockchain, which will usher in significant change. The blockchain is a massive database. Take a look at some of the most frequent features; however, keep in mind that they can change depending on the intended use.

6.2.3.1 A decentralized system

The blockchain differs from conventional digital platforms in that it is a decentralized system, with a copy of the vast record maintained by each member. To avoid forgeries and other threats, there is no central server, only a collaborative administration system. As a result of this disintermediation, costs should be reduced.

6.2.3.2 A transparent system

The system is also completely open: anybody with access to the Internet may look up the register and hence the history of transactions at any moment (or by all network members). As a result, with a blockchain, it is feasible to guarantee complete asset or product tracking. While one individual uses a pseudonym, his actions are fully tracked.

6.2.3.3 A reliable system

The blockchain cannot be tampered with or altered in any way. Information that has been recorded in the blocks cannot be changed or erased after it has been placed there. With this new technology, an electronic document may be just as valuable as paper as a proof document. Because the copies are being multiplied, the decentralized approach provides some protection against piracy as well.

6.2.3.4 An automated system

The blockchain offers complete independence, up to the point of flawless monitoring, without the need for a middleman. Transactions are carried out using computer programs. Self-executing "smart contracts" will be available.

6.2.3.5 An efficient system

All of blockchain's advantages come together to guarantee maximum economic efficiency: time savings and lower costs due to the elimination of middlemen and automation and lower mistake rates and lawsuits. Such assets are understandably attractive when a lack of trust is frequently regarded as a significant impediment to growth. There are disadvantages to these benefits as well. The blockchain revolution must overcome several technological, organizational, and societal obstacles in order to succeed.

6.3 BLOCKCHAIN (BC) FOR CYBER-PHYSICAL SYSTEMS (CPS) APPLICATIONS

There are a lot of conversations going on in the world about blockchain technology. According to Gupta (2017), the blockchain is an information recording system customized with security features that make it impossible to hack attacks or cheat in the system. Abadi and Brunnermeier (2018) indicate a ledger system that decentralizes the records by distributing them across all the blockchain networks. Transactions in the blockchain system are distributed to all the system participants, making it hard to cheat or steal. They further indicate that technology's correctness, decentralization, and cost efficiency make an excellent record-keeping system. Their comparison of the system to the traditional centralized system highlights the tremendous revolution blockchain has brought to the record-keeping industry. One of the blockchain's essential features is the algorithms that permit record-keepers to rewind and undo false reports in the ledger's historical records. Besides the finance industry, the system is quite useful in procurement, internet apps, among other industries where transparency is highly required.

Businesses succeed by improving interaction with their stakeholders. Blockchain technology achieves this by offering a distributed ledger. The strategy allows businesses to utilize a shared database of transactions. The technology applies encryption mechanisms that focus on authentication and authorization of transactions.

E-commerce is one of the major industries that the advancement of blockchain has been enormously beneficial to the continuous and overall growth of the industry. Blockchain innovation is ready to change the internet business industry. It offers an unrivaled mix of security, straightforwardness, and cost-productivity. Entrepreneurs hoping to grow their endeavors should accept this turn of events and reclassify how they work. Blockchain technology has positively disrupted the finance and e-commerce sectors by offering new and effective payments, smart contracts, sufficient trading execution, and smart contracts.

Blockchain technology holds the key to unlocking new possibilities for organizations on a global scale to be more agile and efficient while providing an attractive price and secure environment. Blockchain is a technology enabling digital transactions between a human or an entity and an outside entity. The blockchain is a distributed database that stores information about everything. It is used to store a wealth of information about users, the networks that connect them, and any other connected devices. Each blockchain is called a "wallet" or "blockchain". These wallets store information recorded by the network. This information is known as the "transaction". Blockchain provides a framework for decentralized application developers, allowing users to communicate directly and secure their assets using cryptography. It will enable users to store digital signatures for goods and services securely. They can also send messages to each other. Some of these messages can be used to make payments, but this is still more than an intermediary service. It is the application-level layer where the application can perform operations. The application can be any operating system or application program with a blockchain backend (Ahram et al., 2017).

It is considered that blockchain can create a new way to control transactions and data flow on multiple layers without needing to have an exchange infrastructure and data centers. It allows the developers to add features to it as an efficient, trusted, and efficient solution. It is interesting to understand why and how blockchain works. The concept of blockchain differs from traditional banks as they are created by the people and are made to transact and manage their assets by themselves to avoid risk and make money. Blockchain is a platform that helps to create a central resource that will automatically act as a ledger where these resources and the records could be verified to validate the information.

Blockchain is undoubtedly the major innovation. I have seen massive growth in the application of blockchain to the industry. Not only has it led to the transformation of companies like Airbnb and Dropbox, and many others. This change in the way businesses operate will help drive growth and improve the business's efficiency. It will also help the government to get more people employed, the better quality of services. It has played an essential role for businesses by providing a cost-effective and efficient alternative to cash payments. Blockchain technology allows the payment system to function. It is also a useful feature in several applications, including digital identity, e-commerce, insurance, property management, e-payments, and crowdfunding. The fact that it facilitates the flow of data and information. The ability to verify every transaction made on a network. The ability to do things that are impossible in conventional financial institutions and businesses can achieve in less than two seconds. The speed at which companies and industries can create new products and services.

Blockchain technology is all about consensus, which is where the blockchain works. Blockchain has made a significant impact on businesses and in several industries. For example, the largest IT company in America, Accenture, said they are exploring a blockchain implementation to build blockchain-based applications. As with any technology, there are several uses for blockchain – for example, to enable automated, low-latency bidding through automated contract systems or systems of record for large, complex businesses or to make certain forms of transactions more secure and efficient.

This chapter focuses primarily on emerging blockchain applications for CPSs, namely medical records, transportation, e-commerce, finance, and cyber security.

TABLE 6.2   CPS application domains

SYSTEMS	APPLICATIONS	BENEFITS
Transportation	Automobile electronics, rail systems, road networks, aviation, and airspace management	• Facilitation of complex flow and equipment compliance management • Simplification of payment procedures • Traceability of flows • Reverse logistics
E-commerce	Monitoring and tracking of the supply chain to ensure openness in the market. Redesign of the payments system, secure e-commerce platform, product testimonials for the real deal	• Alternative payment methods • Better order processing • Enhanced payment security • Faster transactions
Healthcare	Automobile electronics, rail systems, road networks, aviation, and airspace management	• Medical data management • Clinical trial optimization • Drug traceability and anti-counterfeiting
Finance	Fraud prevention, financial inclusion, money laundry prevention, trade finance, smart assets and smart contracts	• Uberization of banking services • Facilitation of fund transfers • More secure and efficient transactions
Cybersecurity	Keyless signature infrastructure, user anonymity, validate transactions in CPS s, data authentication	• Permanent data security • Decentralization on a blockchain could replace certification authorities • Advanced authentication

Table 6.2 lists the various systems covered in the study, along with their respective application domains.

6.4 BLOCKCHAIN APPLICATIONS IN CYBERSECURITY

The current techniques available in cybersecurity offer a centralized storage system to authorize access (Koh et al., 2020). However, blockchain uses distributed ledger technology that gives it additional power of not getting compromised quickly. Blockchain achieves trust among the users by applying cryptographic and mathematical algorithms and does not depend on any third party. The characteristics of blockchain technology like authenticity, transparency, and immutability made it applicable to various other sectors. For example, it is applied in Financial Sector, Medical, IoT, Education, and

Cybersecurity. Further discussed are some of the cybersecurity problems addressed by blockchain.

Secure Domain Name Service. The centralized domain name service (DNS) is susceptible to attacks as the core functions of resolving the domain name etc., are located in a centralized location. A map can be established between DNS and hash using blockchain. Users can register, transmit, and revise domain names. Each block represents the public, private key of domain owners and resolved domain names. Since the information is distributed across the nodes, there is no centralized location to attack. Unlike a centralized DNS system, even if a node is attacked, there is no harm to other nodes in the network (Huang et al., 2013).

Keyless Signature Infrastructure. Authentication schemes that rely on keys suffer from key distribution, key updating, and key revocation. Recent research in blockchain resolves this problem by using key signature infrastructure (KSI). Each node in the blockchain stores the state of the data, network, and hash. KSI will constantly monitor the hash value with a timestamp. Any change in the data changes the hash value and helps to detect unauthorized access. There is no need to distribute, retain, or revoke keys when employing a timestamp-based monitoring system. In England, nuclear power plants and flood control systems both use KSI-based security protection system.

Secure Storage. Information regarding finances and medical is usually stored in a centralized location, and unauthorized access brings various problems to the organizations and the users. By using the hash value concept of blockchain, the data can be stored efficiently. Apart from the areas discussed, there are other IoT equipment certification areas, cloud data desensitization, and secure data transmission. Though there are advantages of using blockchain in cybersecurity, there are gaps identified.

Gaps and Resolutions of Security Issues in Blockchain. The frauds that happen in a cryptocurrency network are increasing. The increase in fraud each year is slowing down the cryptocurrency market. Weak security systems and lack of government regulations are blamed for it. Another gap is the increase of quantum power. An increase in quantum power will make hackers break the key used for encryption in the blockchain. It is, therefore, feared to be a cybersecurity threat.

Similarly, one more gap identified is inexperienced users in the blockchain networks. Users who are unaware of safe practices in the blockchain are prone to get attacked by scammers. Thereby they provide insecure access to the blockchain network. Further discussed are three solutions to handle the security gaps identified in the blockchain.

Quantum Computing. The gap-related to quantum computing can be overcome by using a key with a higher number of bits, because quantum computers can crack keys lower number of bits quickly. Therefore, it is better to offer packages with 64 bit, 128 bit, and 256-bit cryptography so that users can choose depending on their requirements.

Dealing with Inexperienced Users. Proper training has to be provided for inexperienced users not to give away their keys to the scammers. Similarly, it is better to add two or three layers of authentication for verification purposes. Another solution is to track transactions using network features, alerting users, and confirm access to their systems.

User Anonymity. The user identity in the blockchain network is hidden. Due to this, scammers and hackers are taking advantage of it. When a public key gets flagged, there should be a possibility to track the user's identity. The tracing also should be enabled to government agencies that deal with cybersecurity. This feature would create fear among scammers, so the probability of fraud might be reduced. Although blockchain has many features to improve cybersecurity, some attacks happened in the blockchain.

6.4.1 Application of Blockchain Technology to Validate Transactions in Cyber-Physical Systems

A relatively new trend in cybersecurity is the development of protection mechanisms and systems based on blockchain technology.

The blockchain ensures transaction integrity in the absence of a reliable central hub. System users' tangible and intangible assets are subject to transactions specified as specific activities taken from a predetermined list. Blocks containing transaction information are linked together using hashing to build a chain. To make it more difficult for an attacker to undermine the blockchain, a specific method known as a consensus algorithm is employed to distribute identical copies of the blocks to all system members.

The main advantage of blockchain, which makes the technology attractive for various data protection applications, is the difficulty of violating the integrity of stored transactions. Any change to a single block might have disastrous consequences for the rest of the chain, and it will have to be rebuilt from scratch. However, the computational complexity of this task minimizes the probability of blockchain hacking (Nakamoto, 2008).

At present, blockchain technology is actively used in CPSs for various purposes. As previously stated, the primary benefit of this technology is the ability to verify a variety of transactions that would otherwise be impossible in an untrusted environment. According to several studies, blockchain technology is crucial for the next fourth industrial revolution (Industry 4.0) (Alladi et al., 2019; Fernández-Caramés & Fraga-Lamas, 2019).

Furthermore, blockchain is being promoted alongside other promising technologies of our time as part of Industry 4.0 (Aceto et al., 2019). The IoT (Fernández-Caramés & Fraga-Lamas, 2018), big data (Zhaofeng et al., 2020), fog computing (Baniata & Kertesz, 2020), and augmented reality (Fernández-Caramés & Fraga-Lamas, 2019) are examples. In general, in the Industrial IoT, blockchain is widely regarded as a key technology, helping transform traditional factories into modern smart factories that use the latest breakthroughs in digital technology.

Let us mention some examples of current research that offer specific scientific and technical solutions to applying blockchain technology to solve security problems in CPSs.

The secure management of diverse assets, including those in CPSs, is an important element of the known works. Blockchain technology was initially used in conjunction with bitcoin. Therefore, this is what happened. With the advancement of blockchain technology, the cryptocurrency industry grew and today plays an essential part in society's daily activities.

Over time, the number of applications of blockchain technology has expanded considerably. For example, a recent paper (Bhushan et al., 2020) analyzes the utility of blockchain in solving the security problems of the smart city, which is an example of a large-scale CPS. The authors consider such components of smart city functioning as transportation, health care, smart grids, financial systems, supply chain management and data center networks, discuss blockchain technology capabilities in relation to these components, and suggest future research directions.

In general, blockchain technology research may be classified into numerous main categories.

The first group of studies is related to supply chain management using blockchain technology. This group is primarily general research, which does not focus on a specific area or a specific class of CPSs, but rather offers a general solution for secure blockchain-based supply chain management and discusses some aspects of the problem. In some cases, the proposed solutions are designed for use in CPSs for different purposes. In some cases, they are not explicitly specified in such a scope of use.

Thus, Saberi et al. (2019) presented the classification of barriers that prevent blockchain technology implementation in supply chain management. Aceto et al. (2019) discussed some of the challenges of overcoming these roadblocks. The precise asset is not provided in either scenario. A wide range of supply chain services and items are included in this set of research as well. Kshetri (2018) described real-world applications of blockchain for tracking raw materials, ingredients, or spare parts in various industries. In many CPSs, the emphasis is on leveraging blockchain technology combined with IoT technologies.

If not to be classified in more detail, the first group includes studies devoted to related tasks arising in organization and management of production. For example, the work by Yu et al. (2020), which presents an architectural solution for data integrity protection in cyber-physical production systems used in co-production.

The second group of studies aims to tackle the problem of risk-free management of a certain asset or service, including supply chain management of the associated assets. Today, there are a plethora of such applications to choose from. Blockchain is used to control sales or distribution of electricity (M. Li et al., 2020), fuel (Lu et al., 2019), computing resources (Seitz et al., 2018), and software.

All of the previous studies have one thing in common: they all involve trading commodities for money. As a result, blockchain-based solutions borrow heavily from cryptocurrency concepts.

The next group includes researches devoted to the problem of the organization of trusted interaction between multiple devices. The specific tasks related to ensuring the integrity of some or other data operated by such devices may differ.

Many papers deal with the interaction of arbitrary IoT devices without reference to specific types of CPSs. Some examples of recent works in this direction are Chi et al. (2020), Koshy et al. (2020), and Luo et al. (2020).

Most of these works focus on the energy efficiency of architectural solutions intended for use in IoT systems, and propose various ways to achieve this property.

In terms of the tasks to be solved, the works under consideration can be divided into those that only ensure the integrity of transactions. Those that, in addition, ensure the confidentiality of the data contained in transactions. For example, in a study by D. Li et al. (2020), data on the location of IoT devices are considered the object of protection. The authors point to the need to ensure the confidentiality of this data, so in the scheme they propose, blockchain is combined with encryption.

Turning from general solutions for the application of blockchain technology for data protection in CPSs, which are based on the IoT technology, to particular cases, it is necessary to note such a class of CPSs as connected vehicles, including unmanned vehicles (Cebe et al., 2018; Qian et al., 2020; Rathee et al., 2019). In 2019–2021, there is an "explosive" growth in the number of journal publications devoted to relevant research, so we can say that the security of this class of CPSs using blockchain technology is an example of a promising direction in the problem area under consideration.

6.4.2 Data Authentication in Cyber-Physical Systems

Digital evidence may be subject to an entire forensic process, encompassing the following stages: identification, collection, examination, analysis, documentation, and presentation (Evsutin et al., 2019). Preservation of digital evidence is an essential principle that should be considered in all stages of this process. For this purpose, blockchain plays an important role in ensuring the integrity and proof of origin of the collected evidence. On the other hand, the complexity existing in the operation scenarios of CPSs imposes, to the security solutions and methods used, restrictive non-functional requirements concerning scalability, computational performance, use of the communication network, among others.

Several blockchain techniques have been proposed in the literature to provide data authentication and prevent cyber-physical attacks. Evsyutin et al. (2019) provide an overview of strategies for embedding information into digital data in the IoT applicable at the end of 2018. As a result, the focus of this review is on new research that has arisen in recent years. At the same time, we should stress that only digital watermark embedding methods will be addressed in the context of this study. In contrast, digital steganography methods are often unrelated to data integrity.

At the outset, it is vital to distinguish between several research projects focused on the development of methods and algorithms for concealing information in digital photographs (as well as other digital objects), to ensure the security of sensitive data in CPSs. Examples of works in this area are Prasetyo et al. (2020) and Qian et al. (2020). Although their authors claim that their solutions aim to ensure data security in the IoT, they don't present any examples of how their algorithms may be used in other domains. In many of these research, the authors are worried about the security flaws in telemedicine systems.

Because such studies are so prevalent, they should be classified as a different class. However, the works in this class do not extend beyond the boundaries of traditional embedding into multimedia data and will not be studied further.

The following set of works also includes traditional data embedding into multimedia products. The authors identify unique data transmission situations specific to such systems and explain the limits associated with them while stressing the applicability of their solutions in CPSs.

This group's works are not as extensively represented, but they should be separated from those in the first group.

A solution for secure picture transmission in telemedicine systems is also presented in Peng et al. (2020). Encrypted confidential pictures are placed in photographs with non-confidential material. In addition, the fingerprint (perceptual hash) of the secret picture is included in the image container for further authentication. The tracking of the picture transmission sequence is a distinguishing characteristic of this approach. To that end, the authors offer the concept of a picture fingerprint chain by analogy with blockchain technology.

The research of Pu et al. (2019) is fairly unique in that it entails embedding secret attachments in graphics used in printed items. On the other hand, this research explicitly describes the potential applications of the proposed approach in IoT systems and the associated situations. These scenarios include, for example, offering data authentication in order to protect products from being counterfeited. There should be an emphasis on the endurance of digital watermark embedding in the authors' discussion on steganographic embedding.

The following works are unrelated to multimedia and deal with inserting digital watermarks in data created and transferred through CPSs. A substantial portion of the work in this group is concerned with inserting digital watermarks in wireless sensor network data for integrity control.

A comparable approach is proposed, among other places, in one of the authors of this review's papers (Evsutin et al., 2019). The ability to alter the degree of distortion generated by embedding is a distinguishing characteristic of this approach. As a result, it applies to sensor data of many physical types.

Hoang et al. (2020) incorporate digital watermarks into wireless sensor network data to protect against clone sensor nodes attacks. The embedding is based on a gamming-like modification of the binary alphabet. It is argued that the algorithm's lightweight provides an advantage.

The algorithms embed the digital watermark components into the sensory data consistently and independently since they are not dependent on the values of these sensory data or some of their features. While traditional digital watermarking methods and algorithms and the problem of wireless sensor networks and the IoT can create a digital watermark based on protected data, the notion is exceedingly wide.

In the simplest example, digital watermark components are created only based on the sensor data elements' values. The embedding approach provided in Xiao and Gao (2019) is an example. This approach generates the digital watermark bit inserted in the next sensor value depending on previous sensor values.

Separate embedding of digital watermark components offers various advantages; nonetheless, this technique poses a challenge with timing. Think about what may happen if a message arrives with the data out of order. The digital watermark extraction will be hampered even if there isn't an active intruder on the communication channel. Wang et al. (2019) offer an answer to this dilemma. Sensor data is divided depending on the key into variable-length groups, as proposed by the authors in their paper. Digital watermark chains are produced and implanted for pairs of adjacent groupings. A series of digital watermarks are used to verify the sensor data. Separators and data synchronization is provided by the second digital watermark chain, which encodes group separators.

Creating a digital watermark that contains sensory quantity values and some of their characteristics is possible in a more complex scenario. Ferdowsi and Saad (2019) proposed a novel watermarking algorithm for dynamic authentication of IoT signals to detect cyber-attacks. Data streams' stochastic features might be extracted and used to create digital watermarks. Spectrum expansion is a technique for incorporating digital watermarks into data streams. In Hameed et al. (2018), it is also addressed how to create a digital watermark using several aspects of the acquired data, such as data length, frequency of occurrence, and time of capture. Nguyen et al. (2019) creates a digital watermark based on CSMA/CA protocol collisions to deter sensor node clone attacks. Furthermore, the way the sensor data is portrayed is a distinguishing characteristic of the study. They are combined to make a matrix resembling a digital image. In general, such a system enables the adoption of methodologies that have proven successful when dealing with digital pictures with sensory data.

Using digital watermarks that represent binary sequences, all of the algorithms in the mentioned study work. Watermarking analog transmissions (particularly modulated signals) to solve signal source authentication is also a field of study. The answers discovered in those works are ideally comparable to those found in digital watermarking. The distinction is solely in the manner in which the signal is represented and, as a result, in the manner in which it is processed.

Sender authentication in systems matching to the Narrow Band Internet of Things (NB-IoT) standard focuses on research (Zhao et al., 2019). The notion of a radio-frequency watermark is used in the investigation. Rather than using binary sequences for future embedding, the watermark is first created as a digital one and then converted to modulated signals. The main benefit of the suggested technique is that it is more reliable since the useable signal and the watermark signal do not conflict with one another.

Watermarks can be used to deter certain sorts of assaults in some instances. Rubio-Hernan et al. (2018) suggested an adaptive control-theoretic technique for detecting cyber replication attempts on networked control industrial systems. This refers to an intruder's effort to tamper with system control by replicating previously intercepted data sequences. The fundamental contribution of this work is not the embedding technique, which is borrowed from prior publications, but rather the approach for employing this algorithm to guard against an intruder.

Huang and Zhang (2019) offer a technique for embedding reversible air signs in signals conveyed in "hard" real-time industrial control systems. The authors choose ship control systems as the most important field of application. A secret key must be delivered in advance through a secure communication channel before embedding can begin. The approach described here can detect attacks that aim to cause signal delay and distortion.

Finally, experiments integrating blockchain with digital watermark technology have begun to emerge as outlined in the preceding section. Different security concerns in CPSs are addressed by blockchain and digital watermarks. Their combined use may produce a better level of security than each of these methods alone. This concept has previously been explored in prior works, but mostly in one aspect, namely the issue of digital rights management (Qian et al., 2020; Zhao et al., 2019). The collaborative implementation of these technologies in other areas (Iskhakov & Meshcheryakov, 2019; Maleh et al., 2019; Sadeghi et al., 2015) is a promising research field whose advancement will benefit cybersecurity. Table 6.3 summarizes the many blockchain uses in cybersecurity.

TABLE 6.3   Blockchain applications in cybersecurity

APPLICATION DOMAIN	APPLICATIONS	CONTRIBUTIONS
Quantum-inspired blockchain (Abd El-Latif et al., 2021)	Smart edge utilities in IoT-based smart cities	Resist potential assaults from digital and quantum computers.
Lightweight blockchain-based cybersecurity (LBC) (Abdulkader et al., 2019)	IoT environments	Address intensive computational requirements and bandwidth consumption overhead.
Blockchain empowered cooperative authentication (Abdulkader et al., 2019)	Vehicular edge computing	Protect and preserve the privacy and confidentiality of data while also ensuring mutual authentication is in place (e.g., reply attack, etc.).
BloCyNfo-share (Badsha et al., 2020)	Cybersecurity information exchange (CYBEX)	Describe how to share private information with other organizations or provide private information to other organizations access.
BBDS (Xia et al., 2017)	Electronic medical records in cloud environments	Aim to disseminate medical data outside of the protected institutions' cloud.
Ancile (Dagher et al., 2018)	Electronic medical records	Preserve the privacy of patients' sensitive information.
Secure and decentralized sharing (Patel, 2019)	Image sharing across domains Personal health data may be processed in a batch using a Hyperledger fabric tree-based system.	Allowing parties to come to an agreement without relying on a single authority.
BlockChain (Dorri et al., 2017)	Interconnected smart vehicles	Address the security and privacy threats that smart vehicles face, such as location tracking and remote vehicle hijacking.

6.4.3 Blockchain in Cryptocurrency and Finance Industry

Many financial networks exist, which include banks, brokers, bonds, and real estate. If they have a car or vehicle and buy fuel, this happens on a blockchain where they own the supply and use a blockchain. In cars with their drivers and their distributed ledgers, anyone on the network can verify anything that goes on there, and they would sell it and repurchase it at a fair price as if it is not there. It is a technology that takes the underlying information that has been used to create the payment system from the banking system and distributes that information to millions of potential customers without any intermediaries that the bank can hold the lead. They can do so using blockchain to create a consensus mechanism, this is what has made this whole technology, and it is a vast revolution. It allows anyone to transact anything to anybody in any block or chain using an Ethereum smart contract. So, in banking and finance, the payment of funds is possible. It may be the next thing to move banks and companies from analog to digital technology (Eyal, 2017).

Banks are trying to provide customer services and financial information in digital format. Banks are trying to replace old banks and financial information with blockchain technology. The banking sector is looking for blockchain solutions to solve its economic problems. The banking and finance industry is about business and technology, about managing money. In the bank and finance industry, the term blockchain refers to dealing with information or a system of transactions that can move money. When they talk about blockchain technology, they can be sure of being part of the banking and finance industry. Blockchain technology creates a secure and reliable system of payments or electronic transactions. This technology is for money generation. It involves ledger-like records. One can read and see the information by using a device called a device with chips. There is no need for any financial information to be stored in a ledger using this technology. They can keep all of the transactions or the blockchain data, and it is not required to have any financial information in the catalog. This technology is related to the banking and finance business; information is simpler than a ledger system. The processes are done automatically on blockchain technology. The server carries out the network to verify all transactions and the data with a chip. It is not required to take the money received, and the information is kept in the blockchain data. As the blockchain data is transparent, there is no need to keep records in a ledger system (Eyal, 2017).

Advancing blockchain is about increasing speed, safety, and availability for financial and banking users. Blockchain is the most scalable, tamper-proof, and secure way to transfer money anywhere. It has already revolutionized how our money is held in the cloud and has been the most disruptive technology for the digital economy. The latest industry is taking this future and applying it to the real world. As part of blockchain technology, it provides a framework that facilitates transactions to and from accounts. As a result, a person or entity of the financial institution may act as an intermediary between bank and customer at one point in the process. As a bank, in the event of a transaction completed by any person, it can act as a transaction broker at the same time. This way, the person, entity acts as a transactor, and the account's funds are released in one or two transactions that would otherwise be delayed. As an institution that wants to develop new technologies, it works to become a blockchain platform provider. It is a good business strategy.

The technology can facilitate the technology companies. It provides a framework for banking companies to create a blockchain and provide transparency and record-keeping. With these changes, banks need to adopt Bitcoin. The advancement of block-chain in the banking and finance industry is much progress. Moreover, now everyone has the technology to build smart contracts that operate entirely on blockchain. The banks can now offer the customers financial products they can make without a central bank. So, this process is accelerating, the pace of changes in this process is improving every day.

What is more, a considerable sector has already started working on what block-chain can be and how to implement it in various industries, where the blockchain itself cannot be used for this purpose. For example, the banking industry, which has a huge problem, is working on smart contracts to manage credit and debt to give customers better banking. Both the credit and debit are stored in a specific virtual account.

The advancement of the blockchain in the banking and finance industry results in many reasons, including high transaction volume, efficient use of the network, rapid pace of payment settlement, and low costs. For the banking industry, there are several advantages like a single ledger of account details provides transparency and ease of access, automated settlement helps in making large transactions quickly and cost less, the rapid scale of payments in financial services makes transactions possible in less time than before, and the fast growth of business in financial services makes it easier for new ideas to advance. Each register is an encrypted archive stored in a distributed ledger called distributed ledger of payment details, which is also a data storage system. These two information systems are complementary. The fact that they are separate from each other is why they are complementary. However, one may prefer to use one over the other. It is a different phenomenon compared to the familiar concept of the ledger of account details.

They contain a copy of the ledger of account details, but these two copies exist on separate machines with their state. It is not easy to know how they are synchronized since they are not synchronized. One may prefer to use a ledger of payment information in the banking and finance industry, allowing transaction speed to be reduced and making transactions cheaper. The difference between banks and finance firms is noticeable. It is a distributed ledger technology that enables instant, decentralized record-keeping that allows an organization, a bank, a medical practitioner. The applications may be used in the finance industry.

Blockchain is an online, distributed ledger that can record everything that ever happened to something. A blockchain ledger, or a distributed ledger, is like a digital currency. Instead of using physical money, one uses computers to create a virtual currency to pay for goods and services. A block is a file; one can write their file in the blockchain and read it later. The blockchain is a record of files, including all Bitcoin network records, the personal bitcoin wallet, and any changes they have made to it, like transactions or mint coins. The blockchain is a platform that allows for a distributed, transparent, decentralized, and secure computing platform for managing all financial information. It offers a peer-to-peer platform for managing digital assets and transactions. It is a secure mechanism by which transactions are recorded, and it acts as a centralized trust to manage digital assets.

This industry deals with a lot of currency, and as a slip of a finger, there are millions of transactions happening worldwide. The blockchain advanced how the financial operations occur; most individuals needed cash, but it was no more complete. The blockchain has introduced more cryptocurrency technologies, but the most known one is bitcoin (Calvão, 2019). Organizations and companies can invest as much as possible; there is no limit to how it happens in the traditional transaction. The traditional transaction has limitations and cannot allow the user or organization to have a certain amount of money in one transaction. However, the blockchain has changed this industry as they can transact as much as possible, and there are no limitations.

Peer to peer global financial transaction is made possible. The traditional transaction has a lot of limitations, and one of them concerns the boundaries. The transaction happening by a third party has limits to the boundary of the nation-state of its origins. For example, the user cannot complete a transaction in the UK for a bank account in France or Spain (Knezevic, 2018). The traditional transaction system works in the country, and in the case of advancement, it works for neighboring countries only. The blockchain has advanced the transitions from the sender to the receiver directly without the third party. It makes the transaction process easy and fast, reducing the time taken to wait for verification. It does not require any third party to validate the process hence confidentiality in the transaction.

Blockchain is useable for protecting market communications from dissimilar clients, strategy holders, and insurance companies. It is useful to exchange, purchase, and record insurance policies. Making a complete transaction is traditionally expensive; the sender must pay the sending fee and the receiver with a withdrawal fee. Blockchain has made the financial industry on another level. Making transaction with the blockchain require less transaction fee, and to some extent, there is no fee to complete a transaction. It has increased the adoption of cryptocurrency to compete for the transaction rather than the traditional way that is not reliable.

The stock of trading is another advancement in the financial industries as a result of blockchain technology. Different nation-states have different currency and are not a problem when it comes to the stock of exchange. The seller may sell the currency to the buyer at a higher price, but the buyer ends up selling it at a lower price due lack of currency standardization. Blockchain has transparency, and the currency remains the same globally. The price of bitcoin currency remains standard in all the nations; if it rises, the impacts apply when there is a drop. It has made the transaction permanent and reduced the cyber activities concerning traditional transactions.

Blockchain technology is essential to all industries and plays a critical role in stimulating productivity. This technology is vet secure when using it due to the encryption mechanisms in cryptography. Only those with perfect encryption keys will be able to decrypt the information. There is no limitation with blockchain technology as a way to complete your transaction. It is available all the time provided there is an internet connection. Indeed, the financial industry has evolved due to the blockchain technology whack allowing you to save as much as you have. Blockchain indeed makes the nay industry successful due to the unlimited number of transactions with lower transaction fees. It also allows more customers to purchase the products in the whole world due to currency standardization.

There are a lot of conversations going on in the world about blockchain technology. According to Gupta (2017), the blockchain is an information recording system customized with security features that make it impossible to hack attacks or cheat in the system. Abadi and Brunnermeier (2018) indicate a ledger system that decentralizes the records by distributing them across all the blockchain networks. Transactions in the blockchain system are distributed to all the system participants, making it hard to cheat or steal. They further indicate that technology's correctness, decentralization, and cost efficiency make an excellent record-keeping system. Their comparison of the system to the traditional centralized system highlights the tremendous revolution blockchain has brought to the record-keeping industry. One of the blockchain's essential features is the algorithms that permit record-keepers to rewind and undo false reports in the ledger's historical records. Besides the finance industry, the system is quite useful in procurement, internet apps, among other industries where transparency is highly required. My focus will be on the finance industry, exploring the technology's advancements in the industry.

6.4.3.1 Fraud prevention

The blockchain has contributed to the reduction of fraud in the finance industry tremendously. The financial organizations dealing with money and assets transactions are highly exposed and susceptible to experiencing losses brought about by fraud or crime. The financial sector has previously depended on a centralized system for record-keeping. Hackers and crime agents are well versed with this kind of design, and it is effortless for them to manipulate it as one access to such a system would give them the ultimate power to do as they please. Blockchain is a secure, non-corruptible technology that depends on a hard decentralized network for attackers to manipulate or penetrate. Each transaction is recorded and stored in the form of a cryptographic mechanism. The mechanism has an almost impossible way of being corrupted, and if corrupted, there are easy ways of tracing the attackers. The difficulty is linking all blocks so that if one breach is detected, they all detect and show the change. The linked blocks also reduce the time of tracing the breach, reducing the time for the attackers to conduct any illegal business in the system.

6.4.3.2 Financial inclusion

The current banking regulations and restrictions highly prevent banks' use by many people who are left looking for an alternative solution. Financial inclusivity is the ability and opportunity for everyone to use a formal financial system for economic growth and development. The low cost associated with blockchain gives start-ups a chance to compete with central banks. The start-ups rely on the alternative that comes with digital identification and mobile devices to access financial services. The hassle-free system has a competitive opportunity for innovators willing to serve small bankers hence achieving financial inclusivity.

6.4.3.3 Money laundry prevention

With the anti-money laundry regulations taking place in most developed and developing economies, knowing your customer policy has made the registration of a customer in a banking institution quite an expensive affair. It is estimated that financial institutions spend between USD.60 million and USD.500 million enrolling a customer to their records. They are required to conduct a background check or what is commonly known as customer due diligence. The process is undertaken to reduce or eliminate global money laundry and curtail criminal organizations such as terrorists and drug groups. Due diligence by one bank or institution on a customer makes the information about the customer access to other financial institutions in the blockchain in the blockchain system. The workload is reduced tremendously, and there is no repetition of efforts from the same industry. This advantage from the blockchain system, highly motivates business leaders in the financial sector to acquire and join the blockchain system to reduce their operations costs, optimizing their organization's profits (Gupta, 2017).

6.4.3.4 Digital currency

As the blockchain system increases financial inclusivity and allowing innovators, the digital currency known as cryptocurrency is the new wave of financial assets. The cryptocurrency highly relies on the blockchain system to increase its credibility and security features. The currency is now used in different parts of the world as an alternative to traditional money. Although the cost of accessing digital currency is currently high, companies' world is overworking to reduce the barrier by providing a continuous exchange of money.

6.4.3.5 Trade finance

Trade finance has been made easier on the blockchain system. Transaction of complex trading in the traditional system is considered a long and tedious process that involves a lot of paperwork and can also be costly. In blockchain technology, trade finance is an essential application that eliminates lengthy processes and involves experts conversing with the system. The experts' role is to engage the traders involved in the complex transaction by signing them in the system, export and import needed ledgers. Once agreed upon, the transaction automatically completes the rest of the task in an impressively short time. All the parties are privy to the activities being conducted in the system. In a practical example, the Barclays Bank in Israel completed a transaction record of four hours. In the traditional design, the transaction would have taken seven to ten days to complete.

6.4.3.6 Smart assets and smart contracts

Smart assets and smart contracts are features in the blockchain system that are automatically executed. A smart asset application in the blockchain is used to store records of asset transactions and eliminate the long process of buying and selling paperwork documentation. Once the transfer of assets is done, the blockchain system holds up this information digitally, updating any information or activity conducted on the system. On the other hand, smart contracts are an application that facilitates the ease of agreements. It enables financial transactions by increasing the speed and simplifying the process to reach or complete a transaction (Sağlam et al., 2020). The application ensures that the information transferred is accurate, and its approval is dependent on the written code. This application's errors and execution time are favorably dropped at the extreme level, and all the parties involved are privy to the transaction.

The blockchain technology is quite a handful of tasks to understand but, once understood, reduces financial fraud in the finance industry, reduces activities by criminal organizations such as the terrorist, makes trading finance a light task, increase the cryptocurrency trading, allow financial inclusivity, and transfers assets and achievement of contracts an easy task. Although there are challenges associated with the system as it is based on peer-to-peer transactions where everyone in the network is privy to the information and allowed to add data, blockchain is a solution to most of the challenges experienced in the financial industry. It has experienced adoption across the globe, and its scalability is expected to open up more opportunities to innovators and financial consumers. The universal adoption of blockchain means that the system will open up cross-border money transfers and scale-up trade across the board.

Cryptocurrency is not one asset but many asset classes. Cryptocurrencies are in many ways like credit cards and stock markets, but they have different characteristics. They are different types of asset classes that provide services to specific groups. Like fiat currencies are used in many cases to control prices, but the money is not limited to that kind of role. Like stocks, crypto can become assets like a bank payment system. The blockchain is a network of digital records, immutable digital copies of all electronic transactions, including paper money. The history of all Bitcoin transactions in the peer-to-peer networks is stored in a database called the blockchain. The blockchain records all of the transactions in Bitcoin. To create a digital asset, one needs to hold bitcoins in an exchange, which is similar to a bank account, so that a user can convert those bitcoins into dollars. The user can transfer those dollars to the person.

It is worth mentioning that many people may not know about it due to the market's low visibility and its lack of development. Since there is nothing wrong with the idea of a blockchain platform, it will be a good idea to write a blog about it. It would help people understand the ecosystem better as it is very technical and might even make them rethink their views. They might start using the services that it provides. Crowdfunding has been a great way to fund projects, and this has helped people with cryptocurrency needs. Since we are beginning the coin economy based on the blockchain, our goal is to increase adoption and decrease entry barriers for anyone interested in cryptocurrencies and technology. We are already working on the coin economy to create the platform to allow anyone with a computer or smartphone to earn tokens from creating projects. Many people have launched their cryptocurrency projects, but with the current market structure, it takes them. Ripple, Bitcoin, and Bitcoin Cash are now the most popular cryptocurrencies in the market. They were even the most significant currencies in the world. Many people are interested in bitcoin, and it seems people are ready to make some progress in the future with it (Aste et al., 2017).

The industry of blockchain is rapidly growing because of its simplicity, ease of use, and flexibility. This technology could be applied to several sectors such as IT, manufacturing, finance, banking, real estate, insurance, education, real estate, health-care, transportation, retail, and more. Blockchain technology enables smart contracts to be validated, making it easier to do business, track and manage the digital assets from start to finish. It also allows the transfer of digital assets through the Internet and creates a new era of investment in digital assets. Blockchain has enabled much innovation in the development of the cryptocurrency market. The community has gone so far as to put in the necessary resources to allow technology development.

Blockchain innovation has made the technology more efficient as its market expands to more prominent industries such as banking, insurance, healthcare, and the IoT.

One exciting aspect of the blockchain is that it allows for a decentralized peer-to-peer financial system. Unlike traditional financial networks, where parties rely on their networks, no central authority provides them with services. As a result, the peer-to-peer network that creates a blockchain has no financial institutions. There have been few breakthroughs in cryptocurrencies since the beginning. Bitcoin has been in this space for quite a while before it caught onto Bitcoin, before it caught onto the crash of the bitcoin bubble that went after its price, then finally it caught onto the Ethereum Bubble. Blockchain has already taken many coins in the space and has given them significant growth that will surely go bigger. The world over, blockchain solutions have been used to build real-time settlements, make real-time payments, provide the backbone for the banking system, verify digital identities, enable financial contracts, and allow digital transactions among people who know each other. With blockchain, it is increasingly apparent that real-time solutions are the currency's backbone. The technology itself provides more applications than just cryptocurrency (Hashemi Joo et al., 2020).

6.5 BLOCKCHAIN LIMITATIONS AND FUTURE DIRECTIONS

Despite their wealth, blockchain promises continue to face many security issues, as seen by the numerous breaches and frauds that have been reported. This is a paradoxical snare to fall into for a system whose key touted attributes are dependability and inviola-bility. Computer assaults, on the other hand, are carried over to all types of interactions with other systems - primarily markets, which are vulnerable to the classic flaws of centralized systems, like banks (Tasatanattakool & Techapanupreeda, 2018).

In general, the speed, throughput, secrecy, scalability, and interoperability issues with blockchains have been shown and well documented. Mining issues, which are at the heart of the proof of work on which the Bitcoin consensus is based, are also the subject of much debate. On the theoretical level, it is a matter of rigorously defining the conditions that will protect against malicious validation nodes. The level of 51% of the computing power held by a malicious entity is certainly considered the reference level. However, this value is the subject of controversy in the research community. The number and distribution of nodes is also a sensitive issue. Economic issues are also beginning to mobilize researchers (Chang et al., 2020). In addition to the monetary and financial aspects (competition between currencies, monetary systems), the themes concern the economics of mining, with the question of cooperative incentives for miners or the evolution of mining capacity. And the debates do not stop at Bitcoin, since many depend on the consensus model chosen to replace the centralized decision-making system. Whatever the case may be, the technological environment for distributed registries will continue to evolve significantly.

The time it takes to complete a transaction on the blockchain is a major drawback. Due to the vastness of the Bitcoin network, this process might take many hours to complete. Using a blockchain like Hyperledger Sawtooth helps reduce this latency since it allows the PoET (Proof of Elapsed Time) consensus process to be used, which is among the fastest and least resource-hungry in terms of reaction time., making it better suited to our current context, which includes networked object data and services (Xu et al., 2021). Second, not everyone should have access to blockchain data. This challenge may be solved by utilizing private blockchains, which can govern blockchain access privileges and transaction execution rights. Second, the blockchain's consensus algorithms, notably the PoW, are extremely energy-hungry in terms of calculations.

Additionally, the redundant data and redundant calculations necessary to decide whether or not a new block may be added to the blockchain are energy-hungry. The blockchain, in the end, represents a sea change in thinking. In other words, the network is becoming decentralized instead of centrally controlled. Customers may have difficulty adopting and integrating this technology into their existing ecosystems as a result of this.

Other limitations of blockchains are regularly invoked, particularly the tension between transparency and confidentiality, between anonymity and identification of stakeholders (see box above on the "dilemmas of blockchain for the financial sector"). Because the register is widely disseminated, stakeholders may easily access the plain language information it includes. When it comes to tracing transactions, this is a benefit, but when it comes to corporate confidentiality, such as in banking or healthcare, it's a redhibitory problem. The market looks for ways to reliably disguise information while engaging in activities that require the disclosure of some and the protection of others (Hashemi Joo et al., 2020).

Another limitation is the high amount of energy required. Using blockchain necessitates a lot of power-hungry verification, validation, and cryptography procedures. If this technique is widely used, it might have significant negative environmental externalities.

Despite the widespread interest in blockchain, it must be recognized that distributed registries are not a panacea. Blockchain is not yet suitable for the fast processing of large amounts of data, especially video and audio, and use in a fast-changing environment for use in fast-changing environments. Blockchain is ideal for the long-term and most as reliably as possible for storing information that changes infrequently. Therefore, the technology is promising for capturing customer data from banks, medical institutions, insurance and logistics companies (Kolb et al., 2020). A distributed transaction registry will benefit patent offices and cadastral offices. Technology is suitable for law enforcement and tax authorities to record personal data. Brokerage and investment firms will benefit from blockchain as a registry of transactions. The technology's current capabilities are just an in-between. The continuous improvement of blockchain opens up prospects for its application in new and new industries. In its evolution, any technology must overcome distrust by conservative and not used to change quickly. Blockchain has already passed that stage and therefore, it will continue to evolve.

6.6 CONCLUSION

Rapid advances in computational and communication technologies drive the scientific community's interest and industry in CPSs. Using sensor, computational, and networking capabilities, CPSs contribute to a new generation of scientific and technical solutions that provide automatic decision-making processes in various fields, from automation of small domestic processes to transportation of materials, factories of the future, and mission-critical industries. Greater efficiency, dependability, and sustainability may be achieved by creating a smart infrastructure that integrates information technology approaches with physical systems like the power grid, transportation system, and supply chain.

An overview of various applications of blockchain in CPSs control protocols is presented. Although each industry has advantages in using blockchain, there are also challenges involved. However, blockchain is well known and adopted for its various benefits in various industries.

This chapter contributes to the thematic area by providing information on a poorly documented topic in the scientific literature. It became clear during the development of the work and deserved further theoretical investigation. The analysis of the results shows that the theme addressed has grown annually and has become of great relevance for the emergence and development of new applications using blockchain for CPSs. It is still too early to say whether blockchain technology is more appropriate in the context of CPS applications and to compare it with other technologies already used.

REFERENCES

Abadi, J., & Brunnermeier, M. (2018). Blockchain economics. *National Bureau of Economic Research, (No. W25407)*. Working Paper 25407. http://www.nber.org/papers/w25407

Abd El-Latif, A. A., Abd-El-Atty, B., Mehmood, I., Muhammad, K., Venegas-Andraca, S. E., & Peng, J. (2021). Quantum-Inspired Blockchain-Based Cybersecurity: Securing Smart Edge Utilities in IoT-Based Smart Cities. *Information Processing & Management*, 58(4), 102549. https://doi.org/https://doi.org/10.1016/j.ipm.2021.102549

Abdulkader, O., Bamhdi, A. M., Thayananthan, V., Elbouraey, F., & Al-Ghamdi, B. (2019). A Lightweight Blockchain Based Cybersecurity for IoT Environments. *2019 6th IEEE International Conference on Cyber Security and Cloud Computing (CSCloud)/2019 5th IEEE International Conference on Edge Computing and Scalable Cloud (EdgeCom)*, 139–144. https://doi.org/10.1109/CSCloud/EdgeCom.2019.000-5

Aceto, G., Persico, V., & Pescapé, A. (2019). A Survey on Information and Communication Technologies for Industry 4.0: State-of-the-Art, Taxonomies, Perspectives, and Challenges. *IEEE Communications Surveys & Tutorials, 21*(4), 3467–3501. https://doi.org/10.1109/COMST.2019.2938259

Ahram, T., Sargolzaei, A., Sargolzaei, S., Daniels, J., & Amaba, B. (2017). Blockchain Technology Innovations. *2017 IEEE Technology & Engineering Management Conference (TEMSCON)*, 137–141. https://doi.org/10.1109/TEMSCON.2017.7998367

Alladi, T., Chamola, V., Parizi, R. M., & Choo, K. R. (2019). Blockchain Applications for Industry 4.0 and Industrial IoT: A Review. *IEEE Access, 7*, 176935–176951. https://doi.org/10.1109/ACCESS.2019.2956748

Aste, T., Tasca, P., & Matteo, T. Di. (2017). Blockchain Technologies: The Foreseeable Impact on Society and Industry. *Computer, 50*(9), 18–28. https://doi.org/10.1109/MC.2017.3571064

Badsha, S., Vakilinia, I., & Sengupta, S. (2020). BloCyNfo-Share: Blockchain Based Cybersecurity Information Sharing with Fine Grained Access Control. *2020 10th Annual Computing and Communication Workshop and Conference (CCWC)*, 317–323. https://doi.org/10.1109/CCWC47524.2020.9031164

Baniata, H., & Kertesz, A. (2020). A Survey on Blockchain-Fog Integration Approaches. *IEEE Access, 8*, 102657–102668. https://doi.org/10.1109/ACCESS.2020.2999213

Bhushan, B., Khamparia, A., Sagayam, K. M., Sharma, S. K., Ahad, M. A., & Debnath, N. C. (2020). Blockchain for Smart Cities: A Review of Architectures, Integration Trends and Future Research Directions. *Sustainable Cities and Society, 61*, 102360. https://doi.org/https://doi.org/10.1016/j.scs.2020.102360

Calvão, F. (2019). Crypto-Miners: Digital Labor and the Power of Blockchain Technology. *Economic Anthropology, 6*(1), 123–134. https://doi.org/10.1002/sea2.12136

Cebe, M., Erdin, E., Akkaya, K., Aksu, H., & Uluagac, S. (2018). Block4Forensic: An Integrated Lightweight Blockchain Framework for Forensics Applications of Connected Vehicles. *IEEE Communications Magazine, 56*(10), 50–57. https://doi.org/10.1109/MCOM.2018.1800137

Chang, V., Baudier, P., Zhang, H., Xu, Q., Zhang, J., & Arami, M. (2020). How Blockchain Can Impact Financial Services – The Overview, Challenges and Recommendations from Expert Interviewees. *Technological Forecasting and Social Change, 158*, 120166. https://doi.org/https://doi.org/10.1016/j.techfore.2020.120166

Chi, J., Li, Y., Huang, J., Liu, J., Jin, Y., Chen, C., & Qiu, T. (2020). A Secure and Efficient Data Sharing Scheme Based on Blockchain in Industrial Internet of Things. *Journal of Network and Computer Applications, 167*, 102710. https://doi.org/https://doi.org/10.1016/j.jnca.2020.102710

Christidis, K., & Devetsikiotis, M. (2016). Blockchains and Smart Contracts for the Internet of Things. *IEEE Access, 4*, 2292–2303. https://doi.org/10.1109/ACCESS.2016.2566339

Dagher, G. G., Mohler, J., Milojkovic, M., & Marella, P. B. (2018). Ancile: Privacy-Preserving Framework for Access Control and Interoperability of Electronic Health Records Using Blockchain Technology. *Sustainable Cities and Society, 39*, 283–297. https://doi.org/https://doi.org/10.1016/j.scs.2018.02.014

Daza, V., Pietro, R. Di, Klimek, I., & Signorini, M. (2017). Connect: Contextual Name Discovery for Blockchain-Based Services in the IoT. *2017 IEEE International Conference on Communications (ICC)*, 1–6. https://doi.org/10.1109/ICC.2017.7996641

Dorri, A., Steger, M., Kanhere, S. S., & Jurdak, R. (2017). BlockChain: A Distributed Solution to Automotive Security and Privacy. *IEEE Communications Magazine, 55*(12), 119–125. https://doi.org/10.1109/MCOM.2017.1700879

Evsutin, O., Meshcheryakov, R., Tolmachev, V., Iskhakov, A., & Iskhakova, A. (2019). Algorithm for Embedding Digital Watermarks in Wireless Sensor Networks Data with Control of Embedding Distortions. In V. M. Vishnevskiy, K. E. Samouylov, & D. V. Kozyrev (Eds.), *Distributed Computer and Communication Networks* (pp. 574–585). Springer International Publishing.

Evsyutin, O., Kokurina, A., & Meshcheryakov, R. (2019). A Review of Methods of Embedding Information in Digital Objects for Security in the Internet of Things. *Computer Optics*, *43*(1), 137–154.

Eyal, I. (2017). Blockchain Technology: Transforming Libertarian Cryptocurrency Dreams to Finance and Banking Realities. *Computer*, *50*(9), 38–49. https://doi.org/10.1109/MC.2017.3571042

Ferdowsi, A., & Saad, W. (2019). Deep Learning for Signal Authentication and Security in Massive Internet-of-Things Systems. *IEEE Transactions on Communications*, *67*(2), 1371–1387. https://doi.org/10.1109/TCOMM.2018.2878025

Fernández-Caramés, T. M., & Fraga-Lamas, P. (2018). A Review on the Use of Blockchain for the Internet of Things. *IEEE Access*, *6*, 32979–33001. https://doi.org/10.1109/ACCESS.2018.2842685

Fernández-Caramés, T. M., & Fraga-Lamas, P. (2019). A Review on the Application of Blockchain to the Next Generation of Cybersecure Industry 4.0 Smart Factories. *IEEE Access*, *7*, 45201–45218. https://doi.org/10.1109/ACCESS.2019.2908780

Gupta, S. S. (2017). Blockchain. *IBM Online*. http://www.IBM.com.

Hameed, K., Khan, A., Ahmed, M., Goutham Reddy, A., & Rathore, M. M. (2018). Towards a Formally Verified Zero Watermarking Scheme for Data Integrity in the Internet of Things Based-Wireless Sensor Networks. *Future Generation Computer Systems*, *82*, 274–289. https://doi.org/https://doi.org/10.1016/j.future.2017.12.009

Hashemi Joo, M., Nishikawa, Y., & Dandapani, K. (2020). Cryptocurrency, a Successful Application of Blockchain Technology. *Managerial Finance*, *46*(6), 715–733. https://doi.org/10.1108/MF-09-2018-0451

Hoang, T., Bui, V., Vu, N., & Hoang, D. (2020). A Lightweight Mixed Secure Scheme Based on the Watermarking Technique for Hierarchy Wireless Sensor Networks. *2020 International Conference on Information Networking (ICOIN)*, 649–653. https://doi.org/10.1109/ICOIN48656.2020.9016541

Huang, H., & Zhang, L. (2019). Reliable and Secure Constellation Shifting Aided Differential Radio Frequency Watermark Design for NB-IoT Systems. *IEEE Communications Letters*, *23*(12), 2262–2265. https://doi.org/10.1109/LCOMM.2019.2944811

Huang, J.-M., Yang, S.-B., & Dai, C.-L. (2013). An Efficient Key Management Scheme for Data-Centric Storage Wireless Sensor Networks. *IERI Procedia*, *4*, 25–31. https://doi.org/10.1016/J.IERI.2013.11.005

Iskhakov, A., & Meshcheryakov, R. (2019). Intelligent System of Environment Monitoring on the Basis of a Set of IOT-Sensors. *2019 International Siberian Conference on Control and Communications (SIBCON)*, 1–5. https://doi.org/10.1109/SIBCON.2019.8729628

Knezevic, D. (2018). Impact of Blockchain Technology Platform in Changing the Financial Sector and Other Industries. *Montenegrin Journal of Economics*, *14*(1), 109–120.

Koh, L., Dolgui, A., & Sarkis, J. (2020). Blockchain in Transport and Logistics – Paradigms and Transitions. *International Journal of Production Research*, *58*(7), 2054–2062. https://doi.org/10.1080/00207543.2020.1736428

Kolb, J., AbdelBaky, M., Katz, R. H., & Culler, D. E. (2020). Core Concepts, Challenges, and Future Directions in Blockchain: A Centralized Tutorial. *ACM Computing Surveys*, *53*(1). https://doi.org/10.1145/3366370

Koshy, P., Babu, S., & Manoj, B. S. (2020). Sliding Window Blockchain Architecture for Internet of Things. *IEEE Internet of Things Journal*, *7*(4), 3338–3348. https://doi.org/10.1109/JIOT.2020.2967119

Kshetri, N. (2018). Blockchain's Roles in Meeting Key Supply Chain Management Objectives. *International Journal of Information Management*, *39*, 80–89. https://doi.org/https://doi.org/10.1016/j.ijinfomgt.2017.12.005

Li, M., Hu, D., Lal, C., Conti, M., & Zhang, Z. (2020). Blockchain-Enabled Secure Energy Trading With Verifiable Fairness in Industrial Internet of Things. *IEEE Transactions on Industrial Informatics*, *16*(10), 6564–6574. https://doi.org/10.1109/TII.2020.2974537

Li, D., Hu, Y., & Lan, M. (2020). IoT Device Location Information Storage System Based on Blockchain. *Future Generation Computer Systems*, *109*, 95–102. https://doi.org/https://doi.org/10.1016/j.future.2020.03.025

Lu, H., Huang, K., Azimi, M., & Guo, L. (2019). Blockchain Technology in the Oil and Gas Industry: A Review of Applications, Opportunities, Challenges, and Risks. *IEEE Access*, *7*, 41426–41444. https://doi.org/10.1109/ACCESS.2019.2907695

Luo, J., Chen, Q., Yu, F. R., & Tang, L. (2020). Blockchain-Enabled Software-Defined Industrial Internet of Things with Deep Reinforcement Learning. *IEEE Internet of Things Journal*, *7*(6), 5466–5480. https://doi.org/10.1109/JIOT.2020.2978516

Maleh, Y., Shojaafar, M., Darwish, A., & Haqiq, A. (2019). *Cybersecurity and Privacy in Cyber-Physical Systems*. CRC Press. https://www.crcpress.com/Cybersecurity-and-Privacy-in-Cyber-Physical-Systems/Maleh/p/book/9781138346673

Melanie, Swan. (2015). *Blockchain: Blueprint for a New Economy*. O'Reilly Media.

Monostori, L. (2014). Cyber-Physical Production Systems: Roots, Expectations and R&D Challenges. *Procedia CIRP*, *17*, 9–13. https://doi.org/https://doi.org/10.1016/j.procir.2014.03.115

Nakamoto, S. (2008). Bitcoin: A Peer-to-Peer Electronic Cash System. *Decentralized Business Review*, 21260.

Nguyen, V., Hoang, T., Duong, T., Nguyen, Q., & Bui, V. (2019). A Lightweight Watermark Scheme Utilizing MAC Layer Behaviors for Wireless Sensor Networks. *2019 3rd International Conference on Recent Advances in Signal Processing, Telecommunications & Computing (SigTelCom)*, 176–180. https://doi.org/10.1109/SIGTELCOM.2019.8696234

Patel, V. (2019). A Framework for Secure and Decentralized Sharing of Medical Imaging Data Via Blockchain Consensus. *Health Informatics Journal*, *25*(4), 1398–1411. https://doi.org/10.1177/1460458218769699

Peng, H., Yang, B., Li, L., & Yang, Y. (2020). Secure and Traceable Image Transmission Scheme Based on Semitensor Product Compressed Sensing in Telemedicine System. *IEEE Internet of Things Journal*, *7*(3), 2432–2451. https://doi.org/10.1109/JIOT.2019.2957747

Porru, S., Pinna, A., Marchesi, M., & Tonelli, R. (2017). Blockchain-Oriented Software Engineering: Challenges and New Directions. *2017 IEEE/ACM 39th International Conference on Software Engineering Companion (ICSE-C)*, 169–171. https://doi.org/10.1109/ICSE-C.2017.142

Prasetyo, H., Hsia, C., & Liu, C. (2020). Vulnerability Attacks of SVD-Based Video Watermarking Scheme in an IoT Environment. *IEEE Access*, *8*, 69919–69936. https://doi.org/10.1109/ACCESS.2020.2984180

Pu, Y., Zhang, N., & Wang, H. (2019). Fractional-Order Spatial Steganography and Blind Steganalysis for Printed Matter: Anti-Counterfeiting for Product External Packing in Internet-of-Things. *IEEE Internet of Things Journal*, *6*(4), 6368–6383. https://doi.org/10.1109/JIOT.2018.2886996

Qian, Y., Jiang, Y., Hu, L., Hossain, M. S., Alrashoud, M., & Al-Hammadi, M. (2020). Blockchain-Based Privacy-Aware Content Caching in Cognitive Internet of Vehicles. *IEEE Network*, *34*(2), 46–51. https://doi.org/10.1109/MNET.001.1900161

Rathee, G., Sharma, A., Iqbal, R., Aloqaily, M., Jaglan, N., & Kumar, R. (2019). A Blockchain Framework for Securing Connected and Autonomous Vehicles. *Sensors*, *19*(14). https://doi.org/10.3390/s19143165

Rubio-Hernan, J., De Cicco, L., & Garcia-Alfaro, J. (2018). Adaptive Control-Theoretic Detection of Integrity Attacks against Cyber-Physical Industrial Systems. *Transactions on Emerging Telecommunications Technologies*, *29*(7), e3209. https://doi.org/https://doi.org/10.1002/ett.3209

Saberi, S., Kouhizadeh, M., Sarkis, J., & Shen, L. (2019). Blockchain Technology and Its Relationships to Sustainable Supply Chain Management. *International Journal of Production Research*, 57(7), 2117–2135. https://doi.org/10.1080/00207543.2018.1533261

Sadeghi, A., Wachsmann, C., & Waidner, M. (2015). Security and Privacy Challenges in Industrial Internet of Things. *2015 52nd ACM/EDAC/IEEE Design Automation Conference (DAC)*, 1–6. https://doi.org/10.1145/2744769.2747942

Sağlam, R. B., Aslan, Ç. B., Li, S., Dickson, L., & Pogrebna, G. (2020). A Data-Driven Analysis of Blockchain Systems' Public Online Communications on GDPR. *2020 IEEE International Conference on Decentralized Applications and Infrastructures (DAPPS)*, 22–31. https://doi.org/10.1109/DAPPS49028.2020.00003

Seitz, A., Henze, D., Miehle, D., Bruegge, B., Nickles, J., & Sauer, M. (2018). Fog Computing as Enabler for Blockchain-Based IIoT App Marketplaces – A Case Study. *2018 Fifth International Conference on Internet of Things: Systems, Management and Security*, 182–188. https://doi.org/10.1109/IoTSMS.2018.8554484

Tasatanattakool, P., & Techapanupreeda, C. (2018). Blockchain: Challenges and Applications. *2018 International Conference on Information Networking (ICOIN)*, 473–475. https://doi.org/10.1109/ICOIN.2018.8343163

Teslya, N., & Ryabchikov, I. (2017). Blockchain-Based Platform Architecture for Industrial IoT. *2017 21st Conference of Open Innovations Association (FRUCT)*, 321–329. https://doi.org/10.23919/FRUCT.2017.8250199

Wang, B., Kong, W., Li, W., & Xiong, N. N. (2019). A Dual-Chaining Watermark Scheme for Data Integrity Protection in Internet of Things. *Computers, Materials & Continua*, 58(3): 679–695, https://doi.org/10.32604/cmc.2019.06106

Xia, Q., Sifah, E. B., Smahi, A., Amofa, S., & Zhang, X. (2017). BBDS: Blockchain-Based Data Sharing for Electronic Medical Records in Cloud Environments. *Information*, 8(2): 1–16. https://doi.org/10.3390/info8020044

Xiao, Y., & Gao, G. (2019). Digital Watermark-Based Independent Individual Certification Scheme in WSNs. *IEEE Access*, 7, 145516–145523. https://doi.org/10.1109/ACCESS.2019.2945177

Xu, L. Da, Lu, Y., & Li, L. (2021). Embedding Blockchain Technology into IoT for Security: A Survey. *IEEE Internet of Things Journal*, 8(13), 10452–10473. https://doi.org/10.1109/JIOT.2021.3060508

Yu, C., Jiang, X., Yu, S., & Yang, C. (2020). Blockchain-Based Shared Manufacturing in Support of Cyber Physical Systems: Concept, Framework, and Operation. *Robotics and Computer-Integrated Manufacturing*, 64, 101931. https://doi.org/https://doi.org/10.1016/j.rcim.2019.101931

Zhang, S., & Lee, J.-H. (2020). Analysis of the Main Consensus Protocols of Blockchain. *ICT Express*, 6(2), 93–97. https://doi.org/https://doi.org/10.1016/j.icte.2019.08.001

Zhao, B., Fang, L., Zhang, H., Ge, C., Meng, W., Liu, L., & Su, C. (2019). Y-DWMS: A Digital Watermark Management System Based on Smart Contracts. *Sensors*, 19(14), 1–17. https://doi.org/10.3390/s19143091

Zhaofeng, M., Lingyun, W., Xiaochang, W., Zhen, W., & Weizhe, Z. (2020). Blockchain-Enabled Decentralized Trust Management and Secure Usage Control of IoT Big Data. *IEEE Internet of Things Journal*, 7(5), 4000–4015. https://doi.org/10.1109/JIOT.2019.2960526

SECTION THREE

Artificial Intelligence for Security Engineering in Cyber-Physical Systems

The Future of Cybersecurity in the Hands of Artificial Intelligence

7

Lisa Devine and Kevin Curran

*School of Computing, Engineering
and Intelligent Systems, Ulster University
Northern Ireland, UK*

Contents

DOI: 10.1201/9781003278207-11

7.1 INTRODUCTION

Security is a major problem with every system in the world. There is always a risk that a specific system will fail to function or be accessed and abused by undesirable persons (Curran & Curran, 2018). This threat is inherent in the world of technology. In the 1950s, the field of cybernetics was developed to create a system of networks that worked to attain specific unified goals. Today, this has been digitalized and the computerized space has evolved progressively since the 1990s. Thus, the risks and vulnerabilities of running cyberspace have evolved with it. A blend of physical and digital infrastructural differences has laid the foundation for creating cyber threats and risks (Blue et al., 2017). Today, the term cyber threat relates exclusively to information security matters and this is based on the possibilities of attacks occurring in a given information system. This relates to security issues that might affect digital signals and digital systems, which could modify the proper functioning of cyberspace. Therefore, a cyberattack is premised on attacks mounted against digital devices with the hope of harming the owners and/or users of the system (Curran et al., 2018). Cyber threats can hit a system directly or affect and influence the functioning of a given system. Ultimately, this will affect an organization and prevent it from meeting its core goals and ends. Thus, governments and businesses take the threat of cybersecurity attacks seriously. Governments in the world have budgets to control cyber risks and build infrastructure and shields to prevent such attacks on cyberspace.

The three most popular motives for cybersecurity threats are (1) financial gains (2) disruption, and (3) espionage. People might want to hack cyberspace to gain information or hold the system owner to ransom. In other cases, cyberattacks might aim at merely disrupting or ending a given activity. An example is a case of an enemy government, hacking the system of an opposing government to force them to negotiate. Then, there is a need to use cyberattacks to gain private information that would allow an external party to gain information they are not allowed to access. Cisco identifies that 31% of organizations have experienced some kind of cybersecurity attack in their lifetime (Kingori, 2019). This includes data breaches, access through illegal applications, and many other issues. Despite this, organizations have increasingly utilized modern and more sophisticated technologies to deal with technology threats. Artificial intelligence (AI) refers to the technology enabling computers and information systems to use technologically-developed cognitive functions to perceive their environments and take actions without waiting for human instructions (SAS, 2019). In other words, AI allows computers to use the sense of thinking, feeling, seeing among others, to detect trends in each system to execute specific actions in response to issues and matters that come up. This means AI allows computers to perceive matters and take actions. This enables computers and information systems to think and do extraordinary things like process large amounts of data and recognize patterns in systems that humans cannot do easily.

This chapter aims to analyze the possibilities of utilizing AI in cybersecurity critically. We evaluate a core question relating to *the use of AI in security*. This will cover important elements of the nature and features of AI and how it can be deployed into systems to solve problems and undertake deductions to predict and minimize risks in cyberspace.

7.2 NATURE OF ARTIFICIAL INTELLIGENCE AND ITS CONNECTION TO SECURITY

The nature of AI is that it automates repetitive learning through information that is programmed into it (Kingori, 2019). The opposite of AI is natural intelligence. Natural intelligence can be found in human beings and animals, and it is all based on the way we learn. In the context of human beings and animals' reaction to danger, we learn to detect risky situations and avoid or ameliorate them over the years of our lives. An antelope in the jungle will perceive danger when it comes face to face with a hungry lion. This leads them to move toward the natural response of flight. It is a natural stimulus based on the antelope's mind. This is also how human minds function. Technology has advanced to the point that computers and systems can also be programmed to perceive specific things they are programmed to see. For instance, some cameras can detect people's faces and link them to a given system's data. This is done through programming and coding to provide the camera and its interlinked computerized system AI. Thus, "if" they pursue a given situation, they are programmed to execute a specific function or outcome. Hence, a computer or system infused with AI can think for itself and react to particular situations and circumstances when the conditions are met.

AI, therefore, constitutes a process of programming that creates specific situations and possibilities that come with specific reactionary outcomes. Advanced AI systems of the 21st century also undertake repetitive learning and discovery through data. In other words, they are programmed to sort through large quantities of data types and gather common features about them. They can sort new information they encounter and undertake specific actions through this. For instance, if AI is integrated into an X-ray system, it can take millions of X-ray scans and corresponding data of the diagnoses that came with each scan. After taking many of these scans, the AI system can take new scans and diagnose patients of different conditions when they "learn" from the different data sets that are fed into them. This is because for every X-ray scan they get, they store the data like a medical doctor would do while handling many diagnoses in their medical practice. Over time, the AI system in the X-ray machine can take new scans and define probabilities of conditions linked to each situation or case. This way, they can provide some reasonable and logical interpretation of any new X-ray scan fed into their system.

The algorithm that is fed into an AI system enables it to predict trends and draw conclusions and inferences based on past experiences. This elevates a system and enables it to develop functionalities that are extremely useful to its owners. Thus, the algorithms involve defining the data structures, rules and classifiers, and predictors that describe the functionality of a given AI system. Once an algorithm system is put in place, it can go deeper and study many more inputs than the human mind. As identified above, an AI system can be fed with millions of X-ray scans. The AI system can interpret this easily in ways that human experts will struggle to emulate. This is the basis of deep learning, which involves going into extreme details that put the AI at a functionality level, much higher than the natural intelligence. Another interesting perspective of AI is that in the past, science has been reserved for answering the "how" questions while philosophy answered the "why" questions (Difesa, 2018). Stated differently, science has been the realm for quantitative data analysis while the qualitative questions were relegated to the arts and philosophical sciences that were more related to questioning with no definite answers. Science always sought to identify things that could be understood and appreciated empirically with hard evidence that could be appreciated in space and time. Philosophy, on the other hand, sought to answer questions relating to the explanatory and metaphysical aspects of things that could not be seen, felt, or ascertained accurately in space and time.

However, the ingenuity of AI is that it brings together the two dimensions of the "how" and the "why". AI allows for the most abstract and inexact things to be measured and evaluated. This is because it gives room for many things that could not be studied tangibly to give measures and values in order to promote their study and quantification. This is because AI is a functionality that is premised on decision-making, and it is important to feed it with inputs and guidelines on how to interpret information quantitatively and qualitatively. AI cannot really do more than what it has been programmed to do although it remains a tool that can take decisions and make choices on the basis of the most minute and extreme circumstances and factors. For instance, in self-driving cars and systems, AI can be deployed over a large number of possible scenarios that a car driver is expected to encounter. This might be in the area of "normal" functionality that every driver can do. However, in some extreme situations and circumstances, an AI will have to take decisions and make choices based on moral dilemmas. This is because the normal human being will go through different scenarios before making a decision on how to react to specific things. An example is the case of the algorithms of a self-driving car, deciding to drive over a cliff to kill its passengers or driving into a crowd, killing ten people. The normal human being is programmed to become sensitive to the realities and take decisions that will ameliorate the losses. On the other hand, AI cannot do much about that. Here, the superiority of natural intelligence in humans is shown clearly.

Despite these inherent limitations of AI, it remains a great and viable option for dealing with cybersecurity risks and issues. This is because cybersecurity risk is premised on the fact that malicious persons seek to do things to a given system in problematic and/or wrong ways. Hence, AI can be programmed to identify these issues as and when they show up and counteract them by providing obvious solutions. This also means that when a human being monitoring a given system is not available to flag and deal with a particular cybersecurity threat, an AI can be trained to flag issues and prevent them from escalating into a serious security breach that could have a far-reaching impact. Therefore, AI is a major tool that can detect and undertake initial filtering and evaluations that can stop security threats within cyberspace.

On the other hand, some writers tend to view AI as a "blessing and a curse" simultaneously (Crane, 2019). This is because the same AI that can be used to defend a given system from cyberattacks can also hack or attack the system. This is because an AI is as ethical or moral as the one using it. Therefore, the purpose for which a given AI system can be used will determine whether it contributes to a security risk or ameliorates it. AI can be used independently to provide security on its own. This includes various methods and mechanisms like speech recognition, search engines, and facial recognition. This can help deal with issues and risks that could plague a given system directly or indirectly. However, AI can be used to analyze, study, and understand cybercrime. When people hack into a system, AI can be deployed to understand the normal functioning of the system and how or why breeches occurred in the system. AI's greatest strength in cybersecurity is its ability to study and understand situations to differentiate the normal from the abnormal. This can be employed in cybersecurity systems analysis and diagnosis. This can also be used in debugging in order to identify where things went wrong and how incompatible things occurred in a given system. AI can also do things to a higher level of precision and faster – to the nanosecond of each functionality (Crane, 2019). Hence, many companies have invested a lot of money into AI as a tool for combatting cybercrimes and their risks to a given system.

On the downside though, cybercriminals have increased their reliance on AI as a tool for committing massive crimes. If an AI is applied, a company that gets a data breach could lose millions of data and transactions within seconds. This can create serious problems for organizations that come under cyberattacks. Therefore, the supply side and demand sides of cybersecurity are both at risk where AI is utilized. The three levels of AI and its subcategories all have direct use in cybersecurity. AI enables algorithms to create "if" questions and situations, which helps a given cybersecurity system to detect security problems. Machine learning, a subdomain of AI, allows for the use of mathematical models and statistics to predict situations and incidents in order to prescribe specific acts in a security issue (NormShield, 2019). Deep learning creates a neural network that links different machine learning systems in order to prevent security risks from spreading through a given system. This way, one unit of a system that comes under a cyberattack can be closed off from other situations and circumstances that might worsen. The most common areas where these three components of algorithms have been applied in cybersecurity in the past include:

1. Spam filtering
2. Fraud detection
3. Network intrusion
4. Botnet detection
5. Hacking incident forecasting
6. Cybersecurity ratings (NormShield, 2019)

Spam filters check new information and messages that enter a given system. The position of AI is that it helps create certain considered actions in response to specific types of things. In other words, it can check the type of material in any given spam and act as appropriate. Fraud detection involves the identification of issues that are suspicious in order to take up actions that would help to prevent them. This includes the ability to detect issues within a given action or procedure. In other words, the AI can use various possible methods of detecting actions and also act in ways that can provide a measured response. The same mechanisms relate to risks such as network intrusion, botnet detection, hacking, and others. AI helps to think and execute actions that the system has been coded to do. This way, an immediate and real-time action is coded into the system that provides solutions that can help protect a particular cyberspace. These practical situations and circumstances apply various levels of AI to detect and handle issues and problems before they get out of hand. This also creates a digital infrastructure that can be improved over time. This explains why organizations release more updated and more sophisticated versions of the infrastructure they use. In most cases, they integrate security factors into these upgrades. Thus, with AI in the backgrounds, it is apparent that cyber systems can be improved and enhanced over time in order to meet goals and ends of preventing security risks and incidents. Figure 7.1 shows the AI technology landscape.

Things like hacking forecasts enable a firm to test their system and undertake simulations using AI in order to identify possible incidents and deal with them before they ever occur. This means AI is deployed in a very proactive manner in order to look out for

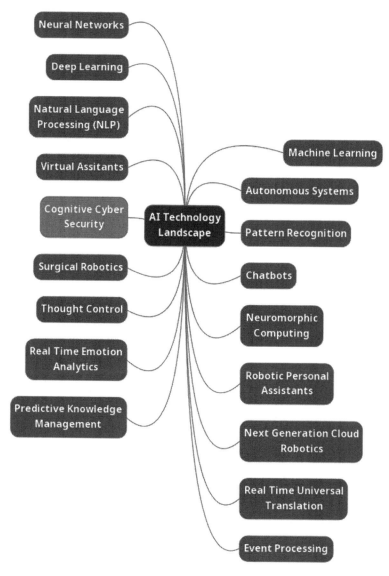

FIGURE 7.1 AI technology landscape.

risks and possible situations so that appropriate action can be executed. AI also allows for the planning and formulation of an appropriate roadmap based on the realities and circumstances of a firm and their possible risks in order to present the right level of action to counter threats (Stephen, 2019). The integration of AI into the system promotes a utilitarian approach that can help to maximize benefits and pursue functionalities that can help an organization to meet its greatest and best goals or ends in cybersecurity and cyber risk analysis and control. AI also helps firms to exchange intelligence on dealing with cybersecurity risks and issues in order to collaborate and stay ahead of hackers (Stephen, 2019). This way, the IT community is enhanced in many ways and forms in order to deal with issues and matters and create industry-wide standards that can put a given community or geographical area ahead of its malicious attackers. This is particularly vital in today's world of ever-increasing security risks and issues that demand proactive attention and responses.

Thus, the possibilities of using AI to enhance or promote security is clear and apparent. There are many possible uses and approaches that can be applied in this process. The actual success of such systems is premised on the nature and features of security threats. This creates the platform for using and applying AI for results.

7.3 SECURITY THREATS AND HOW ARTIFICIAL INTELLIGENCE CAN COUNTER IT

"Security" is a broad term. It is an ocean of possibilities that can hit a given technological system and prevent it from functioning as it should be functioning. Therefore, AI is an important element and feature that can be scaled and applied in order to help a given industry or company that seeks to thrive without these risks and issues. The diversity of cybersecurity risks creates the impetus for AI to be applied and used in order to achieve security goals and ends (Faggella, 2019). This is because security risks, although they are diverse, can be detected by the right persons and groups. AI in the context of security can deploy machine learning to evaluate cybersecurity risks and apply it to control or limit these risks. AI can undertake judgments and can be modified in response to new terms of rules and new regulations, and this can help to create a rule-based system that can promote data integrity and security.

AI is also flexible, and it can be created and re-created in order to meet specific targets in the security context (Faggella, 2019). Therefore, it is a major tool that can be used to respond to the many threats that keep evolving and getting more sophisticated. In other contexts, AI in cybersecurity is standard because cybersecurity risks are also driven by AI. In a survey of some 850 executives in IT roles across 10 countries, the executives identified that they all have an AI-enabled system that assists in their cybersecurity systems (Crane, 2019). This shows that AI is becoming imperative due to the sophistication of cybersecurity risks and their related activities. Of the total number of executives studied, 75% admit that AI helps them to function better and react at a faster rate than they would do if they were dealing with cybersecurity themselves as humans

(Crane, 2019). This shows the importance and vitality of AI as a major source of defense for a given information system. Also, it can be identified that AI improves the level of sensitivity in a given system. This is because AI is about learning and relearning and it can be scaled and adjusted as and where necessary. When the level of risks increases and trust levels fall, AI is often identified as the best method of introducing stronger and stricter methods of enforcing security (Laurence, 2019). AI supports important methods like biometric logins and others that can simply study the dominant cyberattacks and possible risks, create responsive methods, and scale them through the AI's systems. This can help to protect personal information, credit card information and prevent risks of identity theft among others.

AI is also unparalleled in detecting possible issues that are abnormal. This is because they have the functionality to flag a malware and a negative system that enters a particular computer system. AI can also help through pattern recognition and this can help to provide simple but far-reaching solutions to security problems and issues (Laurence, 2019). This means that malware attacks that could happen without given any indication of which changes were made are a thing of the past. Any attack can be traced with AI and used in dealing with the issue and risk.

In spite of AI's numerous potentials, it could also become detrimental in many ways. This includes the possibilities of interfering with normal and legitimate use (Laurence, 2019). In most cases, the first-time deployment of AI into a given organization's systems creates confusion and issues that could potentially lead to the reversal of gains that are made in the use of the existing systems. It also gets increasingly expensive and could create limits and serious exposures which could become a drawback to the existing system. These extra costs are often linked to the need to test and develop and redevelop the existing AI systems. The responsibility reverts back to the hackers who continuously create new systems that render old AI systems futile and ineffective.

Also, the automation of cyberattacks mean that cybercriminals are positioned to do a lot of things with or without AI functionality and systems (Laurence, 2019). This means that human effort in counteracting AI is almost always destined to be futile. This calls on the need to use equally automated systems that can think and react to trends and pointers. This is similar to security in the normal sense where human beings think and analyze the capabilities of their opponents in order to respond to them. In this case, AI becomes the only viable weapon that can be used to counteract the efforts of hackers and other sophisticated cybercriminals. The use of AI as a tool for cybersecurity defense means that a company can be best positioned if they have a responsive system that changes in order to fit the changing landscape for attacks and intrusions into their systems. A cyber defense system that does not respond to the realities on the ground will simply become static and its use will be diminished over time. Therefore, AI becomes the best and most viable option for handling and dealing with issues online. Thus, the three cardinal pointers make it imperative for companies to use AI in their systems, namely:

1. Augmentation of today's cyber threats
2. Development of new threats
3. Variation of the nature of existing threats (Ramachandran, 2019)

This means that a responsive system can best fight the attacks and counteract the intrusions into the system. AI becomes an indispensable tool for the improvement and enhancement of a system to become more robust in dealing with these attacks. Here, AI and machine learning become important tools for drawing on a real-time response that can instantly flag and neutralize some known threats. The use of deep learning can help the nodes of algorithms in a given system to collaborate and interact in order to respond across many different platforms to help an organization deal with its issues and risks. Machine learning, therefore, uses various probability and statistical reviews to analyze risks and deal with these risks. This is something that traditional information systems cannot do to the required level of satisfaction. Therefore, machine learning can be deployed at this level and also, deep learning can be applied to connect different platforms and devices across an Internet of Things (IoT) framework over a group of connected networks. In the past, the application of AI and machine learning has been useful in the following areas:

1. Password protection and authentication
2. Phishing detection and prevention
3. Network security
4. Behavioral analytics of users (Ramachandran, 2019)

This means AI can be a proactive mechanism that can be programmed to deal with any user functionality and activity within a system. This procedure means a responsive and directly accountable system of dealing with actions of hackers, which also provides a strong signal to hackers that a system is protected. Ultimately, the strength of AI is in the fact that it can interpret things and understand the intention of a given high-risk activity or procedure. The essence is that it will have the functionality to interpret things and with that ability to interpret information, the system can also be coded further to take actions that are measured responses to particular situations. This way, there is a positive potential for AI to be used to help act as a kind of watchdog that acts and does things that are proper and appropriate to protect a system. This goes one step further than just launching systems that will merely block threats. Rather, AI creates an avenue for specific actions to be taken in response to particular threats and situations that might affect a given system inappropriately.

7.4 BEST STRATEGIES FOR DEPLOYING ARTIFICIAL INTELLIGENCE FOR SECURITY PURPOSES

This section will focus on the practical elements and considerations necessary for the deployment and optimization of AI in a cybersecurity system. This includes the evaluation of vital issues and pointers that define the success and failure of proper AI use. A firm is best positioned to gain success in AI use when they have a cybersecurity strategy that will integrate AI (Crane, 2019). It is not good enough to acquire AI and deploy it haphazardly in a given system. It is more important to create a strategy that would promote security in a given system without any clear plan. There must be a plan for the digital assets that are at risk and the type of risks that are most likely to occur in the system. This must lead to a vision, mission, and framework for the attainment of cybersecurity in the system. Without this, there is a likelihood of failure and regressive inputs that might not meet the target of protecting the required assets.

AI is often installed in a responsive manner. This way, a firm will set up the AI infrastructure in order to respond to specific risks that are most likely to occur when the system is put in place. This will help the software and hardware of the organization to deal with vulnerabilities and risks. Some writers argue that a firm must not just create a one-off infrastructure without reverting to improve and modify it to meet real-world conditions and circumstances (Fagella, 2019). This is because cybersecurity threats are of an emergent nature and it is necessary to upgrade the existing AI infrastructure in relation to the changes in the conditions and circumstances. Therefore, the initial system that will be deployed will become the basis of the cybersecurity strategy of an organization, and this will be changed as and when the need arises in the system. The most important thing about AI in cybersecurity risk management is that it has to function around the clock and respond to issues as and when they occur (Crane, 2019). The deployment of AI must cover certain important things among others:

1. **Detection of Incidents and Appropriate Responsive Actions**: The primary role of AI is to become responsive to the realities. Thus, the deployment and integration of AI must be based on the ability to function when the existing cybersecurity plan fails. This has to do with the evaluation of circumstances and pointers that could cause the existing system to halt and fail to function. Thus, a backup system and the level of responsiveness to changes must be understood and optimized in order to deal with issues and problems when they ever come up.

2. **Security and Crime Prevention**: This is premised on the need to use AI to secure and detect issues that are malicious. There must be the use of AI to examine what is going on and the type of risks that exist within the system in order to prevent them. AI must provide a reasonable basis of profiling typical crimes that threaten a given system in order to provide solutions that might prevent these crimes from ever happening. This way, there is a predictive policing system that can ensure that new crimes and potential security breaches can be highlighted and treated before they ever materialize.

3. **Privacy Protection**: This is about the need to promote internal systems and ensure their integrity. Hence, there should be aspects of an AI system deployed into an organization's cyber system to gather information about individual privacy breaches and their issues. Once something happens, it must be highlighted by the AI system and given the right level of attention that can be followed up to prevent serious incidents.

4. **Analysis of Emerging Issues**: AI must be deployed in a way that will enable it to analyze information and trend that occur within the system. This has to

do with the ability to proactively monitor trends and create a mechanism for interpreting and acting on information that show up.

5. **Intrusion Detection Systems**: This includes the enhancement of software that is designed to deal with intrusions and their related risks. This includes the use of mechanisms to boost them and enhance their ability to filter issue and apply AI to respond to apparent and obvious risks.

AI must be deployed when a clear plan is put in place to achieve a particular security goal or end. This has to be done on the basis of what the owners of the system want to attain. This becomes the basis for the integration of AI to create a series of actions and processes in order to secure and improve the process. The integration of AI might require testing and training of staff that would use the system. Furthermore, AI will also demand human monitoring to avoid issues that machines and AI cannot achieve to specification.

7.5 RELEVANT ISSUES IN THE APPLICATION OF ARTIFICIAL INTELLIGENCE IN SECURITY

The promise provided by AI is clear and apparent. In spite of these many possibilities, the actual implementation and utilization of AI comes with issues. There are many barriers and limitations that makes it almost impossible to institute and benefit from AI within a system. This means that AI has issues that will have to be taken care of if it has to be used in ways that would give it optimal results. It is identified that the main challenges of AI adoption and utilization include:

1. Costs
2. Resources
3. Training

AI is almost always the intellectual property of a given organization or group. This means it comes at a patent cost that must be paid alongside the normal cost of the system that is acquired. Hence, a firm will have to take reasonable actions in order to acquire the best AI systems and make use of it in ways that guarantee the most optimal outcomes. In many cases, firms struggle with cutting down on costs and this becomes problematic. Also, due to the lack of clear and apparent threats in all situations, AI use could come with challenges. Sometimes, a firm might spend a lot of money on AI infrastructure that will do nothing for them. At the same time, they would encounter a major AI event that could have been solved with a fraction of the layout of the AI system they might have spent money acquiring. At the same time, AI comes with numerous complementary systems and resources. These are resources and systems that must work together to ensure the total protection of a given system. In the absence of such a system and process, all gains in a given AI system could be eroded and this would lead to some undesirable outcomes. Therefore, it is imperative for an AI to be comprehensive and cover all units of a firm; otherwise, the AI would not be useful to the firm.

Furthermore, the institution of an AI system would need training and preparation of staff members to utilize and use the AI system well. An AI system that cannot be optimized by the in-house IT staff is likely to be a wasteful investment. This makes it imperative to make AI an important part of a firm, and the right level of training must be part of the considerations for purchasing the system. In spite of this, AI systems have to be highly responsive to new threats that might develop within a system and this must be ascertained through testing (Saratchandran, 2019). AI will be considered responsive if it has the ability to:

1. Detect an attack.
2. Control access to a targeted unit.
3. Create smart responses that will deal with the issues.

Thus, when implementing an AI system, it is important to create a process whereby fraud detection can be done in real-time. This should be part of the process of building and implementing the system. Real-time attack detection is central to an AI system, and it should be in such a way that the first or a few attacks can be highlighted for quick action to be taken. Thus, in the case of an AI system for a bank, it has to be tested properly to ascertain whether it will respond to threats after a number of attacks are launched. For instance, before implementation, it is important to ascertain the number of transactions that will be launched on a stolen credit card before the attacks are detected. This should be followed by the appropriateness of the response to such a threat – like control of access and limitation of the targeted unit of a given information system. Then, there is the need for smart responses that would be undertaken in order to ameliorate and reverse the negative impacts and destructive influence of a given attack on a system.

There are numerous common trends that have to be watched during the pre-implementation test. This includes things like bypassing filters and the durability of AI detection tools (Polyakov, 2019). This is essential because AI is typically used in ways that respond with specific actions that are meant to achieve a desired end. There is a need to test the number of times and number of steps it will take to break down the defenses in order to judge how durable the system is. Also, hypothetical cases of possible attacks that can bypass the existing limits must be undertaken. This will tell the extent to which an AI system can repel and withstand specific attacks when they are launched. The level of response must be examined and reviewed in ways that would ensure that the system is appropriately strong and can manage or react to attacks of a specific kind. Specific risks in a given industry must form the basis of designing and testing the existing systems (Polyakov, 2019). There must be the review of important challenges in different categories that are most likely to happen. This will shape a view of how well the system is adapted and shaped in dealing with the category of risks and issues that can happen.

Other practitioners identify that there is the need for a functional testing of different risks in order to judge a given AI system. In this process, there must be the review of specific risks including:

1. Data integrity
2. Cloud environment security

3. Third party security issues
4. Digital identity challenges
5. Blockchain or networking challenges (Saratchandran, 2019)

These different pointers create specialized themes that can lead to the testing and evaluation of existing systems in ways that would lead to some diverging outcomes which will make way for proper planning. Data integrity can check the entire impacts of the existing systems on the current data that is kept on-site or in the local networks of an organization. However, cloud environment security can check how the offsite systems will react to an attack. Then, there is the question of what will happen when third party security matters occur. Also, there are risks with the identity of users and the possibility of these users dealing with the existing trends and processes. The connection to external parties and stakeholders also defines an important constituent of AI deployment and its testing. Alternate views of AI system testing include viewing it in three different dimensions, namely, reactivity, proactivity, and preventative (Saratchandran, 2019).

This is an interesting categorization and classification that says a lot about the durability of an AI system. The reactivity index is about how well the AI system detects issues which are presented. Then, there is the question of how well the AI system acts in order to contain a threat and prevents it from becoming a problem for the organization. Then, the preventive category examines how well the AI system can prevent future attacks through actions that can alert the appropriate department to prevent any future recurrence of the event. Hence, there are many dimensions of how AI can be tested and integrated into a system through an iterative mechanism that examines the AI in its functional and other dimensions. A more extreme approach toward testing the efficiency and effectiveness of an AI system is to hire a third party to try to "fool" the machine and system (Polyakov, 2019). Here a robust tester will be brought on board to try to write code that would seek to confuse and interact with the system in ways that would mislead it. This is a human versus machine type of scenario, and the outcomes and results of such a confrontation can be recorded and used as basis for planning and modifying the AI system. This will clearly require some degrees of reasoning and strong IT skills that will be used to test and try to displace the AI system. While this might be very helpful in uncovering vulnerabilities, it could be highly discouraging and might prevent a system from being deployed. This is because the possibilities of attacks being launched successfully is premised on the probabilities and circumstances. This has some random elements that cannot be easily understood. Hence, firms might often want to use this human-attacks on AI systems as a last resort and for the most vital digital assets they might have.

7.6 FUTURE WORK

It is apparent from every indication that AI is here to stay. As such, it is important for organizations to find ways of gaining leverage in their use of AI in cybersecurity. This includes, among other things, the need to combine traditional techniques with AI tools until the AI development community can figure out the best way and approach of developing AI for the best outcomes in cybersecurity (Laurence, 2019). This is because in theory, AI tools can be improved to a level where all cybersecurity issues can be handled by these systems. However, the reality is that a malicious human being who uses AI to pursue cybersecurity projects is most likely to have an upper hand. Therefore, until further notice, any organization that is serious about using AI to end risks and issues in cybersecurity will have to assign human agents to monitor the AI system they are using to defend their cyberspace. AI will have to be observed closely in order to identify its risks and issues in order to react appropriately and gain the best outcomes. This way, malicious actions can be detected, blocked, and monitored as well. This will help the AI system to be upgraded as and when necessary in order to counteract threats. The best way of doing this is through constant auditing of the system in order to react to any emerging cybersecurity issue and matter of interest (Laurence, 2019).

It is also recommended that using a human-AI intervention must not be done randomly. There is a justification to hire experienced cybersecurity professionals with niche skills in order to blend AI with their own knowledge and experience (Klingerman, 2019). This is premised on the fact that cybersecurity risks are niche-specific. As such, it is important to hire the best brains in the industry you operate in, who understand the threats in order to deploy a firm's AI resources in the best way to deal with crimes. Cybersecurity risks are localized and they vary from industry to industry. What the main cybercriminals want in each sector varies. Thus, hiring the most experienced and most advanced persons in the industry helps detect issues and position the AI in the best way that will gain the optimal results. This removes the threat of wasting so much money on an AI system that fails to yield any results or spend money to deal with risks that could not be anticipated. The best persons who can forecast the most relevant risks and provide solutions through AI are those who understand the industry and niche. There is also room for pre-emptive action by cybersecurity professionals to test the system to find vulnerabilities. This means that cybersecurity must not be treated as a one-off incident because a firm has applied AI systems. This does not work. Rather, AI must be checked and re-checked from time to time to ascertain whether it is really helping a firm to meet its needs or not. Another code of best practice in using AI to boost cybersecurity is to have layers of defense and preliminary actions to stop suspicious activities. This is based on the need to build a space where firewalls and malware scanners can be deployed to lay the foundations for an AI system to be optimized in a given system. This way, attention can be given to high-risk areas and areas with high traffic by users in order to avoid issues and risks that might not be detectable and resolvable.

Trend-reading and analysis must be taken seriously because that can help to provide explanations and understandings of major issues. This will require experience and effort from the staff members who deal with AI and its activities. There must be a proper delivery of AI and machine learning among others in order to deal with issues and make the best of a given system. This will have to be done in the shadow of regular audits and evaluation of hardware and software. Also, a partner product or software that is used in a given cyber system must be monitored closely and changed regularly. This is because software system producers like Software as a Service (SaaS) platforms typically upgrade their systems when they detect threats. AI can work best if a firm uses the most recent and most effective version of any software or system. This helps to promote the outcomes and improve results without risks and problems (Klingerman, 2019).

7.7 CONCLUSION

This research identifies that AI has an extremely high and sophisticated application in cybersecurity activities and processes. This is because cybercriminals are getting more sophisticated so cyber threats keep getting more complex and it is no more appropriate to leave these issues unchecked. AI is a system that gives computer systems the ability to perceive things in their environments and act according to a definite pathway that is programmed into the system. AI seem to be the obvious solution to dealing with cybersecurity risks. This is because AI is a responsive version of automated solutions to cybersecurity risks. And with this, it can be programmed to react, prevent, and remain proactive when cybersecurity risks are identified. This means AI takes automated cybersecurity systems to the next level because it provides the ability to get the system to act in specific ways and forms to deal with risks and issues and achieve desired ends. In spite of this, AI comes with a lot of costs and challenges in gaining actual results by way of detecting and dealing with cyber risks. These challenges can be handled through the use of experienced persons who understand the niche to act as human-AI partners to monitor and act appropriately to threats and prevent these threats. AI can be improved through constant monitoring and upgrades in order to make the system better and more efficient and effective.

REFERENCES

Blue, J., Furey, E., Curran, K. (2017) *An evaluation of secure storage of authentication data.* International Journal for Information Security Research (IJISR), ISSN: 2042-4639, Vol. 7, No. 2, pp: 744–754, DOI: 10.20533/ijisr.2042.4639.2017.0086

Crane, C. (2019) "Artificial Intelligence in Cyber Security: The Savior or Enemy of Your Business?" *Hashed Out.* [Online] Available at: https://www.thesslstore.com/blog/artificial-intelligence-in-cyber-security-the-savior-or-enemy-of-your-business/

Curran, J., Curran, K. (2018) *Biometric Authentication Techniques in Online Learning Environments.* Biometric Authentication in Online Learning Environments, IGI Publishing. pp: 266–278, ISBN: 9781522577249, DOI: 10.4018/978-1-5225-7724-9.ch011

Curran, K., Mansell, G., Curran, J. (2018) *An IoT Framework for Detecting Movement within Indoor Environments.* International Conference on Machine Learning for Networking (MLN'2018), Paris, France, November 27-29, 2018.

Difesa, A. (2018) "Explainable Artificial Intelligence: How Does it Work?" *Expert System.* [Online] Available at: https://expertsystem.com/explainable-artificial-intelligence-work/ November 28th Nov 2018.

Faggella, D. (2019) "Artificial Intelligence and Security: Current Applications and Tomorrow's Potentials" *Emerj.* [Online] Available at: https://emerj.com/ai-sector-overviews/artificial-intelligence-and-security-applications/

Kingori, D. (2019). "Top 10 Cybersecurity Risks For 2019" *United States Cyber Security Magazine.* [Online] Available at: https://www.uscybersecurity.net/risks-2019/

Klingerman, S. (2019) "AI and Cybersecurity: Best Practices for Overcoming Security Challenges" *Quest Oracle Community.* [Online] Available at: https://questoraclecommunity.org/learn/blogs/overcoming-cybersecurity-challenges/

Laurence, A. (2019) "The Impact of Artificial Intelligence on Cyber Security" *CPO Magazine*. [Online] Available at: https://www.cpomagazine.com/cyber-security/the-impact-of-artificial-intelligence-on-cyber-security/

NormShield (2019) "Cyber Security with Artificial Intelligence in 10 Question" *NormShield*. [Online] Available at: https://www.normshield.com/cyber-security-with-artificial-intelligence-in-10-question/

Polyakov, A. (2019) "AI Security and Adversarial Machine Learning 101" *Towards Data Science*. [Online] Available at: https://towardsdatascience.com/ai-and-ml-security-101-6af8026675ff

Ramachandran, R. (2019) "How Artificial Intelligence Is Changing Cyber Security Landscape and Preventing Cyber Attacks" *Entrepreneur* [Online] Available at: https://www.entrepreneur.com/article/339509

Saratchandran, V. (2019) "Artificial Intelligence and Machine Learning: The Cyber Security Heroes of FinTech." *Fingent* [Online] Available at: https://www.fingent.com/blog/artificial-intelligence-and-machine-learning-the-cyber-security-heroes-of-fintech

SAS (2019) "Artificial Intelligence What It Is and Why It Matters" *SAS*. [Online] Available at: https://www.sas.com/en_us/insights/analytics/what-is-artificial-intelligence.html

Stephen, M. (2019) Cybersecurity AI: Integrating Artificial Intelligence into your Security Policy. *TechGenix*. [Online] Available at: techgenix.com/cybersecurity-ai/

Cybersecurity-Based Machine Learning for Cyber-Physical Systems

8

Mustapha Belaissaoui
Hassan 1st University, Settat, Morocco

Youssef Qasmaoui, Soufyane Mounir, and Yassine Maleh
University Sultan Moulay Slimane, Beni Mellal, Morocco

Contents

DOI: 10.1201/9781003278207-12

8.1 INTRODUCTION

A wide range of incidents have taken place over several months, from the Equifax data breach to the WannaCry ransomware that crippled numerous English hospitals and companies. The most concerning were those that attacked national security, such as the October cyberattack on the US Army and NATO by a group of Russian hackers alleged to be acting on their behalf and the spyware campaign launched against the governments of India and Pakistan. It was one of the deadliest waves of cyberattacks that the world ever saw in 2017.

Cybersecurity attacks are becoming more frequent as cyber attackers exploit system vulnerabilities for financial gain (Aguilar, 2015). Nation-state actors employ the most skilled attackers to launch targeted and coordinated attacks. Sony, PumpUp and Saks, Lord & Taylor are recent examples of targeted attacks. The time between a security breach and detection is measured in days. Cyber attackers are aware of existing security controls and continually improve their attack techniques (von Solms & van Niekerk, 2013). To extend the range of attacks, cyber attackers have a wide range of tools at their disposal to bypass traditional security mechanisms. Malicious infection control frameworks, zero-day exploits and rootkits can easily be purchased on an underground market. Attackers can also buy personal information and compromised domains to launch additional attacks. (Plonk & Carblanc, 2008).

In these times of paranoia, governments and organizations are investing more than ever in the cybersecurity of defense and aerospace products and services. As cyberattacks have become increasingly sophisticated, with allegations that one country is targeting another country for geopolitical purposes, the rate of investment in cybersecurity in the aerospace and defense market has also increased (Ramalingam et al., 2017).

According to Netscribes' research, the contribution of the global defense and aerospace sector is expected to reach $24.37 billion by 2022. The overall size of the cybersecurity market is also expected to grow strongly over the same period, reaching $125 billion by 2025.

Nowadays, machine learning is one of the most popular topics to detect cyberattacks on Internet of Things (IoT). Because in-depth knowledge-based techniques can offer a robust system for sophisticated attacks. On the contrary, the biggest problem in IoT's security research is the lack of public and updated datasets.

Traditional machine learning techniques, such as Bayesian Belief Networks (BBN) (Janakiram et al., 2006), Support Vector Machines (SVM) (Jha & Ragha, 2013; Kaplantzis et al., 2007; Maleh & Ezzati, 2015; Zhang et al., 2013) have been applied for cybersecurity. However, the generated large-scale data in IoT requires an efficient machine learning-based method, which can be adapted to the IoT specifications.

In this paper, we generated data by real-time simulations due to the lack of public datasets for IoT attacks. Also, the existing datasets such as KDDCup 99 are too old. Simulation-generated raw packet capture files are first converted to Comma Separated Values (CSV) files for processing and are then input into the feature pre-processing module of our system. We identified 28 characteristics as an initial set of features. Then, the normalization of characteristics is applied to all datasets to reduce the adverse effects of marginal values. As a result of this analysis, some features are abandoned in the pre-functional selection process. We have reduced the number of features to 16 main features. The approach used is described in Figure 8.1.

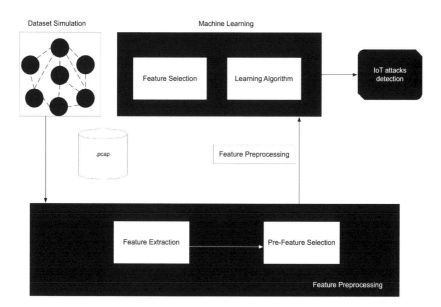

FIGURE 8.1   The proposed methodology.

The energy consumption and calculation capacities of its IoT devices are the most critical constraints of this type of network. Due to these constraints, the security solutions designed for IoT should be both lightweight and efficient, which would reduce the computational load on the devices as much as possible (Yassine Maleh et al., 2016). This chapter proposes a lightweight solution that imposes a minimal load on the IoT network. The overall goals are:

- To generate a new IoT routing attacks dataset
- To build different machine learning algorithms and train them by producing datasets
- To evaluate the different ML models for intrusion detection in IoT

This chapter presents the research background in the next section: the related work in section 3 and the detailed description of the proposed intrusion detection methodology in section 4. Section 5 describes the experiments using the proposed models. Section 6 presents conclusions and future research directions.

8.2 BACKGROUND

8.2.1 Cyber-Physical Systems (CPS)

The modern aerospace systems have a strong link between embedded cyber systems (e.g. processing and communication) and physical elements (e.g. platform structure, detection, activation, and environment). Researchers have begun to explore and exploit "cyber-physical systems" or CPS, defined as "technical systems that are built on and depend on the synergy of physical and computer components" (Atkins & Bradley, 2013). These CPSs consist of interconnected systems of heterogeneous components that can operate autonomously and transparently interact with the physical world through their sensors. For example, a commercial aircraft or a driverless car has thousands of internal and external sensors and actuators on board to provide more efficient and reliable services. Manufacturers can now collect huge amounts of data using these sensors to perform real-time operations and accurately identify hardware, software, and communication failures. Similarly, many new communication standards have emerged to ensure communication between these sensors and actuators for various application scenarios.

CPS contains critical data, conducts research and collaboration activities, and improves quality of life. CPSs are intelligent systems that provide an environment for the cooperation of computer components and things that are well known for their physical activities. The CPS is a kind of bridge that brings the cybernetic and physical domains together and assumes an indispensable responsibility in many areas as clearly as possibly illustrated in Figure 8.2.

The first CPS applications were based on smartphone devices to deploy applications. As a result, personal assistance applications have developed, particularly those

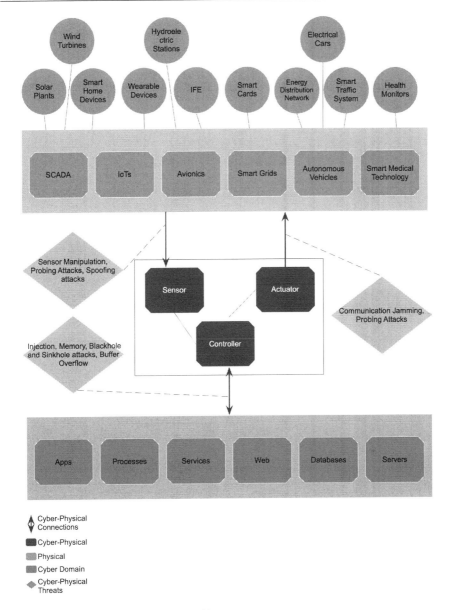

FIGURE 8.2 Cyber-physical system architecture.

focusing on medical assistance. The vision of "connected health" has grown in recent years due to the development of related technologies such as wireless networks or sensors. This has led to the development of Personal Health Devices (PHD), which aim to collect and share information on a local network or the Internet (Berkovich, 2011).

CPSs are cooperating systems, with decentralized control, resulting from the fusion of the real and virtual worlds, with autonomous and context-dependent behaviors, which can be constituted as systems with other CPSs and lead to extensive collaboration with humans (Schuh et al., 2014c). For this purpose, CPS embedded software uses sensors and actuators, connects with human operators by communicating via interfaces, and can store and process information from sensors or the network (Strang and Anderl, 2014). According to (Shi et al., 2011), here are the characteristics attached to a CPS:

- High level of physical integration/cyber
- Processing capabilities in each physical component, because processing and communication resources are generally limited
- Highly connected, via networks with or without wires, Bluetooth, GSM, GPS, etc.
- Adapted to multiple temporal and spatial scales
- Capable of reconfiguration/dynamic reorganization
- Highly automated, in closed loops
- Reliable, even certified in some instances

Cyber-physical systems (CPS) integrate programmable components to control a physical process. They are now widely used in various industries such as energy, aeronautics, automotive, and chemical industries (Humayed et al., 2017). Among the various existing CPS, Supervisory Control and Data Acquisition (SCADA) systems allow the control and supervision of critical industrial installations (Kim, 2012). Their malfunction can cause harmful impacts on the facility and its environment. SCADA systems were first isolated and based on proprietary components and standards. To facilitate the supervision of the industrial process and reduce costs, they are increasingly integrating information and communication technologies (ICT). This makes them more complex and exposes them to cyberattacks that exploit the existing ICT vulnerabilities. These attacks can change the functioning of a system and affect its safety. Security is then associated with uncalculated system risks, and malicious risks, including cyber attacks.(Humayed et al., 2017).

8.2.2 Internet of Things

The IoT consists of sensors connected to the Internet that behave similar to the Internet by making open ad-hoc connections, freely sharing data, and allowing access to various applications so that computers understand the world around them and become the nervous system of humanity (Ashton, 2011).

The IoT is at the center of the attention of consumers and businesses. And for a good reason, the promise of a world populated by connected objects offers countless opportunities through the possibilities offered, both as a user and a service provider. Many studies predict an explosion in the volume of connected objects in the world by 2020 that may reach 26 billion according to Gartner. Although a strong vigilance remains necessary to read these figures, as the perimeter definitions vary, they nevertheless confirm a trend toward the massive deployment of connected objects. The very notion of the IoT, subject to interpretation, deserves to be clarified. For this report, a broad definition of the IoT will be used, corresponding to a set of connected physical objects that communicate via multiple technologies with various data processing platforms, connecting the waves of the cloud and big data. Data and its uses are at the heart of the IoT. These, extracted from the various terminals and sensors, make it possible to inform users about the evolution of their environment in real-time. Beyond the simple provision of information, the aggregation of the diversity of this data from heterogeneous sources makes it possible to quantify the connected environment to identify trends, enrich uses, or consider new ones. The user – individual or company – can act in real-time on his environment – manually or automatically – to optimize processes (for example, optimization of road flows or supply chains in real-time).

The applications of the IoT result in many concrete uses – new or improved – that significantly impact the daily lives of individuals, companies, and communities. The potential benefits are expected to facilitate its adoption by the diversified users. Several sectors, or growth markets, stand out, in particular:

- The so-called "intelligent" territories are at the heart of local authorities' projects and should make it possible to optimize the management of communicating infrastructures (transport, energy, water, etc.) to provide a better service to citizens and respect sustainable development objectives within the territories.
- Thanks to the IoT, housing and workplaces are becoming more comfortable, easier to manage, and less expensive to use. The connected building, including the connected house, offers in particular possibilities for controlling energy consumption, integrating security and comfort systems, and increasing comfort.
- The industry of the future (the use of the IoT to serve the means of production) is gradually developing. The first step is the transfer of information. Feedback and remote control are more complex phases to implement in some areas of activity.
- The connected vehicle, for which first applications have already been developed, has also taken the first step in reading the information thanks to the integration of long-standing onboard electronics. The actors of the automotive industry are now seeking to develop new business models to take advantage of these new opportunities while issues related to responsibilities are emerging.
- Connected health, including the "wellness" segment, is one of the applications the general public is most aware of, mainly thanks to wearables. The aspects related to personal data protection focus attention because of the collection of unusually intimate – or even health – and new personal information by private actors and the stakes involved in their exploitation, particularly by certain services. The technological contributions to the organization of care and the degree of involvement of health professionals are also a subject of attention. The changes made possible by technological developments that are often faster than social and regulatory developments make this sector more challenging to understand and more complex.

To invest in this new field of IoT, protocols must be adapted to new constraints; security must be reinforced because the objects affect the real world and a malfunction can lead to serious consequences. As regards the architecture, it must be the most generic possible to allow interconnection and it must not be linked to a particular purpose.

The 6LoWPAN protocol, for IPv6 Low power Wireless Personal Area Network, is an adaptation of the IPv4 and IPv6 protocols for communications involving connected objects (Shelby & Bormann, 2011). It was developed by the Internet Engineering Task Force (IETF) to be "lighter" than standard IP protocols. Also running on a mesh network model fully supports User Datagram Protocol (UDP) and Transmission Control Protocol (TCP). Mulligan states that the packet headers are very light (2 to 11 bytes) and allow communication between 2^{64} nodes (Mulligan, 2007). Also, most of the work on IDS in connected objects has focused on this protocol (Zarpelão et al., 2017). Like the ZigBee, the 6LoWPAN operates in the 2.4 GHz frequency band, making its integration easier due to current equipment. Thus, the heterogeneity of connected objects within homes makes it much more difficult to propose generic solutions for securing connected objects in this context.

8.2.3 Security Overview in IoT

IoT security is important and routing attacks are a widespread threat to IoT (Maleh, Ezzati, & Belaissaoui, 2018). The security of IoT systems can be exceptionally complex due to a large number of components, a potentially large attack surface and interactions between different parts of the system. Threat modeling is an excellent starting point for understanding the risks associated with IoT systems and how these risks can be mitigated.

Routing Protocol for Low-Power and Lossy Network (RPL) attacks can be classified into three categories according to the vulnerability they aim to exploit (resources, topology, and traffic.) These resource-based attacks are Deny of Service (DoS)-based and aim to deplete energy and overload memory. Topological attacks are intended to interfere with the normal network process. This can lead to the failure of one or more network nodes. Also, these attacks threaten the original topology of the network. Traffic-based attacking nodes aim to join the network like a normal node. Then, these attackers use network traffic information to conduct the attack (Patil & Chen, 2017).

Routing attacks are most common against RPL. Among the most significant routing attacks are hello flood, wormhole, and sinkhole attacks. Figure 8.3 illustrates the location of routing attacks in IoT systems in a physical, cyber environment.

8.2.3.1 Attacks and threats in IoT

With the development of IoT, more devices are becoming connected to the Internet. Every day, these devices are becoming target for several attacks (Suo et al., 2012). To address the security challenges in IoT, the authors need to analyze the security problems in IoT based on four-layer architecture. There are different types of attacks on the IoT. These attacks can be active attacks in which an attacker attempts to make changes to data on the target or data in route to the target, or there can be passive attacks in which an attacker attempt to obtain or make use of information. The attacker can perform various attacks like network jamming, message sniffing, device compromising etc. (Xu et al., 2005).

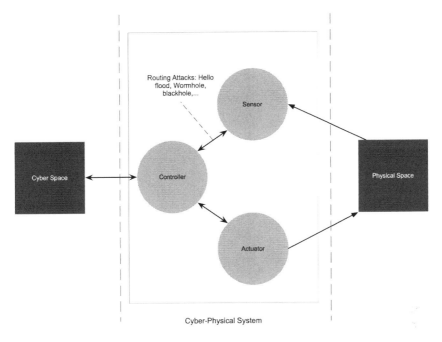

FIGURE 8.3   Routing attacks in IoT-CPS.

8.2.3.1.1 *Security issues in the physical layer*

There are many security issues affecting the physical layer of the IoT system. There is a great need for new technologies to protect energy resources and physical security mechanisms. The devices must be protected against physical attacks. They must also be able to save and optimize energy and be able to rely on battery power in the event of a power failure or interruption of the city's grid. The batteries must be charged long enough and recharged quickly so that the device can continue to operate (Benenson et al., 2007). Common issues in physical layer have been identified in the following sections.

8.2.3.1.1.1 Physical damage   An example scenario in this type of attack is physical devices such as sensors, nodes, and actuators that are physically damaged by malicious entities. This could cause the sensor, nodes, and actuators to lose its expected functionality and become vulnerable to other risks.

8.2.3.1.1.2 Environmental attacks   In this kind of attack, physical devices such as sensors, nodes, and actuators are physically damaged by malicious entities. The sensor, nodes, and actuators could thus lose the expected functionality and become vulnerable to other risks.

8.2.3.1.1.3 Loss of power   Devices that lack energy cannot operate normally, resulting in a denial of service. For example, a common strategy for saving energy is to switch appliances to various energy-saving modes, for example, in different standby and hibernation modes. A sleep deprivation attack makes just enough legitimate requests to prevent a device from entering its power-saving mode.

8.2.3.1.1.4 Physical tampering   In factory automation, the embedded programmable logic controllers (PLCs) that operate robotic systems are integrated into the company's typical IT infrastructure. It is essential to protect these PLCs from human interference while preserving the investment in IT infrastructure and taking advantage of the existing security controls.

8.2.3.1.2 Security issues in the network layer
The network layer connects all things in IoT and allows them to be aware of their surroundings. It can aggregate data from the existing IT infrastructures and then transmit it to other layers. The IoT connects a variety of different networks, which may cause many issues with network issues, security issues, and communication issues. An attack from hackers and malicious nodes that compromises devices in the network is a serious issue. Common threats to network layer have been identified in the following sections.

8.2.3.1.2.1 Selective forwarding attack   Malicious nodes choose the packets and drop them out. They selectively filter certain packets and allow the rest. Dropped packets may carry the necessary sensitive data for further processing.

8.2.3.1.2.2 Hello flood attacks   In hello flood attack, every node will introduce itself with hello messages to all the neighbors that are reachable at its frequency level. A malicious node will cover a wide frequency area, and hence it becomes a neighbor to all the nodes in the network. Subsequently, this malicious node will also broadcast a hello message to all its neighbors, affecting the availability.

8.2.3.1.2.3 Sinkhole attack   In this attack, the malicious node advertises itself as the best path to be chosen as a preferred parent by its neighbors, thus routing traffic through it. As it is, this attack does not appear to be harmful (passive attack). However, it becomes harmful (active attack) if combined with other attacks (Raza et al., 2013).

8.2.3.1.2.4 Blackhole attack   An intruder triggers a blackhole attack by dropping all data packets routed through it. This attack can be considered as a DoS attack. Indeed, the blackhole attack is more dangerous if combined with sinkhole attacks since the attacker is in a position where massive traffic is routed through it. This attack increases the number of exchanged DODAG Information Object (DIO) messages, which leads to instability of the network; data packets delay and thus resources exhaust (Cai et al., 2016).

8.2.3.1.2.5 Selective-forwarding attack   In selective redirection attacks, a malicious node can either actively filter RPL control messages or drop data packets and transfer only control message traffic. The first attack negatively affects the construction of the topology and network functions, which disrupts routing. While the second attack leads to a DoS attack because no data will be transmitted to the destination nodes. These attacks are also known as gray hole attacks, which are a special case of blackhole attacks (Raza et al., 2013).

8.2.3.1.2.6 Wormhole attack   Two or multiple attackers have to connect via wired or wireless links called tunnels to trigger a wormhole attack. Wormhole attack permits an attacker to replay the network traffic in the other ends of the tunnels. In the case of RPL, some attackers can be outside the 6LoWPAN, and thus can bypass the 6LBR. Also, if control messages are replayed to another part of the network, distant nodes see each other as neighbors, distorting routing paths and creating un-optimized paths (Mayzaud et al., 2016).

8.2.3.1.2.7 DoS attack   DoS attack aims to make nodes and/or the network unavailable. These attacks are simple to implement and very common because they have devastating consequences on the network. These attacks can be triggered against any layer of the IoT architecture.

8.2.3.1.2.8 Storage attacks   Vast portions of data containing dynamic user information will need to be stored on storage devices, which can be attacked and the data may be compromised or changed. The repetition of the data coupled with access to different types of people results in the increased surface area for the attacks.

8.2.3.1.3 Security issues in the perception layer
The security threats in the perception layer are at the node level. Because the nodes are composed of sensors, they are prime targets for hackers who want to use them to replace the device's software with their software. In the perception layer, most threats come from outside entities, mainly concerning sensors and other data gathering utilities. Common threats in perception layer have been identified in the following sections.

8.2.3.1.3.1 Eavesdropping   In wireless communication, the communication between devices is wireless and through the Internet, making them vulnerable to eavesdropping attacks.

An adversary can perform an attack scenario, for example, a sensor in the smart home that is compromised can send thrust notifications to users and collect private information from the users.

8.2.3.1.3.2 Sniffing attacks   To acquire information from the device, an attacker puts malicious sensors or sniffers close to the normal sensors of the IoT devices. For example, as human-to-human and human-to-device interactions occur over shared physical networks, services, and social spaces, it is also possible to detect smaller amounts of physical drag from these interactions with a higher degree of sensitivity and accuracy.

8.2.3.1.3.3 Noise in data   As the data transmission takes place over wireless networks covering vast distances, it is probable that the data may contain noise, i.e., false information, missing information. Falsification of data can be dangerous in such scenarios when a lot is dependent on the reliable transmission of data.

8.2.3.1.4 Security issues in the application layer
Due to security issues in the application layer, applications can be easily stopped and compromised. As a result, applications cannot run the services for which they are

programmed or even execute authenticated services incorrectly. In this layer, malicious attacks can cause bugs in the application program code that cause the application to malfunction. This is a critical concern given the number of devices classified as entities at the application level. Threats common to the application layer have been identified in the following sections.

8.2.3.1.4.1 Data authentication   Data authentication could ensure integrity and originality. Data can be collected from any device at any time. Intruders can falsify them. It must be ensured that the perceived data comes only from intended or legitimate users. Also, it is mandatory to check that the data have not been modified during transit.

8.2.3.1.4.2 Malicious code attacks   An example of a scenario in this kind of attack could be a malicious worm spreading to embedded Internet attack devices running a particular operating system for Linux, for example (Kumar et al., 2016). Such a worm could attack a range of small Internet-compatible devices, such as home routers, set-top boxes, and security cameras. The worm would use a software vulnerability known to spread. Such code attacks could enter a car's Wi-Fi, take control of the steering wheel, and cause the car to crash, injuring both the driver and the car.

8.2.3.1.4.3 Tampering with node-based applications   Hackers exploit application vulnerabilities on device nodes and install malicious rootkits. The security design of the devices must be tamper-proof. The protection of specific parts of a device may not be sufficient. Some threats can manipulate the local environment to cause the device to malfunction and cause the environment to heat or freeze. An altered temperature sensor would only display a fixed temperature value, while the altered camera in the smart house would transmit outdated images.

8.2.4 Machine Learning Techniques

Machine learning techniques are based on establishing an explicit or implicit model to categorize classification problems in the target system. A unique feature of these approaches is providing strong data to form the behavioral model. Depending on the organization of these data, we can classify them into three main categories:

- **Supervised Learning**: Training data includes both input features and output decision.
- **Semi-supervised Learning**: The training data only contains the features of the problem to be solved.
- **Unsupervised Learning**: No training data is provided as input.

In many cases, the applicability of automatic learning principles coincides with that of statistical techniques; it focuses on building a model that improves its performance based on the previous results. Therefore, a learning algorithm can modify its execution strategy based on new information about the problem. Although this characteristic may make it desirable to use such schemes for all situations, the major disadvantages are their resource-intensive nature during the learning phase and the sometimes-high error rates, as well as the non-explicit nature of the alarms raised by these models. Other phenomena can impact algorithms by automatic learning. Some algorithms such as decision trees and support vector machines (SVMs) are often subject to overlearning. Thus, we find a largely optimistic estimate of the classifier's performance by evaluating the performance indicators on the training data. Below are the most commonly used models in anomaly detection and their main advantages and disadvantages.

8.2.4.1 K-Nearest neighbors

The K-Nearest Neighbor (K-NN) (Thirumuruganathan, 2010) method is a supervised method. It has been used in statistical estimation and model recognition as a non-parametric technique, meaning that it makes no assumptions about data distribution.

The K-NN algorithm is one of the simplest of all automatic learning algorithms. It is a type of learning based on lazy learning. On the other hand, there is no explicit or very minimal training phase. It means that the training phase is fast enough.

The K-NN technique assumes to have data in a characteristic space. This means that the data points are in a metric space. Besides, the data can be scalar or even multi-dimensional vectors.

The K-NN method was used for classification (Narayanan et al., 2016) and regression.

To find the new case class, the algorithm is based on the following rule: first, it searches for the K-NNs of the latest case, then in the next step, it chooses the closest and most frequent result from the candidates found.

The algorithm searches for the K-NNs among the already classified characters to affect a new character to a class. In this way, the individual is assigned to the class that contains the most individuals among the candidates identified.

This technique focuses on two main parameters: a similarity function to compare individuals in the characteristic space and the number k that determines how many neighbors influence the classification.

The distance is used to test the similarity between two vectors. This makes it possible to measure the degree of difference between the two vectors. Many types of distance exist, including:

Hamming distance:

$$d_{ij} = \sum_{k=1}^{p} \left| x_{ik} - x_{jk} \right|$$

Manhattan distance:

$$d1(p,q) = \left\| p - q \right\| 1 = \sum_{i=1}^{n} \left| p_i - q_i \right|$$

Minkowski distance:

$$\left(\sum_{i=1}^{n} \mid x_i - y_i \mid^p\right)\left(\frac{1}{p}\right)$$

For continuous variables, the most commonly used method is mainly the Euclidean distance, defined by the following formula:

Euclidian distance:

$$\sqrt{\sum_{i=1}^{n}(qi - pi)^2}$$

Euclidean distance can be used for solving problems, where the characteristics are of the same type. To determine the features of the different types, it is recommended to use Manhattan Distance (for example).

In Figure 8.4, an example of classification of K-NN, the test sample (Inside circle) must be classified either in the first class of squares or in the class of triangles. If K = 3 (outside circle), it is assigned to the second class because there are three triangles and only two squares in the inside circle. For example, in K = 5, it is given to the first class (five squares against four triangles).

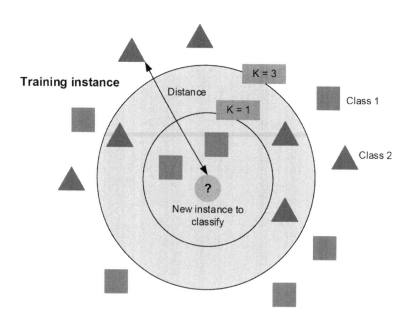

FIGURE 8.4   An example of classification K-NN.

The algorithm of the K-NNs:

k-Nearest Neighbor

Classify (X, Y, x) // X: training data, Y: class labels of X, x: unknown sample

for i = 1 to m do

Compute distance (Xi, x)

end for

Compute set I containing indices for the k smallest distances (Xi, x).

return majority label for {Yi where i ∈ I}

8.2.4.2 Support vector machines

SVMs (Jing & Zhang, 2010) are supervised learning techniques applied to solve classification and regression problems. These are based on two main concepts: the concept of maximum margin and the concept of core function.

Support vector machines can be used to solve discrimination problems, i.e., to decide which class a model is to be included in, or regression, i.e., to predict the numerical value of a variable. To solve these two problems, it is necessary to construct a function f which has an input vector x and corresponds to an output y: $y = f(x)$

SVM learning, which uses a hyperplane to classify the data into two classes, performs a task similar to C4.5, but SVM does not use the decision trees.

A hyperplane is a function like the equation of a line, $y = mx + b$. Well, for a simple classification task with only two functions, the hyperplane can be a line. SVM can make a loop to project the data into higher dimensions. After projecting into larger dimensions, SVM represents the best hyperplane that separates these data into two classes.

For example, let's take a set of squares and triangles samples on a table. If the samples are not very mixed together, we can make a stick and, without moving the samples, separate them with the stick, as shown in Figure 8.5.

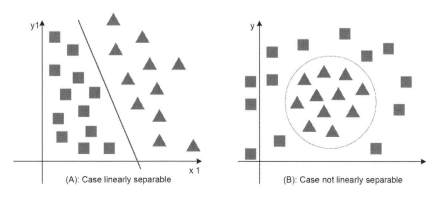

FIGURE 8.5   The problem of two-class classification by SVM.

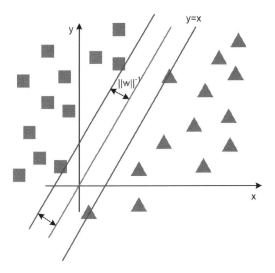

FIGURE 8.6   Optimal hyperplane with maximum margin.

If a new sample is added to the table and knowing which side of the stick is on, we can predict his class. The samples represent data points, and the squares and triangles represent two classes. The stick represents the simplest hyperplane in a line.

There are many possible linear separators for two classes and linearly separable data ash shown in Figure 8.6. SVMs only choose the optimal one, i.e., searching for a decision surface that is as far away as possible from any data point. This distance from the decision surface to the nearest data point determines the maximum margin of the classifier. To obtain an optimal hyperplane, maximizing the margin between the data and the hyperplane is necessary.

To solve separator non-linearity, the idea of SVMs is to increase the size of the data space. In this case, there is likely a linear separator. Indeed, the chance of finding a hyperplane separator rises proportionally with the size of the data space.

This re-dimensioning of space is based on the use of the Kernel function. There are several types of core functions such as Gaussian, polynomial, and sigmoid.

8.2.4.3 Random forest (RF)

Random forest stands for a popular algorithm of machine learning. Data preparation and modeling are not required; however, the results are usually accurate. Random forest is based on decision trees, and more specifically, random forests are sets of decision trees that offer higher predictive accuracy. For this reason, it is called a "forest", consisting essentially of a collection of decision trees (Breiman, 2001).

The main idea is to design several decision trees based on the independent subsets of the dataset (Louppe, 2014). Then, the n variables of the set of characteristics are randomly selected at each node, and the better distribution of these variables is identified.

The random forest algorithm can be summarized as follows:

- The construction of multiple trees is estimated at two-thirds of the training data. Items are randomly selected.
- Multiple predictors are randomly selected from all predictors. After that, only the best splitting on these selected variables can be used to split the node.
- The classification error rate is calculated using the remaining data. This total error rate is calculated as a global out-of-bag error rate.
- Each tree trained is its classification result and gives its own "vote" when the class that has collected the most "votes" is selected as a result.

Random forests inherit many advantages of decision tree algorithms, both applied to regression and classification applications, and are easy to calculate and easily adapted. They also provide better accuracy in general.

Compared with the decision trees, however, it is not very easy to interpret the results. When we examine the resulting tree in decision trees, we can obtain valuable information about essential variables and their outcome. With random forests, this is not possible. However, it can also be described as a more robust algorithm than decision trees – for example, if we change the data a little bit, the decision trees will change, most certainly reducing the accuracy. For random forest algorithms, this will not happen because it is a combination of several decision trees; the random forest will remain more stable. Figure 8.7 shows the random forest algorithm model.

8.2.4.4 Naive Bayes (NB)

The Naive Bayes algorithm is the classification machine learning algorithm built on Bayes' theorem. It may be used for binary and multi-class classification issues

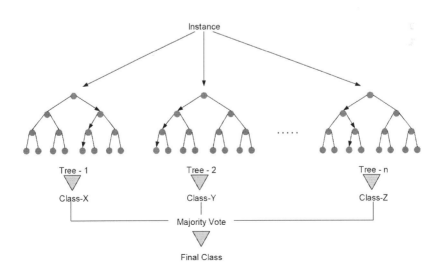

FIGURE 8.7 Random forest algorithm schema.

(Rish, 2001). For the main reason, it is based on the concept of treating each element independently. Naive Bayes evaluates the probability of each element separately, without any correlation, to make a prediction based on the Bayes' theorem of Thomas Bayes, an English statistician, in real-world problems; the attributes often have a correlation level between them.

- To understand the Naive Bayes' algorithm, we must first introduce class probabilities and conditional probabilities.
- Class probability is the probability of a class in the dataset. In other words, if we select a random element from the dataset, it is the probability that it belongs to a particular class.
- The conditional probability is the probability of the value of the feature given to the class.
  1. Class probability is calculated just as the number of samples in the class divided by the total number of samples:

$$PC = \frac{\text{Count (instances in C)}}{\text{Count (instances in N total)}}$$

  2. Conditional probabilities are calculated as the frequency of each attribute value divided by the frequency of instances of that class.

$$P(V \mid C) = \frac{\text{Count (instances with V and C)}}{\text{Count (instances with V)}}$$

  3. Given the probabilities, we can calculate the probability of the instance belonging to a class and therefore make decisions using the Bayes' theorem:

$$P(A \mid B) = \frac{P(B \mid A)P(A)}{P(B)}$$

  4. The probabilities of the item belonging to all classes are compared and the class with the highest probability is selected.

The benefits of this technique are its simplicity and easy understanding. Also, it works well on datasets whose characteristics are not relevant because the probabilities of contributing to production are minimal. However, they are not included in the predictions. In addition, this algorithm generally gives high performance concerning the resources consumed because it only needs to calculate the probabilities of the characteristics and classes. It is not necessary to find coefficients as in the other algorithms. Its primary disadvantage is that each feature is treated independently, but this is not true in many cases.

8.2.4.5 Artificial neural network

The artificial neural network algorithm is based on biological neural networks and is trying to enable computers to learn in the same way as human reinforcement learning

(Jain et al., 1996). Perceptron is the basic unit of a neural network. A perceptron is composed of one or more inputs, a processor, and a single output. A perceptron follows the "feed-forward" model, which means that inputs are sent to a neuron, processed, and output.

A perceptron follows four main steps:

- Receive inputs
- Weight inputs
- Sum inputs
- Generate inputs

Each entry sent to the neuron should be weighted first, i.e., multiplied by a number (between –1 and 1). Generally, the creation of a perceptron begins with the assignment of random weights. Then each input is multiplied by its weight. Finally, the perceptron output is generated by making this sum passed through an activation function. The activation function tells the perceptron with a simple binary output if it must "pull" or not – multiple activation functions to choose from (logistics, trigonometry, step, etc.). For example, we can make the activation function the sign of the sum. Thus, if the sum is a positive number, the output is 1; if it is negative, the output is –1. Besides, there is another factor to consider: bias. Consider that both inputs are equal to zero, so any sum would also be equal to zero regardless of the multiplicative weight.

For this reason, a third input is added, called the bias input, with a value of 1, which avoids the zero problems. Finally, the following steps are used to train the perceptron:

1. Provide the perceptron with inputs for which there is a known answer.
2. Ask the perceptron to guess for an answer.
3. Compute the error (distance from the correct answer).
4. Adjust all the weights according to the error, return to step 1, and repeat.

Now we repeat this until we attain the accepted error. In this way, only one perceptron would function. Then, it is enough to connect several perceptrons in layers, input layer, and output layer to create a neural network. All layers between the input and output layers are called hidden layers. In Figure 8.8, a perceptron is composed of an input layer, two hidden layers, and an output layer.

Popular neural network algorithms are Hopfield, multilayer perception, counter-propagation networks, basic radial function, and self-organized maps, etc.

8.3 THE PROPOSED DETECTION METHOD

The proposed framework for intrusion detection is a hybrid Intrusion Detection System (IDS). The proposed IDS uses the 6LoWPAN compression header based on the machine learning algorithms to learn and classify attacks. Then, the rule or signature created by the machine learning algorithm is set to 6BR. Over time, when a new signature is

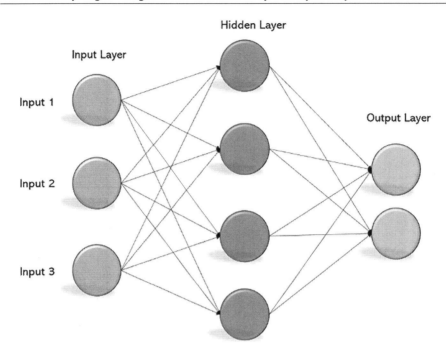

FIGURE 8.8   Multilayer perceptrons neural network perceptrons.

available for routing attacks, 6BR will be updated with the new rule or signature generated by the new features. The proposed DIS framework is divided into three layers, as shown in Figure 8.6. The first layer consists of detection agents that use the Cooja traffic analyzer to capture network data. The captured data is then analyzed and filtered by a second layer model that extracts only the distinct characteristics that distinguish normal and abnormal network activities. The data is classified as normal or malicious (hello flood, wormhole, or sinkhole). The proposed framework for the IDS is illustrated in Figure 8.9.

8.3.1 Module 1: Dataset Generation

The various RPL network communication scenarios were simulated by Cooja simulator. Cooja used the Contiki operating system (Bagula & Erasmus, 2015). The sensor nodes in the network implement the RPL protocol (Winter et al., 2011). Contiki makes it possible to load and unload individual programs and services to the simulated sensors (Dunkels et al., 2004). Figure 8.10 shows a Cooja user interface. To simulate routing attacks such as hello flood attack, wormhole attack, and sinkhole attack, we conducted simulation scenarios of each attack on a large number of IoT nodes, up to 500, with different percentages (10%, 20%, etc.) of malicious sensor nodes as shown in Table 8.1. We, therefore, simulated different routing attack scenarios and processed raw datasets to prepare them for the detection process. Subsequently, we used a Wireshark packet

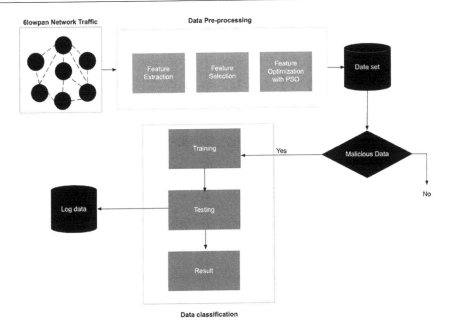

FIGURE 8.9   The proposed architecture.

analyzer to transform Online Court Assistance Program (OCAP) files into comma-separated values (CSV) files. Then, we applied a data pre-processing script to extract the features of the generated CSV files. Finally, we concatenate the same attack datasets to obtain a complete dataset to use in our research.

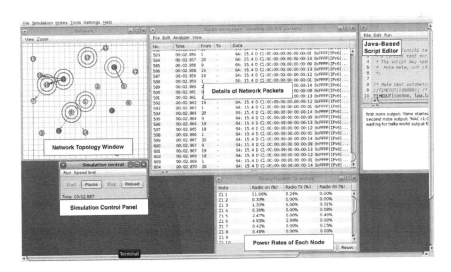

FIGURE 8.10   Cooja user interface.

TABLE 8.1 Datasets scenarios

		MALICIOUS			NORMAL		
DATASETS	SCENARIOS	NB. NODES	NB MALICIOUS/ NORMAL NODES	TOTAL NB PACKET	SCENARIOS	NB NODES	TOTAL NB COUNT
Hello Flood	HF_10	10	2/8	212.134	Normal_10	10	176.286
	HF_50	50	8/50	328.465	Normal_50	50	218.724
	HF_100	100	16/84	416.274	Normal_100	100	310.187
	HF_500	500	50/500	675.765	Normal_500	500	501.075
Wormhole	WH_10	10	2/8	121.126	Normal_10	10	118.172
	WH_50	50	8/50	147.465	Normal_50	50	129.557
	WH_100	100	16/84	317.673	Normal_100	100	238.933
	WH_500	500	50/500	719.764	Normal_500	500	450.193
Sinkhole	SK_10	10	2/8	121.361	Normal_10	10	117.213
	SK_50	50	8/50	227.186	Normal_50	50	165.763
	SK_100	100	16/84	301.392	Normal_100	100	216.031
	SK_500	500	50/500	815.534	Normal_500	500	721.554

8.3.2 Module 2: Data Pre-processing

8.3.2.1 Feature extraction

The Packet Capture (PCAP) files are generated once the situations are simulated. A decomposition into CSV files with Wireshark was performed on these data files. A machine learning algorithm requires the extraction of specified properties from the learning data. The data pre-processing stage involves identifying essential data properties to minimize computation overload and acquire problem-oriented features. For each sort of attack, we ran simulations with various topologies and network sizes. We get the raw datasets as a consequence of the simulation. After the simulation is finished, Cooja outputs the PCAP and CSV files. There is too much information in raw data files to let them stand alone as a starting point for a learning algorithm because of the noise and over adaptation they introduce to the learning process.

As soon as the scenarios are simulated, OCAP files are generated. Wireshark was used to break down these files into CSV files. The PCAP and CSV files are exported by Cooja after the simulation is over. To minimize computation overload and acquire problem-oriented features, the data pre-processing stage involves the extraction of key data characteristics from the dataset. Extracting characteristics from learning data is necessary for machine learning algorithms. The topologies and network sizes for each attack type were varied in our simulations. We can get the original datasets from the simulation results. On the other hand, raw data files do not suffice as an input point into the learning process since they contain information such as source/destination node addresses and packet length, which introduces noise and overadaptation into the system.

8.3.2.2 Data extraction algorithm

Input: *pcap fille*
get Arguments pcap from network traffic;
Loop read each packet;
function
array ← dataset.csv
    Sorted array
    Feature conversion
Feature Extraction:
    5000ms ← Window Size
    Calculate Feature values within the window size
    Labeling the dataset
End
End

It is possible to look at raw data and see both quantitative and qualitative features. However, the algorithm used to learn only accepts numerical values. So, we changed their unified format by changing their characteristics to qualitative characteristics. Destination Advertisement Object (DAO) is used in RPL to make sure that the training destination is only used once because the parents were chosen. A Destination oriented directed acyclic graphs Information Object (DIO) message is the most important type of message in the RPL language. It determines the best route through the base node using specific measures such as distance or countdown (Al-Fuqaha et al., 2015). Another type of message is called DIS, used by the nodes to join the network. One type of message that nodes can use to say thank you is called "ack". Our data also includes Protocol Data Unit (PDU) and Protocol Data Unit (UDP) packets, which are data packets that look like they're from the real world. The extracted features are listed in Table 8.2.

8.3.3 Module 3: Data Classification

The data classification module configured the three routing attacks in the IoT at this layer, namely, hello flood, wormhole, and sinkhole attacks. The essential attacks features are chosen for further analysis. Their packet number is tracked over time to study the behavior of each attack, and a set of rules is then developed. Then, the classes labeled "Normal", "Hello Flood", "Wormhole", and "Sinkhole" are created based on the revised

TABLE 8.2 Extracted features

NUMBER	ABBREVIATION	DESCRIPTION
1	Num	Packet sequence number
2	Time	Time of simulation
3	Src	IP source node
4	Des	IP destination node
5	RT	Rate transmission
6	RR	Rate reception
7	ATT	Average transmission time
8	ART	Average reception time
9	PTC	Packet transmitted count
10	PRC	Packet received count
11	TTT	Total transmission time
12	TRT	Total reception time
13	DIO	DIO packet count
14	DAO	DAO packet count
15	DIS	DIS packet count
16	Tag	Malicious/Normal label

rule. To classify each attack according to the defined classes, we compare six machine algorithms using the R language to find the most efficient algorithm. The algorithms are K-NN, SVM, NB, RF, and Multilayer Perceptron (MLP).

8.4 IMPLEMENTATION

During this step, the research plan is designed and can be implemented in practice. The whole implementation process can be outlined in the following steps:

1. Network traffic record (using Wireshark)
2. Feature extraction and selection (using Python 3.7)
3. Application of the machine learning methods (using R)
4. Evaluation of the results

8.4.1 Evaluation Metrics

Accuracy: The accuracy of detection is measured as the percentage of correctly identified instances. This is the number of correct predictions divided by the total number of instances in the dataset. It should be noted that the accuracy is highly dependent on the threshold chosen by the classifier and may, therefore, vary between different sets of tests. Therefore, this is not the optimal method to compare different classifiers, but it can give an overview of the class. Thus, the accuracy can be calculated using the following equation:

$$Accuracy = \left(\frac{TP + TN}{TP + FP + TN + FN} \right)$$

where:

True positive (TP) = a number of positive samples correctly predicted.
False negative (FN) = number of positive samples wrongly predicted.
False positive (FP) = a number of negative samples wrongly predicted as positive.
True negative (TN) = number of negative samples correctly predicted.

Precision: Precision is defined as the proportion of true positive instances which are classified as positive. The precision tells that how many of the attacks are detected by model. The formula for calculating precision is given here:

$$Precision = TP / (TP + TN)$$

Recall: Recall, also commonly known as sensitivity, is the rate of the positive observations that are correctly predicted as positive. The sensitivity or the true positive rate (TPR) is defined by the following formula:

$$Recall = TP / (TP + FN)$$

Energy Consumption: Energy efficiency is an essential metric to adopt or not a security solution for constrained IoT applications. The evaluation of energy consumption is a key factor in estimating the lifetime of nodes. The following equation shows the energy usage per node:

$$Energy\ (mJ) = \left(\begin{array}{l} Transmit \times 19.5\ mA + listen \times 21.8\ mA + CPU \times 1.8ml \\ + LPM \times 0.0545\ mA \times (3V \div 4096) \times 8 \end{array} \right)$$

Whereas the following equation calculates the average of power consumed per second:

$$Power\ (mW) = \frac{Energy\ (mJ)}{Time\ (s)}$$

Memory Overhead: RAM consumption is defined by statically pre-initialised and pre-zeroed variables, whereas ROM consumption is a size of an image loaded into a board. The obtained results refer to memory consumption for the whole Contiki image, which includes the entire communication stack. The total size of memory consumed in the experiment is calculated according to the following equation.

$$Total\ size = text + data + bss\ where\ bss\ is\ prezeroed\ RAM$$

8.4.2 Experimental Setup

The three routing attacks in the IoT, namely, hello flood, sinkhole, and wormhole, are launched in Contiki's network simulator known as Cooja. Contiki has proven to be a powerful toolbox for building complex wireless systems and has shown a realistic result as in the real network (Napiah et al., 2018; Pongle & Chavan, 2015; Raza et al., 2013). Furthermore, all the data used in the simulation are from the real network environment. In the simulation, Tmote Sky is used as client node, and Cooja mote is used as a 6BR or sink node. Figure 8.11 shows the network setup scenario with 10 nodes

The border router is represented by number 1, the non-malicious nodes are represented by numbers 2–9 and the malicious attack is represented by 10.

As shown in Table 8.1, we test the different ML models through 4 network setups (10 nodes, 50 nodes, 100 nodes, and 500 nodes). In the experimentation part, we will present the results of our experiment with 500 nodes to show the effectiveness of the model proposed in large networks.

8.4.3 Experimental Results and Evaluations

From the experimental results, the best algorithm to classify routing attacks is obtained by analyzing five machine learning algorithms, i.e., K-NN, SVM, NB, RF, and MLP.

8.4.3.1 Hello flood attack

We tested the different machine learning techniques for hello flood attack detection model with the proposed IoT intrusions dataset. The performance metrics are listed in Table 8.3.

The result shows that Random Forest and Naive Bayes have the highest TP rate and can detect 100% of the hello flood attack as shown in Table 8.4. RF reached 100% in terms of accuracy and recall, on the hello flood dataset. The K-NN algorithm is ranked second with a TP rate of 99.64% and an accuracy/precision of 99.97%.

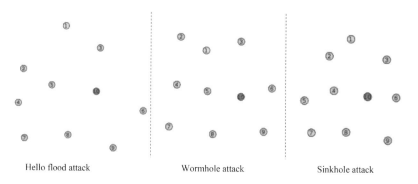

FIGURE 8.11   Network setup scenario with 10 nodes.

TABLE 8.3 Hello flood

	EVALUATION CRITERIA				
CLASSIFIERS	PRECISION	RECALL	ACCURACY	TP RATE	FP RATE
K-NN	99.7%	99.3%	99.7%	99.64%	0.021%
SVM	97.7%	97.6%	97.7%	93.50%	0.063%
RF	100%	100%	100%	99.40%	0.015%
NB	97.1%	96.3%	96.3%	97.80%	0.027%
MLP	98.9%	98.9%	98.9%	96.85%	0.022%

TABLE 8.4 Wormhole

	EVALUATION CRITERIA				
CLASSIFIERS	PRECISION	RECALL	ACCURACY	TP RATE	FP RATE
K-NN	99.6%	99.3%	99.6%	97.36 %	0.048 %
SVM	99.7%	98.8%	99.7%	95.77 %	0.07 2%
RF	100%	100%	100%	98.10 %	0.015%
NB	100%	100%	100%	97.34 %	0.018 %
MLP	100%	100%	100%	97.25 %	0.015 %

8.4.3.2 Wormhole attack

For the wormhole attack RF, NB, and MLP achieve 100% detection, while SVM achieves 99.7% and K-NN achieves 99.6% as shown in Table 8.4.

8.4.3.3 Sinkhole attack

In the Sinkhole attack, RF again attains the best detection performances as shown in Table 8.5, with a 99.74% of precision, recall, accuracy, and TP rate.

TABLE 8.5 Sinkhole

	EVALUATION CRITERIA				
CLASSIFIERS	PRECISION	RECALL	ACCURACY	TP RATE	FP RATE
K-NN	94.3%	95.7%	95.2%	95.17 %	0.067 %
SVM	93.2%	93.7%	93.5%	94.15 %	0.085 %
RF	99.5%	99.6%	99.7%	99.74 %	0.004 %
NB	93.7%	94.2%	93.6%	94.20 %	0.072%
MLP	95.7%	95.8%	96.3%	96.85 %	0.045 %

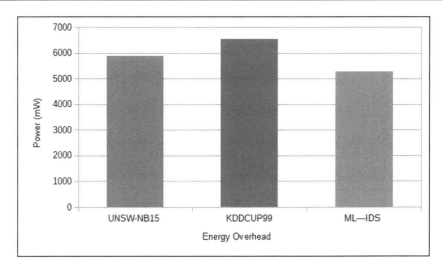

FIGURE 8.12   Energy overhead.

8.4.3.4 Energy and memory consumption

To measure the energy efficiency of our dataset with the proposed ML detection models, we compared the combined machine learning IDS (ML-IDS), with the most popular public datasets that are preferred to be used in intrusion detection researches. UNSW-NB15 (Moustafa & Slay, 2015) and KDDCUP99 (Tavallaee et al., 2009) are considered in this evaluation. The energy and memory consumption of each dataset with the combined ML techniques are compared to inspect their efficiency in a real environment implementation. Figure 8.12 shows the comparison of energy overhead for

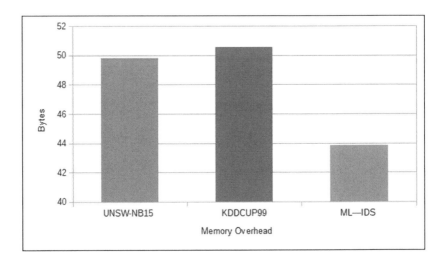

FIGURE 8.13   Memory overhead.

each IDS in a Tmote Sky node. The energy consumption of the proposed ML algorithms combined is 5840 mW.

Typically, constrained devices in IoT applications have limited memory. Thus, memory consumption is evaluated to assess the feasibility of IDS methods in constrained devices. In this assessment, the consumed memory of combined ML is 43.8 Kbytes as shown in Figure 8.13.

8.5 CONCLUSION AND FUTURE WORKS

IoT-6LoWPAN network nodes in cyber-physical systems are vulnerable to a wide range of threats. Hello flood attacks, wormhole attacks, and sinkhole attacks can be easily detected by the ML detection models that we've made, so they can be prevented. Another important thing this chapter does is fill in a big hole in the detection of routing attacks for IoT, which can be very dangerous. In these kinds of fields, the biggest problem is that there isn't enough data, and the datasets that are there are too old. In this case, we used real data from IoT-6LoWPAN network traffic that was recorded by network sniffers like Wireshark. Also, we've used machine learning techniques to build a detection model, train it with the routing attack datasets we've made, and make different detection models for different types of attack. We tried K-NN, SVM, NB, RF, and MLP. RF is chosen for the proposed IDS because it has the best accuracy, precision, and positive rate of all the algorithms. The proposed IDS, which used machine learning techniques, was able to identify both individual and new anomaly attacks that were caused by the combination of routing attacks.

There will be more experiments done in the future to see how well the dataset used in this chapter works with more attacks and normal node rates. We want to add new routing attacks to our IoT attack dataset. This will make our dataset more complete. Our goal is to improve the model's ability to predict three routing attacks by adding more routing attacks.

REFERENCES

Aguilar, L. A. (2015). The need for greater focus on the cybersecurity challenges facing small and midsize businesses. *Public Statement, US Securities and Exchange Commission.*

Al-Fuqaha, A., Guizani, M., Mohammadi, M., Aledhari, M., & Ayyash, M. (2015). Internet of Things: A Survey on Enabling Technologies, Protocols, and Applications. *IEEE Communications Surveys & Tutorials, 17*(4), 2347–2376. https://doi.org/10.1109/COMST. 2015.2444095

Atkins, E. M., & Bradley, J. M. (2013). Aerospace Cyber-Physical Systems Education. In *AIAA Infotech@Aerospace (I@A) Conference.* American Institute of Aeronautics and Astronautics. https://doi.org/doi:10.2514/6.2013-4809

Bagula, B. A., & Erasmus, Z. (2015). *Iot Emulation with Cooja. March*, 1–44. http://wireless.ictp. it/school_2015/presentations/firstweek/ICTP-Cooja-Presentation-version0.pdf

Benenson, Z., Cholewinski, P. M., & Freiling, F. C. (2007). Vulnerabilities and attacks in wireless sensor networks. *Wireless Sensor Network Security*, 22–43. https://cris.fau.de/converis/ portal/publication/110268004?lang=en_GB http://books.google.com/books?hl=en&lr=&i d=pA2XUtdwewAC&oi=fnd&pg=PA22&dq=Vulnerabilities+and+attacks+in+wireless+s ensor+networks&ots=EWSDVSXYOF&

Berkovich, S. (2011). Physical World as an Internet of Things. *Proceedings of the 2Nd International Conference on Computing for Geospatial Research & Applications*, 66:1–66:2. https://doi. org/10.1145/1999320.1999389

Breiman, L. (2001). Random Forests. *Machine Learning*. 1–33. https://doi.org/10.1017/ CBO9781107415324.004

Cai, R. J., Li, X. J., & Chong, P. H. J. (2016). A Novel Self-checking Ad Hoc Routing Scheme against Active Black Hole Attacks. *Security and Communication Networks*, 9(10), 943–957. https://doi.org/10.1002/sec.1390

Dunkels, A., Gronvall, B., & Voigt, T. (2004). Contiki - A Lightweight and Flexible Operating System for Tiny Networked Sensors. *29th Annual IEEE International Conference on Local Computer Networks*, 455–462. https://doi.org/10.1109/LCN.2004.38

Humayed, A., Lin, J., Li, F., & Luo, B. (2017). Cyber-Physical Systems Security—A Survey. *IEEE Internet of Things Journal*, 4(6), 1802–1831. https://doi.org/10.1109/JIOT.2017.2703172

Jain, A. K., Mao, J., & Mohiuddin, K. M. (1996). Artificial Neural Networks: A Tutorial. *Computer*, 29(3), 31–44. https://doi.org/10.1109/2.485891

Janakiram, D., Reddy, V. A., & Kumar, A. V. U. P. (2006). Outlier Detection in Wireless Sensor Networks using Bayesian Belief Networks. *2006 1st International Conference on Communication Systems Software & Middleware*, 1–6. https://doi.org/10.1109/ COMSWA.2006.1665221

Jha, J., & Ragha, L. (2013). Intrusion Detection System Using Support Vector Machine. *International Journal of Applied Information Systems*, 2013(Icwac), 25–30. https://doi. org/10.5120/758-993

Jing, R., & Zhang, Y. (2010). A View of Support Vector Machines Algorithm on Classification Problems. *2010 International Conference on Multimedia Communications*, 13–16. https:// doi.org/10.1109/MEDIACOM.2010.21

Kaplantzis, S., Shilton, A., Mani, N., & Sekercioglu, Y. A. (2007). Detecting Selective Forwarding Attacks in Wireless Sensor Networks Using Support Vector Machines. *2007 3rd International Conference on Intelligent Sensors, Sensor Networks and Information*, 335–340. https://doi.org/10.1109/ISSNIP.2007.4496866

Ashton, K. (2011). That "Internet of Things" Thing. *RFiD Journal*, 22(7). https://www. rfidjournal.com/that-internet-of-things-thing

Kim, H. (2012). Security and Vulnerability of SCADA Systems over IP-based Wireless Sensor Networks. *International Journal of Distributed Sensor Networks*, 2012. https://doi. org/10.1155/2012/268478

Kumar, S. A., Vealey, T., & Srivastava, H. (2016). Security in Internet of Things: Challenges, Solutions and Future Directions. *2016 49th Hawaii International Conference on System Sciences (HICSS)*, 5772–5781. https://doi.org/10.1109/HICSS.2016.714

Louppe, G. (2014). Understanding random forests: From theory to practice. *ArXiv Preprint ArXiv:1407.7502*.

Maleh, Y., & Ezzati, A. (2015). Lightweight Intrusion Detection Scheme for Wireless Sensor Networks. *IAENG International Journal of Computer Science*, 42(4), 1–8.

Maleh, Yassine, Ezzati, A., & Belaissaoui, M. (2016). DoS Attacks Analysis and Improvement in DTLS Protocol for Internet of Things. *Proceedings of the International Conference on Big Data and Advanced Wireless Technologie*s, 54:1–54:7. https://doi. org/10.1145/3010089.3010139

Moustafa, N., & Slay, J. (2015). UNSW-NB15: A Comprehensive Data Set for Network Intrusion Detection Systems (UNSW-NB15 Network Data Set). *In Military Communications and Information Systems Conference (MilCIS)*, 1–6.

Napiah, M. N., Idris, M. Y. I. Bin, Ramli, R., & Ahmedy, I. (2018). Compression Header Analyzer Intrusion Detection System (CHA - IDS) for 6LoWPAN Communication Protocol. *IEEE Access, 6*, 16623–16638. https://doi.org/10.1109/ACCESS.2018.2798626

Narayanan, B. N., Djaneye-Boundjou, O., & Kebede, T. M. (2016). Performance Analysis of Machine Learning and Pattern Recognition Algorithms for Malware Classification. *2016 IEEE National Aerospace and Electronics Conference (NAECON) and Ohio Innovation Summit (OIS)*, 338–342. https://doi.org/10.1109/NAECON.2016.7856826

Patil, H. K., & Chen, T. M. (2017). Wireless Sensor Network Security. In John R. Vacca (Ed.), *Computer and Information Security Handbook* (pp. 317–337). Elsevier. https://doi. org/10.1016/B978-0-12-803843-7.00018-1

Plonk, A., & Carblanc, A. (2008). *Malicious software (malware): A security threat to the internet economy.*

Pongle, P., & Chavan, G. (2015). Real Time Intrusion and Wormhole Attack Detection in Internet of Things. *International Journal of Computer Applications, 121*(9), 840–847.

Ramalingam, T., Christophe, B., & Samuel, F. W. (2017). Assessing the Potential of IoT in Aerospace. In A. K. Kar, P. V. Ilavarasan, M. P. Gupta, Y. K. Dwivedi, M. Mäntymäki, M. Janssen, A. Simintiras, & S. Al-Sharhan (Eds.), *Conference on e-Business, e-Services and e-Society* (pp. 107–121). Springer International Publishing.

Raza, S., Wallgren, L., & Voigt, T. (2013). SVELTE: Real-time Intrusion Detection in the Internet of Things. *Ad Hoc Networks, 11*(8), 2661–2674. https://doi.org/https://doi.org/10.1016/j. adhoc.2013.04.014

Rish, I. (2001). An Empirical Study of the Naive Bayes Classifier. *In IJCAI 2001 Workshop on Empirical Methods in Artificial Intelligence, 3*(22), 41–46.

Shelby, Z., & Bormann, C. (2011). *6LoWPAN: The Wireless Embedded Internet - Shelby - Wiley Online Library*. John Wiley & Sons. http://onlinelibrary.wiley.com/book/10.1002/9780470 686218;jsessionid=1BDEF8F5F70E795897585F984C9D5ECA.f03t03

Tavallaee, M., Bagheri, E., Lu, W., & Ghorbani, A. A. (2009). A Detailed Analysis of the KDD CUP 99 Data Set. *2009 IEEE Symposium on Computational Intelligence for Security and Defense Applications*, 1–6. https://doi.org/10.1109/CISDA.2009.5356528

Thirumuruganathan, S. (2010). A Detailed Introduction to K-Nearest Neighbor (KNN) Algorithm. *WWW Document. Available at*: https://Saravananthirumuruganathan.Wordpress.Com/ 2010/05/17/a-Detailed-Introduction-to-k-Nearest-Neighbor-Knn-Algorithm/

von Solms, R., & van Niekerk, J. (2013). From Information Security to Cyber Security. *Computers & Security, 38*, 97–102. https://doi.org/http://dx.doi.org/10.1016/j.cose.2013.04.004

Winter, T., Thubert, P., Brandt, A., Clausen, T. H., Hui, J. W., Kelsey, R., Levis, P., Pister, K., Struik, R., & Vasseur, J. (2011). Rpl: Ipv6 routing protocol for low power and lossy networks. *Work In Progress)*, http://Tools.Ietf.Org/Html/Draft-Ietf-Roll-Rpl-19, July, 1–164. https://doi.org/10.2313/NET-2011-07-1

Zhang, Y., Meratnia, N., & Havinga, P. J. M. (2013). Distributed Online Outlier Detection in Wireless Sensor Networks Using Ellipsoidal Support Vector Machine. *Ad Hoc Networks, 11*(3), 1062–1074. https://doi.org/https://doi.org/10.1016/j.adhoc.2012.11.001

Mitigation of Malware Using Artificial Intelligence Techniques

A Literature Review

9

Farhat Lamia Barsha
Tennessee Tech University, Cookeville, Tennessee

Hossain Shahriar
Kennesaw State University, Kennesaw, Georgia

Contents

DOI: 10.1201/9781003278207-13

9.1 INTRODUCTION

Malicious software that causes damage to a computer framework without consent and informing the owner is known as malware. This malware is named computer virus or retrovirus or researchers [1]. Malware started its journey in 1982 through the first computer virus called Elk Cloner, which was discovered on Mac and the first PC-based malware was released in 1986 named Brain. After that, malware software increased rapidly day by day as the security field was not that much developed, so attacking was quite easy.

Hackers use malware to steal personal information from users' computer. It can be a piece of single person information or an organization's information and sell them to a third party in exchange for money. This information includes user password browsing history or any other sensitive details. Malware holds a large space in hardware storage, slowing down computer speed. When malware enters a system, it replicates itself and spreads throughout the network system, deletes files, or restricts files [2].

Innovative methods and techniques make malware detection stronger than before. Different techniques were applied to develop anti-malware software and the first anti-virus product was supposed to be developed in 1987. After that, various developments occurred in this field.

Detection and prevention of malware keep users away from unwanted software. Malware detection is a way to identify if a system is malicious or benign. And malware prevention includes establishing antimalware systems. In 1987, Ross Greenberg invented the first anti-malware system, Flushot Plus, to prevent viruses from bringing changes to user files [3].

Malware detection and prevention systems are available on various platforms such as mobile devices, servers, gateways, and workstations. Several manual or automated tools run malware detection technology and provide updates of the detection process [4]. After detection, the prevention process starts with being proactive. Users need to be aware of these kinds of attacks. Users can keep themselves safe only when they recognize malicious links or software. Also, anti-malware software is developing widely nowadays [5].

The primary purpose of this book chapter is to analyze malware detection and prevention methodologies from the perspective of artificial intelligence (AI). We will provide a detailed overview of AI applications in current malware detection systems, their limitations, scope to improve, and finally, propose ideas to overcome current limitations.

The book chapter will be organized as follows: Section 9.2 will present details on AI techniques and malware. Section 9.3 will give an overview of techniques used for malware detection using AI. Section 9.4 will discuss the limitations of existing techniques and future research directions. Finally, Section 9.5 concludes the chapter.

9.2 ARTIFICIAL INTELLIGENCE AND MALWARE

9.2.1 Artificial Intelligence

AI refers to the capacity of an advanced computer or robot to perform chores associated with human intelligence. Intelligence has been characterized in numerous ways: the capacity for augmentation, conception, consciousness, investigation, enthusiastic information, thinking, arranging, innovation, and problem-solving [6]. AI is widely used in developing projects based on intellectual processes.

AI applies machine learning, deep learning, and other strategies to solve real issues. A closely related term of AI is machine learning. Both are not the same; rather machine learning is an application of AI which assists computers in attaining AI. Machine learning is based on the thought that machines ought to be able to understand and learn through circumstances. AI refers to a broader thought where machines can execute assignments "intelligently." Figure 9.1 illustrates different fields of AI.

With the advancement of AI, researchers are applying AI to develop anti-malware systems to overcome limitations of existing prevention technology. In "Artificial Intelligence in Malware – Cop or Culprit?" Pan and Chun discussed how AI is applied in both malware and anti-malware systems [7].

9.2.2 Malware

Malware is a short form of malicious software used to hack any system to get access to sensitive data. Depending on how malware can affect any system, it is divided into three categories worm, virus, trojan.

A worm is an autonomous type of malicious software that spreads from one computer to another by reproducing itself. A virus is a code that puts itself in another autonomous system and then forces the system to act maliciously and spread itself. A trojan can't reproduce itself but attract users to activate it. In this way, they do damage to the system and spread. Malware can be categorized in other aspects too. Ransomware, Rootkit, Adware, and Spyware are different kinds of malware. Rootkit combines two words "root" and "kit." A rootkit is a malicious software, which provides access to a computer or any personal information to unauthorized users. Hackers use it to gain access to system users [8].

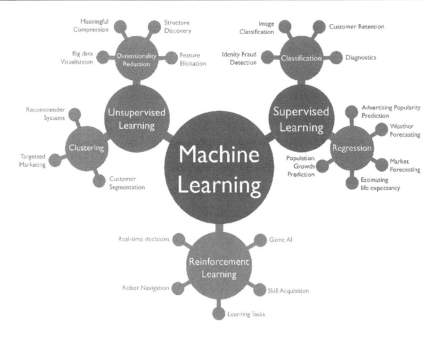

FIGURE 9.1 Fields of artificial intelligence.

Ransomware is another malicious software that hacks users' computers and gives messages demanding money if they want to work their system again. So, it is a money-making software. Ransomware can enter anyone's computer from email or files from malicious sites. Spyware is a software that gathers information from any person or any organization and gives that information to an unauthorized person who can harm them by violating the privacy of their system.

Malware can be installed on a system physically by hackers if they somehow get access to the computer. It can also enter into the user system from other sources like downloading files from a malicious website. Table 9.1 compares different kinds of malware [5].

9.3 LITERATURE REVIEW

The purpose of malware detection is to protect the system from various kinds of attacks by following detection and prevention policy. There are various existing algorithms to detect malware but for better performance using AI is more preferable.

For malware detection purposes, finding malware source code is the first step. Rokon et al. [9] proposed SourceFinder to identify malware source code repositories in their paper. SourceFinder is the largest malware source code database. At first, they showed that their approach identifies malware repositories with 89% precision and 86% recall.

TABLE 9.1 Malware families' comparison

COMPARISON FACTORS	MALWARE FAMILY	SPYWARE	ADWARE	COOKIES	TRAPDOOR	TROJAN HORSE	SNIFFER	SPAM	BOTNET	LOGIC BOMB	WORM	VIRUS
CREATION TECHNIQUES	Pattern	✓	✓	✓	✓	✓	✓	✓	✓	✓	✓	✓
	Obfuscated	✓	✓	✓	✓	✓	✓	✓	✓	✓	✓	✓
	Polymorphic	✓	✓	✓	✓	✓	✓	✓	✓	✓	✓	✓
	Toolkit	✓	✓	✓	✓	✓	✓	✓	✓	✓	✓	✓
EXECUTION ENVIRONMENT	Network	✓	✓	✓	✓	×	✓	✓	✓	✓	✓	×
	Remote Execution Through web	✓	✓	✓	✓	✓	✓	✓	✓	×	×	×
	PC	×	×	×	×	×	×	×	×	✓	✓	✓
PROPAGATION MEDIA	Network	✓	✓	✓	✓	✓	✓	✓	✓	✓	✓	✓
	Removable disks	✓	✓	✓	✓	✓	✓	✓	✓	✓	✓	✓
	Internet downloads	✓	✓	✓	✓	✓	✓	✓	✓	✓	✓	✓
NEGATIVE IMPACTS	Breaching confidentiality	✓	×	✓	×	✓	✓	×	×	×	×	×
	Inconveniencing users	×	✓	×	×	×	×	✓	×	×	×	×
	Denying services	×	×	×	✓	×	×	✓	✓	✓	✓	✓
	Data corruption	×	×	×	✓	×	×	✓	✓	✓		✓

Secondly, they identified 7504 malware source code repositories using SourceFinder and finally, they analyzed properties and characteristics of repositories.

Machine learning techniques have been used in malware detection for a long time. Naser and Zhu [10] have proposed a machine learning algorithm developed by using permission and API calls to detect malware for the Android mobile platform. They extracted permission from profile information of App's and extracted API from the App by using packages. After that, by using permission and API they analyze whether an app is malicious or benign. To validate the method's performance, they applied their method on more than 1200 malware and 1200 benign samples. As mobile devices and applications are increasing rapidly, security in this sector is also a major point [7]. Dargos [11] presented a framework to distinguish malware and clean files using ML. He worked with cascade one-sided perceptrons and cascade kernelized one-sided perceptrons. At first, they applied their algorithm on medium-sized malware and benign files and later they submitted it to the scale-up process, which enabled them to work with a large dataset.

Sanjay Sharma [12] proposed an approach based on opcode occurrence to detect malware. They have used a dataset from Kaggle [13]. They have found that five multiple classifiers (LMT, REPTree, Random Forest, NBT, J48Graft) can successfully detect malware with an accuracy of 100%.

However, there are many challenges to applying machine learning in intrusion detection, like unconventional computing paradigms and unconventional evasion techniques, which Sherif [14] discussed in their paper titled "The Curious Case of Machine Learning in Malware Detection" with proposed solutions.

Besides machine learning, other technologies are also used in malware detection like cloud computing, network-based detection system, virtual machine, or hybrid methods and technologies. In [3], the authors briefly described those techniques with current malware detection situations and techniques.

Nowadays, deep learning and AI are actively applied in malware detection. Irina Baptista [15] presented a new way of malware detection using binary visualization and self-organizing incremental neural networks and achieved 91.7% and 94.1% of accuracy in Portal Document File (.pdf) and Microsoft Document Files (.doc) files, respectively.

Syam and Vankata [16] proposed a detection way where a virtual analyst was developed by using AI to defend threats and take appropriate measurements. They have categorized supervised and unsupervised data, and later converted unsupervised data to supervised data with the help of analyst feedback and then auto-updated the algorithm. It develops the algorithm to become more efficient.

Cong and Ivan [1] published a survey that aims to demonstrate AI on malware detection in digital space. They have discussed both sides of how AI can be issued to develop viruses and how researchers can apply AI to fight against viruses. A complete overview of AI against AI is presented in this chapter.

This chapter will discuss AI-based techniques to detect malware, shortcomings of currently used strategies, and ways to overcome the shortcoming to improve performance.

9.3.1 Malware Detection Techniques

Researchers develop detection systems, keep track of malicious and benign software, and analyze them. Malware detection techniques can be classified into three categories: signature-based, anomaly-based, and heuristic-based. In this section, we discuss existing malware detection systems along with their limitations. Figure 9.2 illustrates various malware detection techniques.

These malware detection techniques work in a flow that includes data processing, feature selection, classifier training, and malware detection. At first, we need to collect a dataset consisting of malware and benign websites, the dataset is available on the Kaggle website [13]. Then, we have to develop a malware detection system in such a way that will process malware datasets, and analyze malware to understand its feature. Fisher Score (FS), Chi-Square (CS), Information Gain (IG), Gain Ratio (GR), and Uncertainty Symmetric (US) are used to select 20 features. After that, the system will train the classifier by comparing different classifiers on FS, CS, IG, GR, and US to detect unknown malware. Different classifiers are better to use to get more

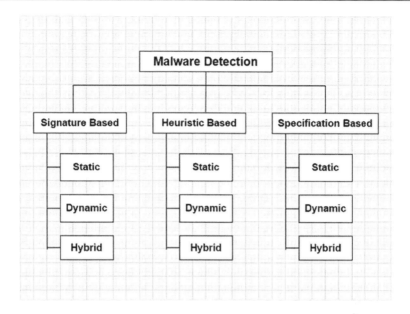

FIGURE 9.2   Malware detection techniques.

accuracy [12]. Figure 9.3 shows a flow of unknown malware detection using artificial intelligence.

9.3.1.1 Signature-based detection technique

In the signature-based method, developers use a database containing signatures of viruses. While searching for malware in a file, scanner software scan the file and evaluate information with that database. If the information matches the database's data, the file contains viruses. The main advantage of this method is its effectiveness, but this technique cannot detect unknown malware [17]. In Figure 9.4, we can see that intrusion detection system (IDS) keeps a statistical model of traffic, which is a database. IDS accepts traffic from various sources and matches it with statistical traffic to determine whether it is malicious and then provides the result to the administrator.

9.3.1.2 Anomaly-based detection technique

An anomaly-based malware detection system later solved this problem. This method can detect any known or unknown malware by applying classification method over activities of a system, where signature-based used to depend on the pattern for malware detection. So, a transformation from pattern-based detection to classification to identify normal or abnormal behavior is a huge development [18]. Figure 9.5 shows anomaly-based IDS scheme.

Here, IDS has a connection with a database that consists signatures of known attacks, matches signatures coming from different packets with that database, and lastly,

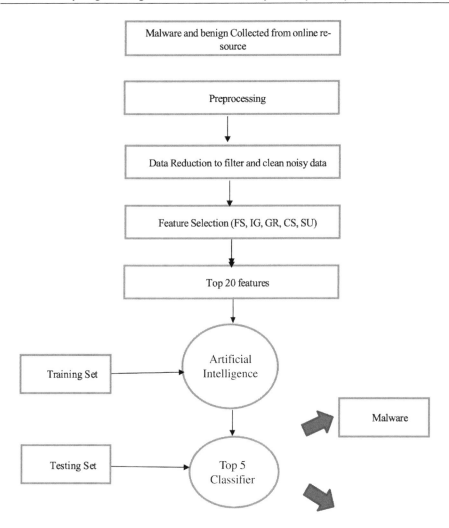

FIGURE 9.3   Flow chart of malware detection.

alerts the system admin if the unknown signature matches with known signature mean malware detected.

9.3.1.3 Heuristic-based detection technique

After that AI was applied over the signature and anomaly-based detection system to improve detection efficiency. To adopt environmental change and improve prediction ability, neural network was applied. A machine learning algorithm named genetic algorithm was applied over malware detection system to improve the classification method. This algorithm applies characteristics such as inheritance, selection, and combination. The main advantage of this system is without any previous knowledge about the system.

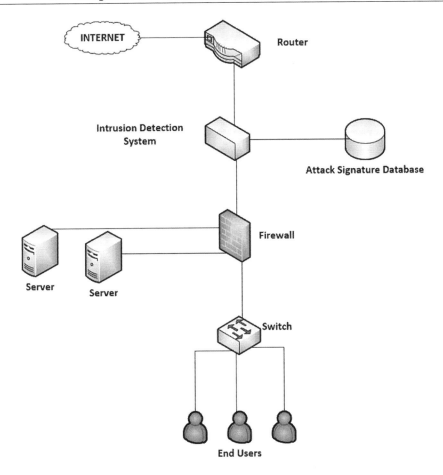

FIGURE 9.4   Signature-based intrusion detection system.

It is possible to attain optimum solution from multiple directions [19]. Combining statistical and mathematical techniques improved the heuristic method from previous methods.

9.3.2 Malware Detection System

In 2003, Tal and Mendel proposed a virtual machine monitor to detect malicious software. They presented an architecture that maintains the host-based IDS, but for larger attack resistance, they kept the IDS away from the host. They also claimed to gain the distinct ability to moderate interactions between host and principal software by using virtual machine monitors. But, the negative factor of their system is at risk of errors and tamper resistance [20].

In [21], the authors analyzed the distributed aspects of the IDS system and emphasized the use of client-based IDS system over host-based IDS system. They proposed

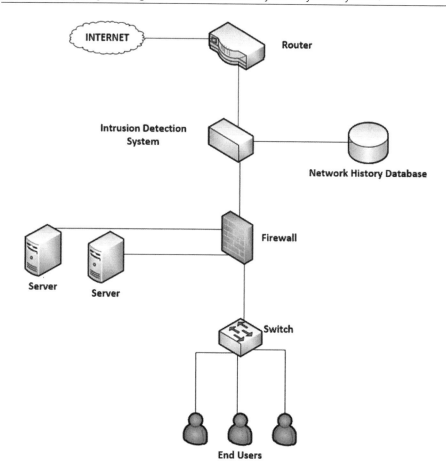

FIGURE 9.5   Anomaly-based intrusion detection system.

that network or client-based IDS systems protect inside and outside the system. But adaption and extensibility lacking is a limitation.

Many developed malware detection technology for the PC domain, but in 2008, Deepak and Hu proposed a malware detection method for mobile devices based on signature matching technology. Their method works on lower memory and provides high-speed scanning. This method is effective for known malware system detection but fails to detect new ones [21].

In a specification-based intrusion detection framework for mobile phones, the authors used a specification-based method for malware detection. For detecting new malware, they introduced touch screen interrupt to identify malware and human activity separately [21].

In their chapter, anomaly-based network intrusion detection: techniques, systems, and challenges, the authors focused on anomaly-based IDSs for detecting new malware using AI or statistical analysis techniques [18].

9.4 LIMITATIONS

Analyzing the limitations of detection systems is a significant part of thinking about new ideas. Previously we discussed different kinds of malware detection techniques. Those techniques came one after another, solving the limitations of previous techniques.

9.4.1 Static Signature-Based Method

The major limitation of the static signature-based method is the failure of new malware detection. This method cannot detect unknown viruses whose signature is not present in the database. The solution to this problem is to update the database regularly with new viruses, which will make the system able to detect new viruses. For this, researchers need to have the proper knowledge to analyze and understand the characteristics of new viruses [3].

However, some viruses modify their code inside their body after infecting any system. Updating the database cannot make this method detect these types of viruses. Virus developers also need to update their code to detect this type of virus, which is a time-consuming system [22].

9.4.2 Generic Signature Scanning

Generic signature scanning solved the limitation of the static signature-based method. Generic signature scanning can detect unknown viruses, but the limitation is this method cannot clean the affected file. This method uses a wildcard to scan signatures of databases [22].

9.4.3 Heuristic Analysis

Heuristic analysis is divided into two parts – static and dynamic. Static heuristic analysis performs code mapping, which is difficult as many characteristics of a virus can be implemented in various ways. Dynamic heuristic analysis is better than static analysis but is a slow process. And the limitation of dynamic processes may not detect viruses that became active in a certain situation, like a user performing any operation or pressing a key, etc. Again, some viruses are active in a particular date or time. Dynamic heuristic analysis cannot detect this type of virus [23].

9.4.4 Integrity Checking

Integrity checking solved the limitation of dynamic heuristic analysis, able to detect viruses with certainty, but the problem is accuracy. The integrity checking process has a record of a large number of failure cases.

Another limitation is integrity checking always assumes that the starting state of a file is unaffected, but this can be false. Slowness is another lacking of this method.

9.4.5 Scope of Improvement

Malware detection techniques are working simultaneously to detect malicious software. With progress, they have some limitations also. To improve the efficiency of malware detection techniques, improvement of existing limitations is a major fact. To improve the static signature-based method, database needs to be updated with newly invented malware's signature [24]. Dynamic solutions need to reduce malware feature analysis time and a more sophisticated approach should be applied to detect malware [25]. Ahmed proposed a malicious software detection method based on API call graph to reduce the computational complexity of malware detection system and their proposed system gained 0% false-positive rate [26]. Menaham proposed combining separate classifiers into one to improve malware detection accuracy. They used five different types of inducers into five malware datasets and the goal was to improve accuracy and execution time [27]. Yi Bin Lu used multi-feature and grouped different classifiers to implement a hybrid classifier to improve the malware detection system [28].

9.5 CONCLUSION

This chapter presented a detailed review of malware detection techniques. At first, we tried to provide a clear concept of malware and AI. Malware or malicious software is causing damage to files along with the system and selling sensitive data to a third party. Ensuring the safety of clients' data is a major issue that rises malware detection. Various fields of AI are effectively used in the development of anti-malware systems. An overview of existing malware detection systems was discussed. After that, we identified the limitations of existing systems and found that no system is fully perfect. Every system has some limitations and facilities and improvements from the previous one. We proposed some ideas to overcome those limitations. Further development in this field will make stronger antivirus to protect a system.

REFERENCES

1. C. T. Thanh and I. Zelinka, "A survey on artificial intelligence in malware as next-generation threats," *Mendel*, vol. 25, no. 2, pp. 27–34, 2019.
2. B. Larison, "What happens if your computer is infected by malware?," *Consoltech.com*, 31 January 2019. [Online]. Available at: https://consoltech.com/blog/what-happens-if-your-computer-is-infected-by-malware/ [Accessed 18 January 2021].

3. I. A. Saeed, A. Selamat, and A. M. A. Abuagoub, "A survey on malware and malware detection systems," *International Journal of Computer Applications*, vol. 67, no. 16, pp. 25–31, 2013.

4. C. Binnie, "Malware Detection," in *Linux Server Security*, Indianapolis, IN: John Wiley & Sons, Inc., USA, 2016, pp. 85–98.

5. Digital Guardian. 2020. *What Is Malware? A Definition & Tips for Malware Prevention.* [Online] Available at: https://digitalguardian.com/blog/what-malware-definition-tips-malware-prevention [Accessed 26 December 2020].

6. Encyclopedia Britannica. 2020. *Artificial Intelligence – Reasoning.* [Online] Available at: https://www.britannica.com/technology/artificial-intelligence/Reasoning [Accessed 26 December 2020].

7. A. B. M. Kamrul Riad, et al., "Plugin-based tool for teaching secure mobile application development," in *Proceedings of the EDSIG Conference ISSN.* vol. 2473. 2020.

8. J. Pan, Y. Jonathan, and C. Fung, *Artificial Intelligence in Malware – Cop or Culprit*, 2008. position paper, Murdoch University, Perth, WA, Australia.

9. M. O. F. Rokon, R. Islam, A. Darki, V. E. Papalexakis, and M. Faloutsos, "SourceFinder: Finding malware source-code from publicly available repositories," *arXiv [cs.CR]*, 2020.

10. N. Peiravian and X. Zhu, "Machine learning for android malware detection using permission and API calls," in *2013 IEEE 25th International Conference on Tools with Artificial Intelligence*, 2013, pp. 300–305.

11. D. Gavrilut, M. Cimpoesu, D. Anton, and L. Ciortuz, "Malware detection using machine learning," in *2009 International Multiconference on Computer Science and Information Technology*, 2009, pp. 735–741.

12. S. Sharma, C. R. Krishna, and S. K. Sahay, "Detection of advanced malware by machine learning techniques," *arXiv [cs.CR]*, 2019.

13. Kaggle, "Microsoft malware classification challenge (BIG 2015)," *Microsoft*, Available at: https://www.kaggle.com/c/malwareclassification [Accessed 10 December 2016].

14. Saad, W. Briguglio, and H. Elmiligi, "The curious case of machine learning in malware detection," *arXiv [cs.CR]*, 2019.

15. I. Baptista, S. Shiaeles, and N. Kolokotronis, "A novel malware detection system based on machine learning and binary visualization," in *2019 IEEE International Conference on Communications Workshops (ICC Workshops)*, 2019, pp. 1–6.

16. S. A. Repalle and V. R. Kolluru, "Intrusion detection system using AI and machine learning algorithm," *International Research Journal of Engineering and Technology (IRJET)*, vol. 4, no. 12, pp. 1709–1715, 2017.

17. Y. Ye, et al., "Intelligent file scoring system for malware detection from the gray list," in *Proceedings of the 15th ACM SIGKDD International Conference on Knowledge Discovery and Data Mining*, 2009, ACM: Paris, France, pp. 1385–1394.

18. D. Bolzoni and S. Etalle, *APHRODITE: An Anomaly based Architecture for False Positive Reduction*, 2006, Enschede: Centre for Telematics and Information Technology, University of Twente.

19. S. M. Bridges and R. B. Vaughn, "Fuzzy data mining and genetic algorithms applied to intrusion detection," in *Proceedings of the National Information Systems Security Conference (NISSC)*, 2000.

20. T. Garfinkel and M. Rosenblum, "A virtual machine introspection based architecture for intrusion detection," in *Proceedings of the Network and Distributed System Security Symposium, NDSS 2003*, 2003, San Diego, CA, 3, pp. 191–206.

21. F. Basicevic, M. Popovic, and V. Kovacevic, "The use of distributed network-based IDS systems in detection of evasion attacks," in *Proceedings of the Telecommunications, 2005. Advanced Industrial Conference on Telecommunications/Service Assurance*, 2005.

22. G. H. Deepak Venugopal, "Efficient signature based malware detection on mobile devices," *Mobile Information Systems*, vol. 4, no. 1, pp. 33–49, 2008.

23. A. Chaugule, Z. Xu, and S. Zhu, "A specification-based intrusion detection framework for mobile phones," in *Proceedings of the 9th International Conference on Applied Cryptography and Network Security*, 2011, Springer-Verlag: Nerja, Spain, pp. 19–37.

24. A. Thengade, A. Khaire, D. Mitra, and A. Goyal, "Virus detection techniques and their limitations," *International Journal of Scientific & Engineering Research*, vol. 5, no. 10, pp. 1334–1337, 2014.

25. Zahra Bazrafshan, et al., "A survey on heuristic malware detection techniques," in *the 5th Conference on Information and Knowledge Technology*, IEEE, 2013.

26. Ammar Ahmed E. Elhadi, Mohd Aizaini Maarof, and Bazara Barry, "Improving the detection of malware behaviour using simplified data dependent API call graph," *International Journal of Security and Its Applications*, vol. 7, no. 5, pp. 29–42, 2013.

27. Eitan Menahem, et al., "Improving malware detection by applying multi-inducer ensemble," *Computational Statistics & Data Analysis*, vol. 53, no. 4, pp. 1483–1494, 2009.

28. Yi-Bin Lu, et al., "Using multi-feature and classifier ensembles to improve malware detection," *Journal of CCIT*, vol. 39, no. 2, pp. 57–72, 2010.

AI Techniques in Blockchain Technology for Fraud Detection and Prevention

10

Yogesh Kumar
Chandigarh Group of Colleges, Mohali, India

Contents

DOI: 10.1201/9781003278207-14

10.1 INTRODUCTION

The emergence of machine learning or deep learning algorithms in various domains is evident. These algorithms have provided immense power in analyzing the collected data and making decisions using that data. But, for the model to be efficient and accurate requires training with an enormous amount of data. Data sharing within organizations can lead to threats like tampering, attack by various hackers, and decentralization of data. Another technology, blockchain, can overcome all the described shortcomings. The amalgamation of these technologies results in systems resistant to ticketing, robust, decentralized, and secure. One such application of such techniques has been studied in this chapter, fraud detection and prevention using blockchain and machine learning or deep learning algorithms. An unknown group, Satoshi Nakamoto, behind bitcoin, described the importance of blockchain technology in solving the maintaining order of transactions. Bitcoins consist of blocks which are constrained-size structures containing transactions. These blocks are connected with the help of hash values [1], present in the previous blocks. As described, blockchain was formerly originated to prevent fraud in digital currency exchanges. As blockchain refers to a collective ledger that is decentralized and unaffected to any sort of tinkering, it gives the confirmed contributors the access to store, view, and share the digital information in a situation that is rich in safety, which in turn supports in development trust, liability, and transparency in business relations. To capitalize on this specified assistance, companies have now started exploring how blockchain technology could prevent fraud in numerous industry verticals. Figure 10.1 describes the structure of the blockchain. It is visible from the figure that each block is a collection of transactions occurring at the same timestamp. It also contains the hash value of the next block in a chain.

Protection from identity theft and fraud is an endless challenge for everyone to elaborate on buying and selling. Merchants, consumers, issuers, and acquirers know there are susceptibilities in how payments and data are secured. Hackers and fraudsters learn

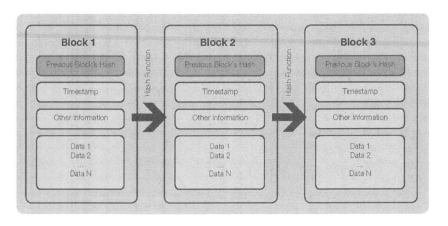

FIGURE 10.1   Structure of blockchain.

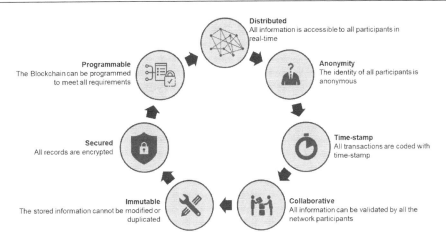

FIGURE 10.2   Properties of blockchain.

to outsmart the technology with each novelty in security technology and breach these networks. Blockchain seems to possess capabilities that help to overcome the described problems.

Figure 10.2 displays the various properties of blockchain:

- **Programmable:** Blockchain uses the concept of smart contracts (SCs). SCs can be defined as: "a computerized transaction protocol which helps in executing the terms of a contract", minimizing external risks. In the context of blockchain, SCs can be defined as scripts that run in a decentralized manner [2] without relying on third parties.
- **Distributed:** This is one of the biggest strengths of blockchain. All the computers (nodes) in a network have a copy of the full ledger to ensure transparency.
- **Immutable:** The data present in the ledger cannot tamper. Hence, making the blockchain robust.
- **Consensus:** Since the data present in the ledger is transparent and distributed, all the nodes in a network agree to the validity of the records.
- **Secure:** All the records present in the blockchain are encrypted individually.
- **Time-Stamped:** All the records present in the ledger are time-stamped. These timestamps are also stored in the ledger with their corresponding records.
- **Anonymous:** Blockchain doesn't reveal the user's information, keeping them anonymous.

Sensing devices like IoT devices, web applications, etc., have led to massive data production [3]. The data produced can be effectively analyzed with the help of various algorithms of machine learning and deep learning [4]. But, such algorithms in application work on centralized models where different organization servers can access this model on their specific data, without sharing it [5]. But, this centralized nature of models leads to the problem of tampering with data [6]. Moreover, data authenticity cannot be verified [7]. So, the outcomes of these models cannot be trusted completely. We can say that:

Decentralized AI = Blockchain + Machine Learning / Deep Learning Algorithms

Such systems allow secure, shared data and help better personal data analysis. This allows authentication of the data source and stores data in a highly secure manner.

The structure of the chapter will comprise a framework for automatic fraud detection systems using blockchain, the motivation of the work, different benefits of fraud prevention, and detection using blockchain technology, applications, and role of learning models in blockchain for fraud prevention and detection. The chapter's primary concern is to highlight the various features in the blockchain that can prevent the different types of fraud from occurring. Another focus is to highlight the different types of frauds, identify theft, and supply chain, which can be prevented and detected using blockchain technology. This chapter will also cover the various implementation challenges to prevent fraud and the importance of machine learning and deep learning for fraud detection in blockchain technology. The machine learning models for blockchain include the anomaly transaction detection system, bitcoin fraud detection, and other types of fraud detections.

10.2 BACKGROUND STUDY

This section of the chapter gives information about the blockchain framework, the different types of frauds, the importance of machine and deep learning in blockchain, benefits associated with the work, and most importantly, the research challenges.

10.2.1 Automatic Framework of Blockchain

This section of the chapter describes the blockchain framework for an automated transaction.

Figure 10.3 explains the flow of transactions in a blockchain-based framework. Suppose A requests B for the transaction. This request is broadcasted via peer-to-peer. The algorithms are used to validate transactions and users by the nodes (computers in a network). Once the transaction is verified, it can involve cryptocurrencies, records, or confidential information. A new block is created in a ledger added to the existing blockchain, immutable and permanent. This addition of the block to the blockchain marks the completion of the transaction.

There are many industry-specific frameworks of blockchain. Some of them are:

- **Exonum:** It's an open-source project given by the Bitfury group and developed in Rust. It has applications in fintech and legal tech.

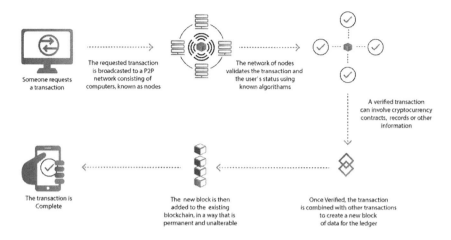

FIGURE 10.3 Blockchain framework for automated transaction.

- **Hyperledger:** It's an open-source project given by the Linux Foundation and developed in python. It has applications in the cross-industry.
- **Openchain:** It's an open-source project given by Coinprism and developed in Javascript. It has applications in the cross-industry.
- **Graphene:** It's an open-source project given by Cryptonomex and developed in C++. It has applications in cross-industries.
- **Corda**: It's an open-source project given by R3 Consortium and developed in Kotlin, Java. It has applications in the financial services industry.
- **Multichain**: Coin Science's open-source project and developed in C++. It has applications in the financial services industry.

All of the frameworks mentioned above allow SCs and are generally private. Most of them enable regular updates. Only a few are not active. Only hyperledger and graphene are public.

10.2.2 Types of Fraud

The technological advancements have also posed immense threats like phishing, malware, and many more. There are nine types of frauds:

- **Mail Fraud:** It is a fraudulent activity that revolves around postage mail. It involves a letter sent to scam money or steal a person's personal information. In simple words, mail fraud consists of the use of mail.
- **Driver's License Fraud:** At first glance, this fraud doesn't seem to cause a lot of harm to anyone but, it has an immense capability to ruin someone's life. A driving license can help in fraudulent activities like opening a bank account in someone's name, boarding a plane, etc.

- **Health Care Fraud:** In this type of fraud, insurance information is used by any other individual for personal gain. To avoid such frauds, it is necessary to keep updated on all medical bills, personal information, and insurance claims.
- **Debit and Credit Card Fraud:** One of the most common fraudulent activities we all encounter. It happens when a number present on the card or the card itself is stolen. Continuous monitoring of bank accounts every week is crucial to prevent this fraud. One should keep their cards safely and not display the number present on the card. Never save card numbers online, instead use e-wallets for the purpose. These days, hackers are also using "skimmers" to tamper information.
- **Bank Account Takeover Fraud**: Getting account information is comparatively easy. Personal information required to access an account can be obtained by getting access to the cheque in the cheque box or through an email scam, or maybe with the help of malware. It is necessary to keep a check on account statements. Never login to the bank account using unsecured Wi-Fi.
- **Stolen Tax Refund Fraud:** It is one of the top scams encountered by the IRS. When someone steals a Social Security number and fills the taxes themselves, this leads to receiving a refund by a thief. It is necessary to be vigilant to whom we provide our information.
- **Voter Fraud:** This broad term includes various malfunctions like voting under a false identity, buying votes, voting twice, and voting a felon.
- **Internet Fraud:** As it sounds, it is the type of fraud that occurs via the Internet. It includes breaching of data, EAC (email account compromise), phishing, and malware. Every year, millions of dollars are stolen through the Internet. It is necessary to keep an anti-virus update for your system to prevent malware and viruses from entering your system. Always read links to ensure that you are directed to an official site.
- **Elder Fraud:** Senescence makes the person more susceptible, kind-hearted, and trusting. All these qualities of an elder person are extorted by scammers and lead to illegal activities like phone scams offering lottery winnings, health care services. These activities help them to gain access to their personal information.

10.2.3 Importance of Deep Learning and Machine Learning Model for Blockchain in Fraud Prevention and Detection

Machine learning is a paradigm that automatically learns from the data fed. It gains knowledge by observing the data provided to it. Various patterns are analyzed and inferences are made based on those observations. The efficiency of the model is dependent on large volumes of data. There are two phases in the machine learning process: training and validation. During the training phase, labeling of a large amount of data is fed to the system whereas, during the testing of trained models is validated by cross-checking the predicted labels of the data. It helps the system understand complex perception tasks trying to achieve maximum performance. The deep learning model consists of various layers, including a non-linear processing unit for feature extraction.

Learning can be classified into three types:

- Supervised learning
- Unsupervised learning
- Reinforcement learning

Applications of deep learning include: biological image classification, deep vision systems, healthcare, parking systems, object detection, medical applications, document analysis and recognition, data flow graph, remote sensing, stock market analysis, semantic image segmentation, synthetic aperture radar, person re-identification, and many more.

Machine learning applications are image recognition, speech recognition, medical diagnosis, automatic language translation, online fraud detection, stock market trading, email spam and malware filtering, virtual personal assistant, self-driving cars, traffic prediction, product recommendation, and many more.

Some of the work of the various researchers using machine learning or deep learning for fraud detection has been discussed below:

- To control corruption in governmental bodies.
- Automatic digital signature during a transaction with the help of machine learning.
- It helps solve the access control problem of IoT.
- It is helpful to protect customers from online fraud ratings.
- It helps remove the anonymity in the blockchain which leads to illicit activities. Supervised machine learning technique is useful by providing 80.2% accuracy.
- It is useful in detecting suspicious activities using various algorithms like XGBoosting, Support Vector Machines, Random Forest, and many more.
- It helps detect frauds with the help of various graphs with considerably high results.
- Various clustering techniques are also helpful in detecting suspicious activities and frauds.
- By detecting fraudulent machine learning also helps an organization to increase profits.
- Frauds in telecommunication can be precisely detected with the help of fuzzy logic with an accuracy of 97.6%. It also helps organizations to divide customers into various categories.
- By analyzing a series of transactions a problem of high false-positive rates can be successfully addressed. Algorithms like SVM and LSTM-RNN are helpful by giving AUC as 89.322% and 95%, respectively.
- GANs help increase the data available for the minority class. This helps reduce the problem of overfitting and increase the model's performance.

Considering the above-provided results, we can considerably check that the results of deep learning and machine learning are significant in fraud detection. They help detect the fraud and also the associated problems with it. So, it is no brainer to merge these two emergent techniques with blockchain.

Bringing AI and blockchain together can result in a revolutionized paradigm. Blockchain, on the one hand, is a distributed ledger that is transparent and immutable, whereas AI (machine learning and deep learning) can result in the study of the enormous data gathered in the blockchain. Machine learning and deep learning can help analyze the data gathered more efficiently. It can be fruitful in enhancing the security feature of the chain. Since blockchain works on a decentralized ledger, enormous data can be gathered for training the machine learning model, creating a robust model. Their amalgamation has resulted in various frameworks for fraud detection like credit cards, insurance, and many more.

The proposed work of many researchers in this field is demonstrated in the reported work section of the article where we will come across advantages their merger has posed.

10.2.4 Benefits of Blockchain

Blockchain has many advantages: blockchain possesses three main features that increase its robustness and makes it suitable for fraud detection. Those three features are Distributed Networks, Immutable, and Permissible. As a result, the relevance of blockchain technology is increasing exponentially [8]. According to a survey conducted by IBM in 2017, almost 33% of executives are engaged with blockchain. With the advancements, three generations of blockchain have been witnessed [9].

- It provides more efficient performance for security and transactions [10–11]. Since, blockchain is transparent, and transactions are digitally signed and encrypted, they are highly secured.
- It inhibits the involvement of third parties so no involvement of hidden fees. Blockchains have made the involvement of third parties or settlers zero because all the users in a network can check the ledger. All the activities are transparent and blockchain also involves usage of SCs.
- It provides transparency. It means that all the associated nodes (computers) in a network can see the ledger instantly. All the transactions are known to everyone connected in a network.
- Since it is based on distributed ledger, it creates a sense of trust among its participants or connected nodes in a network.
- Highly cost-effective. Since, it expedited the involvement of third parties.
- Transactions are cryptographically signed and verified. All the transactions made in blockchains require users to sign them digitally and all the transactions are encrypted after that.
- It provides security against hackers as the data present in the ledger cannot be tampered.

- It provides high speed. Since blocks in the blockchain are connected via hash values, it is easy and faster to navigate between them.
- It helps to check fraudulent activities like corruption because of its transparent and distributed characteristics.

10.2.5 Research Challenges

This section discusses the challenges faced to bringing blockchain and AI together. Some of the main issues are listed below:

- **Privacy:** The data stored in ledgers of blockchain are publicly available. But making the data private can lead to inefficient performance of AI models. It can lead to harm to privacy.
- **Blockchain Security:** Blockchain is susceptible to cyber-attack by 51% [12]. Issues related to security are more evident in public blockchains like bitcoin and Ethereum. Decentralized characteristics of blockchain make it more prone to attacks.
- **Trusted Oracle:** Smart contacts cannot pull data from the outside world. It cannot trigger an event automatically. Trusted oracles, commonly known as third parties, come into play [13].
- **Scalability and Side Chains:** Bitcoin can complete 4 transactions in a second, whereas Ethereum can complete 12 transactions. Side chains are useful in enhancing scalability [14]. These days, researchers are working significantly on improving the scalability of the blockchain [15].
- **Fog Computing:** It allows localized computation of the gathered data. It helps to prevent long delays which can be faced in cloud computing.
- **Lack of Standards, Interoperability, and Regulations:** No standards have been devised. Many bodies are working towards it.
- **SCs Vulnerabilities and Deterministic Execution**: SCs should be error-free and secured against various vulnerabilities. For instance, DAO was hacked in 2016, which resulted in a loss of 3.6 million Ethers.
- **Governance:** It is crucial to manage, deploy, and construct blockchain effectively among its participants.
- **Quantum Computing:** Blockchain requires a digital signature that is cryptographically stored. It is estimated that Quantum computing to grow by 50 per cent per year until 2027. So, sound research that can solve blockchain's scalability, security, and breakability issues using quantum computing should be worked on.

10.2.6 Various Features of Fraud Detection/ Prevention Systems

- **Real-Time Transaction Screening and Automated Review:** Machine learning helps monitor incoming data. This real-time processing of data allows employees to review data.

- **Deep Insights on User Behavior:** Machine learning or deep learning-based systems help better understand user behavior and analysts work accordingly.
- **Reduction in False-Positives:** It means the decline of legitimate transactions. Accuracy can be maintained beyond the transaction amount and the user's location.
- **Real-Time Operations Tracking and Reporting:** Customers can track their performance in real-time. Analysts use various fraud patterns using visualization software to find user behavior. They can also check various information like location, channel, payment method, etc.
- **Automation Level:** Organizations have two choices: either entirely rely on automated fraud detection models or consider taking an additional service of analysts to comply with the model's results.
- **Comprehensiveness and Self-learning Capability:** Systems used for fraud detection must be versatile. The systems used by organizations must be comprehensive to cover all the information systems. These systems should automatically learn from the data gathered in the organization so that known and yet-to-be-discovered threats can be discovered.
- **Multiple Protection Layers:** Gartner group suggested a five-layer approach to detect fraud and prevent it. Figure 10.4 describes five layers.
- **Integration and Deployment:** Organizations should encourage discussions and reviews on their products to work on the pitfalls. They should also be focused on integrating current facilities in their software.
- **Compliance with Security Standards:** Organizations should maintain the document of their requirements handy. They must ensure that every customer complies with these presented requirements of the organization.
- **Cost:** The cost of fraud detection software varies according to the organization's expectations. For example, fraud screening tools are comparatively less expensive than full-service fraud tools. The choice is between: having fixed subscription plans and flexible pricing according to the requirements [16].
- **Customer Support:** Organizations should provide robust and easily accessible customer support services. They should work on a document that describes the technical support customers can get from the service provider in case of difficulty, the response time, and the contact authority.
- **Approval Rates and False-Positive Handling:** It is necessary to evaluate how the software handles cases of false declines which are initially legitimate.

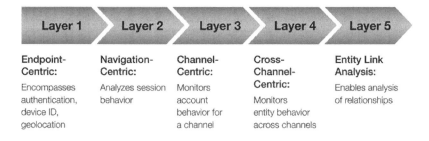

FIGURE 10.4   Five-layer architecture for fraud detection/prevention.

10.3 REPORTED WORK

This section illustrates the findings of different researchers for fraud detection and prevention using blockchain technology. This section also highlights how deep and machine learning techniques have been used in blockchain technology for fraud detection and prevention.

10.3.1 Fraud Detection Using Blockchain

In research by Joshi et al. [17], a framework was worked out to prevent frauds among various governmental organizations. Their work was generic and developed a layered architecture for the disbursement of funds through various government bodies. They addressed the problems of corruption, which occur at various levels, leading to economic losses to the country. They employed blockchain because of its transparent, decentralized, and immutable characteristics. They used a complete graph to model cash flow across various levels in government. The information generated at any level is broadcasted on a network. The proposed model has four levels: sub-departments, district government, state government, and central government. Their model can be deployed on Ethereum. In their model, central authorities could deploy the SCs, whereas other levels could only update it. Their objectives were transparency, time complexity improvement, complete utilization of funds, immutability, security, promptness, and eco-friendly. Podgorelec et al. [18] proposed an automated blockchain transaction signing using machine learning. They also proposed personalized anomaly detection in their work. Data storage in a blockchain ledger can be done only with the help of a digital signature, but this technique is time-consuming. They proposed a machine learning-based method for the automated signing of blockchain transactions to address this issue. An analysis has been done using Ethereum.

Customers are susceptible to fraud ratings in online shopping. Cai et al. [19] addressed the problem of fraud ratings and discussed blockchain effectiveness in objective rating and its leggings in subjective ratings. In their study, they checked the performance of blockchain under the two types of attacks: ballot-stuffing and bad-mouthing. They found that blockchain is more robust for bad-mouthing as compared to ballot-stuffing. Outchakoucht et al. [20] amalgamated machine learning and blockchain to address the problems associated with access control in IoT (Internet of Things). IoT is related to the problem of decentralization and dynamicity, which have been discussed in their work with the help of blockchain and machine learning respectively. Their proposed framework was based on smart contract and reinforcement learning. They used reinforcement learning to make agents learn from the environment and update the smart contract as per the results. Yin et al. [21] used supervised machine learning to remove anonymity from the bitcoin blockchain. Bitcoin has enabled widespread illicit activities due to its high degree of anonymity. They used 385 million transactions to train the model and built a classifier to categorize it into 12 categories. Their proposed model had the capability of detecting the yet-unidentified entities. They used a Gradient Boosting algorithm with parameters set with default values. They achieved a mean accuracy of 80.42%, F1-score of 79.64%. In their article, they predicted a set of 22 clusters that might be related to cyber-crime and also classified 153,293 clusters to estimate the bitcoin ecosystem.

An attempt to address the needs of the ever-growing insurance market, Dhieb et al. [22] proposed a blockchain-based framework to detect frauds and increase monetary profits. Since the framework was based on blockchain, it allows secure transmissions among various agents. They employed extreme gradient boosting to provide insurance services and compared the performance with other algorithms. They used the auto-insurance dataset and found an increment of 7% invalidation compared to the robust decision trees. They combined the proposed machine learning model with the hyperledger fabric composer to implement a blockchain-based framework.

Pinquet et al. [23] detected suspicious users and transactions with the help of graphs which were generated with the help of the blockchain network. In graphs, nodes were represented as users or transactions. They used many algorithms like Support Vector Machines, k-means clustering, and Mahalanobis distance. They also extended their study with the help of Densification Laws and Power Degree and used unsupervised learning methods like Local Outlier Factor. They also applied Random Forests, Support Vector Machines, and XGBoost to detect fraudulent activities in the famous Ethereum blockchain network.

Monamo et al. [24] used a K-means clustering technique for anomaly detection in the records. It validated the model's performance on the Ethereum network, gained better results, and detected more fraudulent transactions.

10.3.2 Fraud Prevention Using Blockchain

Estevez et al. [25] designed a system to prevent fraud in fixed telecommunication. They addressed the problem associated with the long-distance impact factor. They designed both classification and prediction modules. They classified subscribers into 4 different categories: fraudulent, normal, insolvent, and subscription fraudulent based on their history. Whereas the prediction module was proposed to find a fraudulent customer. They employed fuzzy logic on a database with more than 10,000 subscribers residing in Chile. The database considered for the study had a fraud prevalence of 2.2%. Multilayer perceptron was used for the prediction of potential fraudulent customers. The model was robust enough, which identified 56.2% using only 3.5% of the test data. For the total dataset, it gave a tremendous result of 97.6%.

Wiese et al. [26] addressed the problem of high false-positive rates using dynamic machine learning algorithms. They suggested rather than analyzing single transactions, a series of transactions must be analyzed for the detection purpose. The use of biased machine learning methods was done to achieve better results. They used Support Vector Machines and Long Short-Term Memory Recurrent Neural Network. The authors considered the European cardholder dataset for their study, with 30,876 transactions collected over 12 months. PERF Release 5.10 was used to determine performance metrics in each case. They used 41 features out of the total feature set for classification. The AUC valued 95% confidence using 30 trials. The maximum value of AUC was recorded as 99.216 and the minimum as 91.903. With the help of SVM they achieved AUC as 89.322, it was also found that SVM took a shorter duration for classification.

GANs can mimic minority classes as flexible, general, and powerful generative deep learning models. Fiore et al. [27] exploited GANs to increase the training dataset. As a result, the performance of the classifier considerably improves. The generator and discriminator were both of 3 layers each. Using GAN, they successfully addressed the class imbalance problem by producing great results – specificity as 99.998% and sensitivity as 70.229%. Rushin et al. [28] used a dataset with 80 million transactions gathered over 8 months for credit card fraud detection. The considered dataset has 69 attributes containing information related to account, transactions, and account holder. The dataset also suffered from imbalance class problems as it consists of 99.864% legitimate credit card holders and only 0.136% as frauds. They used autoencoder and domain expertise to obtain a feature set for building the model. They created 6 different feature sets using original features, autoencoder features, and the ones generated by the domain expertise. They tested the performance of all the six datasets with the help of the following classifiers, deep learning models, logistic regression, and Gradient Boosted Trees. Deep learning models outperformed most of the cases, and the other two classifiers gave presentable results.

10.4 COMPARATIVE ANALYSIS

This section of the chapter compares the performance of various machine learning and deep learning algorithms in blockchain technology for fraud detection.

As stated in Table 10.1, we can see that different machine and deep learning algorithms have been used in different fraud detections and tested the performance on various parameters such as accuracy, the area under the curve, confidence rate, true positive, and false negative.

10.5 CONCLUSION AND FUTURE WORK

In this chapter, we have walked through the combination of machine learning or deep learning algorithms with blockchain to prevent and detect fraud. We have studied the blockchain framework, the various types of frauds committed by fraud, the benefits associated with the blockchain, and the research challenges. We also checked the contributions of different researchers to detect fraud using various algorithms. This study shows that bringing AI (machine learning/deep learning) and blockchain together results in tremendous systems that have the following capabilities: secure, transparent,

TABLE 10.1 Comparative analysis for fraud detections using blockchain technology

AUTHOR	FRAUD TYPE	DATASET	TECHNIQUE	RESULT
Awoyemi et al. [29]	Financial fraud	ULB Machine Learning Group	Naïve Bayes, K-nearest neighbor and Logistic Regression	Accuracy = 97.92%, 97.69%, and 54.86% respectively
Maes et al. [30]	Credit card fraud	Serge Waterschool	ANN, Bayesian Networks	Accuracy = 70%, 74% respectively
Yee et al. [31]	Credit card fraud	WEKA	K2, Tree Augmented Naïve Bayes, and Naïve Bayes, logistics and J48	Accuracy = 95.8%, 96.7%, 99.7%, 100.0%, 100.0% respectively
Ford et al. [32]	Energy fraud	WEKA	ECB neural network	TN: 75.00% TP: 93.75% FN: 6.25% FP: 25.00%
Bahnsen et al. [33]	Credit card fraud	From European card processing company	Logistic Regression (LR), and Random Forest (RF)	Bayes gave g savings of 23% more as compared to Random Forest
Bauder et al. [34]	Medicare fraud	2015 medicare PUF data	DNN, GBM, RF	Confidence = 95%
Randhawa et al. [35]	Credit card fraud	European Card Holders	AdaBoost	Accuracy = 99%
Khare et al. [36]	Finance fraud	European Card Holders	Logistic Regression, Decision Tree, Random Forest and SVM	Accuracy = 97.7%, 95.5%, 98.6%, 97.5% respectively
Estévez et al. [25]	Fixed telecommunication fraud	DICOM	A multilayer perceptron neural network, fuzzy logic	Accuracy = 97.6%
Wiese et al. [26]	Credit card fraud	European card holder	Support Vector Machines, Long short-term memory	AUC as 89.322%, 99.126% respectively

(Continued)

TABLE 10.1 (*Continued*) Comparative analysis for fraud detections using blockchain technology

AUTHOR	FRAUD TYPE	DATASET	TECHNIQUE	RESULT
Thennakoon et al. [37]	Credit card fraud	Fraud transactions log file and all transactions log file	Support Vector Machine, Naive Bayes, K-Nearest Neighbor and Logistic Regression	74%, 83%, 72%, and 91% accuracy respectively
Yap et al. [38]	Technical loss fraud	Pre-Populated Database (PPD)	Support Vector Machines, Genetic Algorithm	Accuracy = 94%
Viaenese et al. [39]	Auto-claim fraud	PIP claim data	Bayesian Neural Network	NA
Dornadula et al. [40]	Credit card fraud	European credit card dataset	Isolation Forest, local outlier factor, SVM, LR, DT, RF	Accuracy = 90.11%, 89.90%, 99.87%, 99.90%, 99.94%, 99.94%, respectively
Viaene et al. [41]	Credit card fraud	Claims during 2000	Logistic regression	Accuracy = 99.42%
Pinquet et al. [23]	Credit card fraud	Claims during 2000	Backpropagation	NA
Panigrahi et al. [42]	Credit card fraud	NA	Decision Tree Naïve Bayes	Avg. Accuracy = 98%

decentralized, robust, encrypted, analytical, accurate, precise, and many more. We can see from the presented related work that machine learning and deep learning algorithms can precisely catch fraudulently. We have also seen that these technologies counter each other. There are many such described limitations of these technologies which can be rectified using the other. The disadvantages associated with one can be remedied by the other. For example, a model requires a large amount of data to create better results and the limitation of data can be rectified using blockchain. Since, the model uses personal and private information, there is a grave fear of tampering with data. But since, blockchain ledgers are tampering free and decentralized, this makes the task easy and suitable.

Blockchain and AI show the signs of being a new emergent field that can help establish systems that people didn't even think of. The researchers should work to bring down the associated cost so that the majority can access this technology. Untouched domains like genetics and evolution should also be explored using these technologies to suffer from the disadvantage of limited and private data.

REFERENCES

1. Crosby, M., Pattanayak, P., Verma, S., & Kalyanaraman, V. (2016). Blockchain technology: Beyond bitcoin. Application or Innovation, vol. 2, pp. 6–10.
2. Christidis, K., & Devetsikiotis, M. (2016). Blockchains and smart contracts for the internet of things. IEEE Access, vol. 4, pp. 2292–2303.
3. Gilad, Y., Hemo, S., Micali, G., Vlachos, & Zeldovich, N. (2017). Algorand: Scaling byzantine agreements for cryptocurrencies. IACR Cryptology ePrint Archive, 1, pp. 454.
4. Anjum, A., Sporny, M., & Sill, A. (2017). Blockchain standards for compliance and trust. IEEE Cloud Computing, vol. 4, no. 4, pp. 84–90.
5. Koch, M. (2018). Artificial intelligence is becoming natural. Cell, vol. 173, no. 3, pp. 531–533.
6. Kakavand, H., Sevres, N., & Chilton, B. (2017). The blockchain revolution: An analysis of regulation and technology related to distributed ledger technologies. SSRN Electronic Journal, Available at SSRN: https://ssrn.com/abstract=2849251
7. Kiktenko, E., Pozhar, N., Anufriev, M., Trushechkin, A., Yunusov, R, Kurochkin, Y. V., Lvovsky, A., & Fedorov, A. (2018). Quantum-secured blockchain. Quantum Science and Technology, vol. 3, no. 3, pp. 035004–035013.
8. Rodenburg, B., & Pappas, S. P. (2017). Blockchain and quantum computing. MITR, pp. 1–8.
9. Zhao, J. L., Fan, S., & Yan, J. (2016). Overview of business innovations and research opportunities in blockchain and introduction to the special issue. Financial Innovation, vol. 2, pp. 1–28.
10. Zyskind, G., Nathan, O., & Pentland, A. S. (2015). Decentralizing privacy: Using blockchain to protect personal data. Proceedings – 2015 IEEE Security and Privacy Workshops, SPW, pp. 180–184.
11. Yamada, Y., Nakajima, T., & Sakamoto, M. (2017). Blockchain-LI: A study on implementing activity-based micro-pricing using cryptocurrency technologies. ACM International Conference Proceeding Series, pp. 203–207.
12. Qi, Y., & Xiao, J. (2018). Fintech: AI powers financial services to improve people's lives. Communications of the ACM, vol. 61, no. 11, pp. 65–69.

13. Li, X., Jiang, P., Chen, T., Luo, X., & Wen, Q. (2017). A survey on the security of blockchain systems. Future Generation Computer Systems, 107, pp. 1–13.
14. Stradling, A., & Voorhees, E. (2018). System and method of providing a multivalidator oracle. US Patent App. 15/715,770.
15. Hwang, G., Chen, P., Lu, P., Chiu, C., Lin, H., & Jheng, A. (2018). Infinitechain: A multi-chain architecture with distributed auditing of side chains for public blockchains. International Conference on Blockchain. Springer, pp. 47–60.
16. Boyen, X., Carr, C., & Haines T. (2018). Graphchain: A blockchain-free scalable decentralised ledger. Proceedings of the 2nd ACM Workshop on Blockchains, Cryptocurrencies, and Contracts. ACM, pp. 21–33.
17. Joshi, P., Kumar, S., Kumar, D., & Singh, A. K. (2019). A blockchain-based framework for fraud detection. Conference on Next Generation. IEEE, pp. 1–5.
18. Podgorelec, B., Turkanović, M., & Karakatič, S. (2019). A machine learning-based method for automated blockchain transaction signing including. Sensors, vol. 20, no. 1, pp. 147–165.
19. Cai, Y., & Zhu, D. (2016). Fraud detections for online businesses: A perspective from blockchain technology. Financial Innovation, vol. 2, no. 20, pp. 1–16.
20. Outchakoucht, A., Es-Samaali, H., & Leprosy, J. P. (2017). Dynamic access control policy based on blockchain and machine learning for the Internet of Things. International Journal of Advanced Computer Science and Applications, vol. 8, no. 7, pp. 417–424.
21. Yin, H., Langenheldt, K., Harlev, M., Mukkamla, R., & Vatrapu, R. (2019). Regulating cryptocurrencies: A supervised machine learning approach to de-anonymizing the bitcoin blockchain. Journal of Management Information Systems, vol. 36, no. 1, pp. 1–24.
22. Dhieb, N., Ghazzai, H., Besbes, H., & Massoud, Y. (2020). A secure AI-driven architecture for automated insurance systems: Fraud detection and risk. IEEE Access, vol. 8, pp. 58546–58558.
23. Pinquet, J., Ayuso, M., & Guillén, M. (2007). Selection bias and auditing policies for insurance claims. The Journal of Risk and Insurance, vol. 74, no. 2, pp. 425–440.
24. Monamo, P., Marivate, V., & Twala, B. (2016). Unsupervised learning for robust Bitcoin fraud detection. Proceedings of the 2016 Information Security for South Africa (ISSA); Johannesburg, South Africa. 17–18 August 2016; pp. 129–134.
25. Estevez, P. A., Held, C. M., & Perez, C. A. (2006). Subscription fraud prevention in telecommunications using fuzzy rules and neural networks. Expert Systems with Applications, vol. 31, pp. 337–344.
26. Wiese, B., & Omlin, C. (2009). Credit card transactions, fraud detection, and machine learning: Modelling time with LSTM recurrent neural networks. Innovations in Neural Information Paradigms and Applications, SCI, vol. 247, pp. 231–268.
27. Fiore, U., De Santis, A., Perla, F., Zanetti, P., & Palmieri, F. (2017). Using generative adversarial networks for improving classification effectiveness in credit card fraud detection. Information Sciences, 479, pp 1–20.
28. Rushin, G., Stancil, C., Sun, M., Adams, S., & Beling, P. (2017). Horse race analysis in credit card fraud—Deep learning, logistic regression, and Gradient Boosted Tree. Systems and Information Engineering Design Symposium (SIEDS), pp. 117–121.
29. Awoyemi, J. O., Adetunmbi, A. O., & Oluwadare, S. A. (2017). Credit card fraud detection using machine learning techniques: A comparative analysis. International Conference on Computing Networking and Informatics (ICCNI), IEEE, pp. 1–7.
30. Sam, M., Tuyls, K., Vanschoenwinkel, B., & Manderick, B. (1993). Credit card fraud detection using Bayesian and neural networks, In: Maciunas RJ, editor. Interactive image-guided neurosurgery. American Association Neurological Surgeons, 1: 261–270.
31. Yee, O. S., Sagadevan, S., & Malim, N. (2018). Credit card fraud detection using machine learning as data mining technique. Journal of Telecommunication, Electronic and Computer Engineering, vol. 10, pp. 23–27.

32. Ford, V., Siraj, A., & Eberle, W. (2014). Smart grid energy fraud detection using artificial neural networks. IEEE Symposium on Computational Intelligence, pp. 1–6.
33. Bahnsen, A. C., Stojanovic, A., Aouada, D., & Ottersten, B. (2013). Cost sensitive credit card fraud detection using Bayes minimum risk. 12th International Conference on Machine Learning and Applications, pp. 333–338.
34. Bauder, R. A., & Khoshgoftaar, T. M. (2017). Medicare fraud detection using machine learning methods. 16th IEEE International Conference on Machine Learning and Applications, pp. 858–864.
35. Randhawa, K., Loo, C. K., Seera, M., Lim, C. P., & Nandi, A. K. (2018). Credit card fraud detection using AdaBoost and majority voting. IEEE Access, vol. 6, pp. 14277–14284.
36. Khare, N., & Sait, S. (2018). Credit card fraud detection using machine learning models and collating machine learning models. International Journal of Pure and Applied Mathematics, vol. 118, no. 20, pp. 825–838.
37. Thennakoon, A., Bhagyani, C., Premadasa, S., Mihiranga, S., & Kuruwitaarachchi, N. (2019). Real-time credit card fraud detection using machine learning. 9th International Conference on Cloud Computing, Data Science & Engineering (Confluence), pp. 488–493.
38. Nagi, J., Yap, K. S., Tiong, S. K., Ahmed, S. K., & Nagi, F. (2011). Improving SVM-based nontechnical loss detection in power utility using the fuzzy inference system. IEEE Transactions on power delivery, 26(2), 1284–1285.
39. Viaenese, S., Dedene, G., & Derrig, R. (2005). Auto claim fraud detection using Bayesian learning neural networks. Expert Systems with Applications, vol. 29, no. 3, pp. 653–666.
40. Dornadula, V. N., & Geetha, S. (2019). Credit card fraud detection using machine learning algorithms. Procedia computer science, *165*, 631–641.
41. Viaene, S., Ayuso, M., Guillen, M., Gheel, D., & Dedene, G. (2007). Strategies for detecting fraudulent claims in the automobile insurance industry. Elsevier, European Journal of Operational Research, vol. 176, no. 1, pp. 565–583.
42. Panigrahi, S., Kundu, A., Sural, S., & Majumdar, A. K. (2009). Credit card fraud detection: A fusion approach using Dempster–Shafer theory and Bayesian learning. Elsevier, Information Fusion, vol. 10, no. 4, pp. 354–363.

Index